Readers of the Quilt

Essays on Being
Black, Female, and Literate

UNDERSTANDING EDUCATION AND POLICY
William T. Pink and George W. Noblit
Series Editors

Readers of the Quilt

Essays on Being
Black, Female, and Literate

Joanne Kilgour Dowdy

Kent State University

HAMPTON PRESS, INC.
CRESSKILL, NEW JERSEY

Printed in the United States of America

Library of Congress Cataloging-in-Publication-Data

Readers of the quilt : essays on being black, female, and literate / [edited by] Joanne Kilgour Dowdy.
    p. cm. -- (Understanding education and policy)
   Includes blbliographic references and indexes.
   ISBN 1-57273-608-9 -- ISN 1-57273-609-7
   1. African American women--Education. 2. African American women--Race Identity--Social aspects--United States. I. Dowdy, Joanne Kilgour. II. Series.

LC2717.R42 2005
302.2'244'082--dc22

2005041915

Cover photo by Matthew Weinstein
Cover design by Darryl Crosby

Hampton Press, Inc.
23 Broadway
Cresskill, NJ 07626

To all the learned men and women who
I have met in all walks of life

Contents

Series Preface

Books in this series, Understanding Education and Policy, examine various perspectives to better understand the aims, practices, substances, and contexts of schooling, and the meaning of these analyses for educational policy. Our primary intent is to redirect the language used, the voices included, and the range of issues addressed in the current debates concerning schools and policy. In so doing, books in this series explore the varied conceptions and experiences that surface when analysis includes racial, class, gender, ethnicity, sexual orientation, and other salient differences. As a result, books in this series span the social sciences (anthropology, history, philosophy, psychology, sociology, cultural studies, etc.) and research paradigms.

Books in the series will be grounded in the contextualized lives of the major actors in school (students, teachers, administrators, parents, policymakers, etc.) and address major theoretical and methodological issues. The challenge our authors have taken upon themselves is to fully explore life-in-schools, through the multiple lenses of various actors and within the contexts in which these actors and education are situated. The range of empirically sound and theoretically sophisticated works that have been included in this series contribute to a fundamental and necessary rethinking of content, process, and context for school reform. They underscore the reform that all too often disadvantages some for the benefit of others. The challenge we see in these books is that educational policy has a complexity that few are willing to engage. This in turn requires that studies of education and policy have a critical yet constructive stance.

In *Readers of the Quilt*, Joanne Kilgour Dowdy and her colleagues have recontextualized literacy. Literacy to their way of thinking includes traditional definitions of reading and writing but reminds us that these same definitions emanate from positions of white power, from social institutions that reproduce the existing social hierarchies and ideologies. If you are Black and female, being literate involves being subject to such oppression. However, it also means that Black women have had to be literate in much more than just the words written or spoken. Being literate under oppressive conditions, means being able to read power, racism, and sexism as well as the texts through which they are transmitted. This is a higher form of literacy for which Black women have met the standard and Whites are hard pressed to understand. What whites cannot understand is precisely what is elucidated here—that literacy is embedded in the contexts of life and to know words is to know one's power and one's subjugation. We are hopeful that including it in this book series will help this message be understood both for the power it brings and for the critique it entails.

About the Authors

Sunny-Marie Birney is a doctoral candidate whose area of concentration is Multicultural and International Education, particularly African-Centered Education. She is a grassroots community activist, entrepreneur, and educator who taught within the public school system.

Mandi Chikombero was born in what is now Harare, Zimbabwe. After completing her dissertation in Communication Studies, she would like to teach organizational communication, as well as mass media/advertising effects, and particularly the effects of media on women.

Sharon M. Darling is an Assistant Professor at Boise State University in Idaho, where she prepares teachers to work with young children who are typically developing and those with delays or disabilities and their families. Her research interests include inclusion, family involvement, and early and family literacy, especially among people of color.

Joanne Kilgour Dowdy is an Associate Professor of Adolescent/Adult Literacy at Kent State University in the department of Teaching, Leadership, and Curriculum and Instruction. Her major research interests include women and literacy, drama in education, and video technology in qualitative research instruction.

Wanda J. Franklin, MS, RN, is currently a doctoral student and teaching assistant in the joint PhD in Nursing Program at the University of Akron and Kent State University. Her professional nursing focus is community health, disparities in health status in Black Americans, and breast cancer screening in Black American women.

Sandra Golden is a doctoral student with interests in Adult Literacy and Multicultural Education. She is presently the project director for the Ohio Literacy Resource Center, GED Scholars Initiative of Kent State University.

Bessie House-Soremekun is an award-winning author and poet, administrator, entrepreneur, and Associate Professor in the Department of Political Science at Kent State University. Her latest book, *Confronting the Odds: African American Entrepreneurship in Cleveland, Ohio*, is the recent recipient of the coveted Henry Howe Book Award from the Ohio Genealogical Society.

Christina McVay has degrees in Russian, German, and Comparative Literature. She currently teaches in the departments of English and Pan-African Studies, as well as the honors College, at Kent State University.

Leonie C. R. Smith is a Doctoral Student in Health Education and Promotion at Kent State University. Her major areas of interest are Women's Health and HIV Prevention, and she plans to do HIV Prevention research about Blacks in the United States.

Lillie Gayle Smith was born and raised in the Alabama "Black Belt." After leaving Alabama, she taught English Literature for 30 years at Kent Roosevelt High School in Kent, Ohio. She is now completing her PhD in Cultural Foundations of Education at Kent State University.

Esther Yvette Walters received her doctorate in Teaching and Learning from Georgia State University. She is currently an educator for the Atlanta Public Schools System in Georgia.

Carol Marie Webster (MarieGrace) is currently a master's degree student at the Katholieke Universiteit Leuven in Belgium. She was born in Jamaica, after which she and her family migrated to New York City. Her career as a dancer, choreographer, and performance artist led her to the field of theology.

Robin Wisniewski is a school psychologist in Upper Arlington City Schools in Columbus Ohio and Adjunct Graduate Faculty at Kent State University. Her teaching, administrative leadership, and seminars have included topics of college literacy, counseling strategy, large-scale testing, reading and attention disabilities, and the transition to college learning.

Joan T. Wynne, a former high school English teacher, is Associate Director of the Center for Urban Education & Innovation and a Professor in the Department of Educational Leadership and Policy Studies at Florida International University in Miami, Florida.

Introduction

Joanne Kilgour Dowdy

I
JUNE PLUM ROOTING
GRACE MARIE

Dash wey mi heart
Dash wey mi tongue
Dash wey the sweet horizon
Of my umbilical home.

Almond fruit and mango trees
Ackee, saltfish and breadfruit dreams
June plum veins dem line mi belly
Rooting Jamaica deep in mi cells re-memory

The Eagle flies high over the blue ocean of jungle trees
Leaving my familiar ways of people that stir of the sea
Settling in its niche of concrete skies and tarred streets
A foreign me de, my tongue's captivity.

Say *this*, not *dat*.
They can't hear mi when my sound sings like the breeze
Kissing longingly bamboo leaves
Or, when sugar cane spills sweet
From the corners of mi island mouthpiece.

The white ones look
To dissect, experiment, project, test, prod,
And write about me on leaves.
The black ones look to disgrace and bury me.
The yellow, brown, and off-white
Fly east, west, north and south side
Praying wah mi have no contagious from air, rain,
Or, through the life mi breathe.

A fight mi fight
In concrete skies and tarred streets
And, I am different from the fight
But, the blue ocean of jungle trees still know me
And, the mysterious way of my people, who stir the sea
Is why I can stand here proud
With this island mouthpiece
June plum veins rooted deep in mi belly
Pumps Jamaica's breath to every part of me.

Mi ancient re-memory reveal to mi hear and tongue
No one can dash wey the essence of what makes me whole
My umbilical cord pulsates to the stirring of the Caribbean sea,
And whether mi dede or dya the rhythm is me.
The sweet horizon's in me, in me is my home.

II

Long before emancipation was proclaimed, Black women like Grandeson were known to be conducting literacy classes in the dark of night, out in the forest where they could not be seen or heard by their slave masters (Davis, 1983). Soon after the slaves were freed, Black and White women began their literacy campaign in earnest (Perkins, 1983). Names like Anna Julia Cooper, the Coppin sisters, and Mary McLeod Bethune stud the list of luminaries who blazed a path in education for the newly freed masses in the southern states (Giddings, 1994). It is to these women's fortitude and unshakable faith in the talent and promise of free Blacks at the end of Emancipation that we must turn if we are to understand the legacy of the literate Black woman in the United States of the 21st century.

An understanding of the term *literacy* is useful for any investigation of the ways and means by which Black women become literate and use their education in our country. Cervero (1985) talked about literacy in terms of the ability to act within a certain context. In this broad description of a practical application of literacy, we can begin to sketch in the efforts made by Black women from the beginning of their lives on this soil. Fingeret (1983, 1991), in contrast, talked about book knowledge—the ability to use and create information that is produced through reading and writing—and therefore aids us in understanding how the literate slaves like Harriet Tubman and Harriet Jacobs were able to facilitate the illiterate slaves along the Underground Railroad on their way to freedom in the northern states like Ohio (Harley & Terborg-Penn, 1997).

What does it mean to be Black, female, and literate? Black women find that the answers to this question can be as varied as the circumstances in which they find themselves. Whether they are trying to become literate in the sense described as book smart, as is required by the education system, or when they decide to break with traditional ideas of literacy and establish their spiritual relationship with their maker as Sojourner Truth and Jarena Lee (Andrews, 1986), Black women are continually evolving in their quest for advanced forms of literacy. Because they see themselves as part of a community, and therefore answerable to that communal need (Dowdy, 2003), they judge themselves by the highest standards of book knowledge and common sense (Hine & Thompson, 1988). Following the tradition of the community mothers (Meyers, Dowdy, & Paterson, 2001), Black women like Dr. Lisa Delpit, Dr. Maya Angelou, and Dr. Toni Morrison ensure that they are role models in the field of formal education for young and old students.

The collection of chapters in this book is, in fact, a documentation of the many ways in which Black women see themselves as literate, productive citizens. Their stories, as well as their writing of these documents, represent another phase in the journey of Black women's literacy in this country (Sterling, 1984). Whether the women write about functional literacy (Gowen, 1992), school literacy (Fingeret, 1991), media literacy (Harste, Woodward, & Burke, 1984), maternal literacy (Hayes, 2000), traditional literacy (Schmidt, 1992), workplace literacy (Gowen, 1992), or computational literacy (Moses & Cobb, 2002), the writers find themselves seeking ways to share their knowledge and widen the degree of agency that they exercise in this society. Further, the women enumerate the ways in which we must now become aware of the Black woman's part in the evolution of literate practices and the role that literacy plays in the development of all aspects of our society.

Readers of the Quilt: Essays on Being Black, Female, and Literate represents several aspects of the journey of race, gender, and education as it is embodied in Black women in the United States of America in the last 50 years. Just like the slaves who had to learn to follow the directions sewn into the design of quilts that would help them escape from plantations in the southern United States to the safe harbors in the industrial north, Black women continue to read directions to their financial, social, and emotional freedom in the *quilt* that is formal education. The authors in this book have created a quilt from their experience of being descendants of Africans who were brought to these shores in the 16th century (McFeely, 1991). The ability to read and write the English language, learning to speak standard English in an acceptable form for mainstream society's acceptance, and then pass on the culture that has evolved from overcoming the cruel legacy of slavery, are all pieced together in this volume of literacies.

The reality for many Black people and others of non-White heritage is that they find public schools alienating places full of White middle-class values (Delpit, 1995). I know why the "caged bird sings," as poet Paul Laurence Dunbar (Braxton, 1993) told us in his famous poem.

To be Black and female in this country is to bear the burden of racism, sexism, and classism (Lerner, 1972). It means that you have to challenge the societal expectations that say you are incapable of rising to a level of excellence that other members of society can achieve (Harley & Terborg-Penn, 1997). The status of the Black female, in the words of Anna Julia Cooper (1976), is always influenced by the consciousness of representing her community "when and where" she enters. This tradition, a direct descendant of slavery and its ravages, causes Norris (1992) to describe the Black American woman as "the most resilient" among her sisters in the world. As a result of the legacy of slavery, our skin color leaves us vulnerable to the slights and scourges that society metes out to those who are African descendants. This legacy of disrespect includes lower wages, less health care, more children living in poverty, a greater likelihood of ending up in jail on lesser charges than our White counterparts, and a minimum level of education (Gregory, 1999).

To be Black and a woman also means that you strive to resist the narrow limits of traditional expectations, for those of your kind, in a country with Eurocentric values. It means that you must continually reach back in history and remember the examples set by women such as Sojourner Truth, Harriet Tubman, Phyllis Wheatley, Fannie Lou Hamer, Septima Clarke, Wilma Rudolf, and Marian Anderson (Igus, 1991). Whether a preacher, teacher, revolutionary, or athlete, every Black woman who has set a standard for excellence that cuts across race, class, and national boundaries established a standard for all others to reckon with. Each one of the women who did their work in our society's unsupportive environment created a role model for the sisters of the quilt in this book.

Quilt gives voice to women who would otherwise not be heard, or not choose to speak or write, because they might be misunderstood by those who do not know about making or even reading quilts in the Black tradition. Graduate students, professors of education, and artists have come together to speak with each other and listen to the individual experiences connected with formal and nontraditional types of literacy. Although the chapters unveil personal experiences, they are couched in academic language or use research lenses that allow the writers a greater level of confidence in telling their tale. This style of reporting allows the reader to stand in the shoes of the writer and see how the story being shared fits into a larger framework of literature by and about women of color.

In the chapters where White women share their stories of becoming literate around issues concerning Black women in their classrooms, the focus shifts to the kind of unveiling that takes place when teachers put themselves in the place of students. Wynne, Wisnewski, and McVay share their stories of learning as teachers in the midst of their Black female students. These women leave us with the realization that they are much richer for taking the time to listen to their Black, female students, unpack their stories of learning and growth as professionals, and then learn to count these significant lessons as important parts of their teacher toolboxes.

Reading the quilt in the situations described by this group of authors means that the writers have stopped to ponder about the nature of the experience of gaining education in a formal setting while negotiating life in a culture that otherwise deems women, and especially Black women, invisible and unworthy beings (Larson, 1992). *Quilt* represents a safe space devoid of the judgmental atmosphere that too often accompanies conversations around race, gender, and formal education. The freedom of the community of writers makes it possible for the women to speak to their experience in the personal way that they do. The pieces by Lillie Smith, Sandra Golden, and Bessie House-Soremekun represent the personal journeys that brought them their knowledge of the challenges confronting Black women in academic settings. Each woman writes her way into a confident stance regarding her personal delivery from self-doubt, social stigma, resistance to the stereotypes that impact the lives of Black women negatively, and, finally, a resolution to "sing their song in a strange land."

What does it mean for the Black women who are considered illiterate in our society to make their way in a constructive life? What do we understand, in other words, about those female citizens who are consistently at the bottom of the ladder in health, education, and financial independence, as inheritors of this legacy? I put this question to my doctoral students and found that they, like Sharon Darling who wrote *Literacy and Black Women* in this collection, were surprised when they read about the resilience of Black women in the face of the tremendous obstacles they encounter on a daily basis. In the words of Darling, the Black woman in our society "has been and remains a member of the underclass." However, she continues to struggle so that she may "refute" claims made against her and she still achieves many significant goals associated with literacy.

These writers' perspectives on life and the various forms of literacy that inform our choices compel us to look more closely at ourselves and the people around us. We begin, through the journeys of the women who share their stories, to appreciate the many forms of brilliance that human beings represent.

The authors also draw attention to their high level of formal literacy, as female citizens functioning successfully in our society, and make us thankful that they did survive and benefit from many of the challenges they endured.

Considering that throughout the course of this country's history most Blacks have lived near or below the poverty line (Farley, 1997), we should not be surprised at the herculean effort that Black women must make to overcome tremendous disadvantages. A study by Critzer (1998) found that Black women's income did not improve significantly as a result of the wealth of a state, the number of women legislators, party competition, or the number of Black state legislators. The author also emphasized that any further reduction in state support for affirmative action would represent a continued decrease in income parity for minorities and women (i.e., Black women would continue to be at the bottom of the social and economic food chain). As early as 1980, Wilson delineated the ways in which economic restructuring had discouraged urban industrial development and consequently provided fewer manufacturing jobs for Black women with low skills. Until 1995, Black women were still earning only 90% of the median incomes of White women (Farley, 1997). From 1980 to 1990, the odds of minorities being unemployed relative to Whites increased significantly compared with previous years (Farley, 1997), and the positive impact of the unionization of jobs in manufacturing industries (Grant & Parcel, 1990; Maume, 1985) created the few openings for Black female mobility in an otherwise bleak employment picture. Even if Black women could get their foot in the door of a business, a federal commission on the status of women and minorities in the largest private industries reported that the leaders of these businesses held to an unspoken law that kept this group of citizens out of the highest ranking jobs in the country (U.S. Federal Glass Ceiling Commission, 1995). Men and women who did not fit the corporate image of White men faced a glass ceiling constructed to keep them out of the highest levels of decision making. Overall, then, the grim picture for Black women's employment severely limits the opportunities for these women to pursue literacy beyond the rudimentary levels in grade school.

Therefore, it is imperative that we consider (a) the fact that there is a need for the transformation of Black women's labor, presently tied to the structure of the state and economy as well as to features of the racial/gender division of labor (Critzer, 1998; Epstein, 1973); and (b) the reality of Black women being mostly employed in federal jobs, at lower wages than whites, if not totally unemployed (Beggs, 1995), to understand the context in which Black women might seek literacy instruction.

The first section of the book presents three chapters that use a historical lens to set the stage for the authors' stories on the changes they have experienced as literate Black women.

Sharon Darling's chapter uses a historical lens to set the background of the Black woman's struggle for literacy and its benefits in this society. Darling shows how society is set up to thwart most efforts at self-improvement through the lack of formal education for Black women. The chapter also outlines the ways in which Black women have historically resisted many of the forms of disenfranchisement that society creates to hold Black women in servile positions. Darling goes on to recommend ways in which communities can organize successful literacy organizations to cater to the most pressing needs of poor, dedicated women who want to improve their circumstances and those of their children and family.

Sunny-Marie Birney reaches back into the past, hers and our collective history as teachers, to show how the pedagogy of her most inspiring Black teachers has impacted her life. In *Voices of our Foremothers: Celebrating the Legacy of African-American Women Educators,* she lays out the legacy of influences of the Black women leaders in education across time and reminds us that it is their practices as visionaries that have kept the Black academic community alive and thriving over the last two centuries. Although these women might not call themselves feminist or liberatory educators, Birney points out the ways the Black women's ideals for their community in the era after emancipation can be traced in the work of such modern educators as Paulo Freire and Jacky Jordan Irvine.

In the piece on Black welfare women, Golden tells a personal story that unfolds the truths about Black single-parent women who have survived and are surviving the welfare system. The work reveals the ways in which Black women are willing, capable, and determined to create a life of self-sufficiency for themselves and their children through their acquired social, informal, and formal literacies. The reader is also informed about the impact of the welfare reform law, and Golden goes on to make recommendations to help address some of the inequalities that Black women now face while navigating the welfare system.

Lessons Learned in a Cotton Field by Lillie Gayle Smith brings us into the experience of a Black woman who comes to value her education in a family that engaged practical experience as a learning tool. Smith allows us to listen closely to the kind of thinking that one Black woman was trained to do in school and to witness her journey many years later as she struggles to excavate those lessons learned in the cotton field. The author salvages her respect for her parents' attitude toward education from her lofty academic stance and puts the cotton field pedagogy in perspective as she adjusts her lens gained from mainstream ideas of literacy.

Lessons From Down Under focuses attention on the development of different literacy types in rural Alabama during the years immediately following the civil rights movement. Using her personal story of growing up in a small town in Alabama when the country was undergoing radical changes in its conception and practice of civil rights, Bessie House-Soremekun argues that many African Americans' ability to become literate was influenced by two sets of rules at play in society. The social circumstances not only included historical factors interwoven in the plantation economy, but also the written and unwritten rules of behavior mediated on both formal and informal levels of southern society.

The second strand of the book opens with *Literate Black Women Peer Counselors: Transformations of College Literacy Perspectives and Practice* by Robin Wisniewski. As the director of a college literacy program where peer counselors contribute to the literacy learning of their colleagues, Wisnewski experienced a marked change in her theoretical orientation to leadership. Her changed perspective took place as she moved from a cognitive leadership style to one that is inquiry based and democratic. Wisniewski exposes White privilege in college literacy, her biases as a White literacy leader, and her decision to take on the charge of recognizing and ending the perpetration of a neutral stance in literacy research and practice. Placing Black women as central to the exploration of transformative college literacy contributes to a growing number of studies of women's literacy that exposes the assumption of *Whiteness* as central and normal.

The second chapter in this section features an interview with veteran teacher Christina McVay. After more than 20 years of English instruction in a department of Pan African studies, McVay pauses to consider what it means to teach Black women about their literary legacy and to coax them to see their own language, Black English, as a necessary and important part of their history and education. In the face of the pressure to perform in Standard English or *concensus English*, as McVay calls it, the veteran teacher makes a safe space for students to discuss the beauty and value of the Black literary heritage and to consider the impact that studying this literature has had on her life and pedagogy.

Finally, Joan Wynne discusses the changes that she witnessed and enjoyed as part of the Urban Teacher Leaders program she created with Dr. Lisa Delpit. The story of uncovering racist notions among the group of Black teachers, and Wynne's own consideration of her heretofore unrevealed racist thinking, should give the reader a rich prompt for discussion of the issues that impact teachers and students within the education system. As Wynne says: "Over a year into the program, however, after listening to these teachers and reflecting on their experiences, I now realize that reckoning with the ravages of racism has been the central focus in the lives of the participants as well as mine—and the most important impact of the program." It is her willingness to grapple with the implications of this realization, and the way it has forced her to talk about the issues with White and Black professionals since the Urban Teacher Leaders program was conceived, that make this piece important to the discussion of literacy and its implications for Black women.

The third section of the book uses the lens of oral history, literature, and film to analyze issues of Black women's socialization and the impact of literacy on their lives. Franklin and Dowdy's *Storytelling* chapter discusses the importance of teaching and learning about values and life experiences of all people, especially Black women, through stories. Black women have used their stories to make sense out of chaotic and hurtful life events and also to teach children about spirituality, life lessons, and nature. Tall tales with good punch lines like "Tongue Brought Me Here" and the history based on *Mary Lou Thorton: My*

Family are used to teach family values, the value of racial struggle, political protest, and survival. *Storytelling* also discusses how this art form facilitates literacy learning and the ways in which it can serve the documentation of important research in the Black community.

Women and Literacy in Alice Walker's The Color Purple by Yvette Walters integrates the five women's ways of knowing constructed by Belenky, Clinchy, Goldberg, and Tarule (1986) to examine the role that literacy plays in the quest for self in Alice Walker's *The Color Purple*. Through Celie, Walker's protagonist, we witness the recursive phases of knowing that both promote and hinder the Black woman's ability to become self-actualized. As a result, strong implications for further expanding the notion of literacy emerge, and we are treated to an analysis of the ways in which a woman who is "poor, black, can't cook, and [is] ugly" survives a life of sexual abuse on her way to becoming spiritually fulfilled. It is an invitation to look closely, again, at the ways in which women, not just Black women, make sense of their world and use learning to enhance their lives.

Dysfunctional Literacies of Exclusion: An Exploration of the Burdens of Literacy in Tsitsi Dangarembga's Nervous Conditions by Mandy Chikombero brings us to a world set in Zimbabwe. She looks at the literacies established by tradition, colonial society, and academic culture enshrined in the novel. In this analysis of Dangarembga's novel, Chikombero also discusses the *double* burdens of being poor and female in a black country and how these burdens overwhelm and eventually cripple the characters under her analysis. She does not shrink from the challenge of excavating and then demonstrating how the huge price that Black women pay to learn new forms of literacy eventually points the way to their exclusion from traditional society.

Reel Women: Black Women and Literacy in Feature Films analyzes the literacy levels or *school literacy*, of Black female characters in nine feature films, including "Passion Fish," "Wit," "The Color Purple," "Losing Isaiah," "The Josephine Baker Story," "Clara's Heart," "Music from the Heart," "Sarafina," and "Eve's Bayou." I discuss the ways in which these films can be used by teachers to enhance the critical thinking skills of students of literacy and suggest that a multigenre representation of the themes and issues raised in the films can provide many opportunities for community-wide projects that involve youth in the creation and production of new works. It is also recommended that the films be used as a jump-off point for discussion and critical analysis of the role that stereotypes play in feature films, and that teachers encourage students to do historical research so they will not be held captive by the films' beauty and sophistication.

Finally, Leonie Smith writes a haunting autobiographical account of what it means to survive various forms of oppression to be successful at formal literacy and functional literacy in mainstream American society. *To Be Black, Female, and Literate: A Personal Journey in Education and Alienation* chronicles Smith's life from Antigua in the Caribbean to Brooklyn in the United States.

She reminds us of the importance of reading and writing skills, book literacy, in the pursuit of young women's dreams for independence from their men and families. More important, Smith shows the resilience that is the birthright of Black women regardless of their socioeconomic standing in the face of the obstacles that less literate members of society construct to keep us at the bottom of the social, economic, political, and educational ladders.

REFERENCES

Andrews, W. L. (Ed.). (1986). *Sisters of the spirit*. Bloomington: Indiana University Press.

Beggs, J. J. (1995). The institutional environment: Implications for race and gender inequality in the U.S. labor market. *American Sociological Review, 60*, 612-633.

Belenky, M. F., Clinchy, B. M., Goldberg, N. R., & Tarule, J. M. (1986). *Women's ways of knowing: The development of self, voice, and mind*. New York: Basic Books.

Braxton, J.M. (Ed.). (1993). *The collected poetry of PLD*. Charlottesville: University Press of Virginia.

Cervero, R. M. (1985). Is a common definition of adult literacy possible? *Adult Education Quarterly, 36*(1), 50-54.

Cooper, A.J. (1982). *A voice from the south*. Xenia, OH: The Aldine Printing House.

Critzer, J. (1998). Racial and gender income inequality in the American states. *Race & Society, 1*(2), 159-176.

Davis, A. Y. (1983). *Women, race, and class*. New York: Vintage Books.

Delpit, L. (1995). *Other people's children: Cultural conflict in the classroom*. New York: The New Press.

Dowdy, J. K. (2003). *GED stories: Black women and their struggle for social equity*. New York: Lang.

Epstein, C. F. (1973). Positive effects of the multiple negative: Explain the success of Black professional women. *American Journal of Sociology, 78*, 912-935.

Farley, R. (1997). Racial trends and differences in the United States 30 years after the civil rights decade. *Social Science Research, 26*, 235-262.

Fingeret, A. (1983). Social network: A new perspective on independence and illiterate adults. *Adult Education Quarterly, 33*(3), 133-146.

Fingeret, H. A. (1991). Meaning, experience, and literacy. *Adult Basic Education, 1*(1), 4-11.

Giddings, P. (1984). *When and where I enter: The impact of black women on race and sex in America*. New York: Bantam.

Gowen, S. G. (1992). *The politics of workplace literacy: A case study*. New York: Teachers College Press.

Grant, D. S., & Parcel, T. L. (1990). Revising metropolitan racial inequality: The case for a resource approach. *Social Forces, 68*, 1121-1142.

Gregory, S. T. (1999). *Black women in the academy: The secrets to success and achievements*. Lanham, MD: University Press of America.

Harley, S., & Terborg-Penn, R. (Eds.). (1997). *The Afro-American woman: Struggles and images*. Baltimore, MD: Black Classic Press.

Harste, J. C., Woodward, V. A., & Burke, C. L. (1984). *Language stories and literacy lessons*. Portsmouth, NH: Heinemann.

Hayes, E. (2000). Social contexts. In E. Hayes & D. D. Flannery (Eds.), *Women as learners: The significance of gender in adult learning* (pp. 23-52). San Francisco, CA: Jossey-Bass.

Hine, D. C., & Thompson, K. (Eds.). (1988). *A shining thread of hope: The history of Black women in American*. New York: Broadway Books.

Igus, T. (1991). *Book of black heroes: Vol. 2. Great women in the struggle*. East Orange, NJ: Just Us Books.

Larson, C. R. (1992). *An intimation of things distant: The collected fiction of Nella Larsen*. New York: Doubleday.

Lerner, G. (Ed.). (1972). *Black women in White America: A documentary history*. New York: Random House.

Maume, D. J., Jr. (1985). Government participation in the local economy and race- and sex-based earnings inequality. *Social Problems, 32*, 285-299.

McFeely, W. S. (1991). *Frederick Douglass*. New York: Simon & Schuster.

Meyers, B., Dowdy, J., & Paterson, P. (2001). Finding the missing voices: Perspectives of the least visible families and their willingness and capacity for school involvement. *Current Issues in Middle Level Education, 7*(2), 59-79.

Moses, R. P., & Cobb, C. E. (2001). *Radical equations: Civil rights from Mississippi to the algebra project*. Boston: Beacon.

Norris, J. (1992). *Presenting Rosa Guy*. New York: Dell.

Perkins, K. A. (1983). The impact of the Cult of True Womanhood on the education of black women. *Journal of Social Issues, 39*, 17-28.

Schmidt, E. (1992). *Peasants, traders, and wives: Shona women in the history of Zimbabwe*. London: James Currey.

Sterling, D. (1984). *We are your sisters: Black women in the nineteenth century*. New York: Norton.

U.S. Federal Glass Ceiling Commission. (1995). *Good for business: Making full use of the nation's human capital*. Washington, DC: Author.

Wilson, W. J. (1980). *The declining significance of race: Blacks and changing American institutions* (2nd ed.). Chicago: The University of Chicago Press.

Section I

1

Literacy
and the Black Woman

Sharon M. Darling

The Black woman represents strength and endurance, yet she also represents what we consider to be at risk and poverty. Oxymoronic as these concepts are, she represents them all. She occupies a tier of society that binds us all, yet she is the most ignored within the structure of society. Because she represents aspects of our being that many wish to ignore, she then is overlooked. Cumulatively, her sense of being is approaching a sense of anonymity. The question that has been asked in regard to women (i.e., does being a woman make you poor?) brings the answer of a resounding *yes*. The new question with regard to poverty and women is: What does being a Black woman make you? The possibilities of an answer to this question are equally negative. The point of crisis where the Black woman now finds herself has been hundreds of years in the making.

Historically, she has been and remains a member of the underclass. From the period of slavery through today, she has been perceived as nothing much. The myth is "through literacy, all can be overcome" (Lim, 1996, p. 1). The truth is that the Black woman has much more to endure in our society. This chapter examines the education and literacy of the Black woman, historically tracing it from the period of slavery through today. Based on this history, the Black woman finds herself an overrepresented member of the society's bottom tier. She heads the list for groups who are considered illiterate, those who are impoverished, and those who are underemployed.[1] The implications of this position are astounding to the student of Blacks, women, and education. Issues of economic status, cycles of illiteracy and poverty, access to jobs, and family needs are viable for today's Black woman. How these issues can be addressed, (i.e., via the use of effective literacy programs,) is also be examined.

HISTORICAL PERSPECTIVE

Many citings in the literature that refer to the education of women references to the education of White women. Benzel (1983) detailed this deficit of material. Did the Black woman not exist when the education of women was taking place? Physically she existed, but from the narrowed lens of White society she did not (and does not) exist. As it is for other aspects of the history of people of color, this is no exception. People of color, including the Black woman, have had to rely heavily on the oral tradition to preserve their history. Lim (1996) stated that the Black woman comes from "societies rich with oral traditions in which knowledge and wisdom are transmitted by word of mouth, through recitation, song, and drama, from generation to generation" (p. 2). Stories are told of women who were enslaved and despite fear for their lives, dared to learn to read and educate their babies.

Schoolhouse was held in the wee hours of the morning because the importance of reading and writings skills was recognized early on. The ability to read was an important division between those who were enslaved and their oppressors in the pre-emancipation era. The Black woman realized early that literacy was a valued skill to be possessed. The difficulties faced by the Black woman during the period of slavery were worse for her than for her counterpart, the Black man, because he was primarily viewed as the *workhorse*. She was viewed as the *workhorse with liabilities*; one of her liabilities was her ability to bear children and thus be burdened by rearing children. Perhaps this is why the Black woman recognized the value of the necessity for a change in her educational situation early in her time on this country's soil. Some women of the period of slavery, like Sojourner Truth and Harriett Tubman, epitomize the image of what Black women endured to become who we are today. Is it possible, then, that a people who have survived the atrocities of slavery cannot begin to thrive? The answer is uncertain at best. It is difficult to respond positively because hundreds of years later the Black woman still finds herself struggling for survival.

Prior to emancipation or, more accurately, the legislated end to slavery, the formal education of Blacks was nonexistent. Laws existed that forbade slaves from learning how to read and write (Ihle, 1986a, 1986b). What then was the lit-

---

[1]Adeshehiah (1990), Fitzsimmons (1991), Safman (1986), and United Nations (1990).

eracy level of Blacks? If *literacy* is narrowly defined as just being able to read and write, the number who would have been considered literate is negligible. Ihle noted that after the Civil War illiteracy was the rule rather than the exception. A broader definition is necessary to recognize the contributions of Blacks to the development of the economy and cultural life of the United States. Runaways who were counted as enslaved people and who were able to guide themselves to freedom *must* be considered literate. The changes brought about by activities during reconstruction showed, however, an attempt to alter the view of literacy in reference to Blacks, especially Black women.

After 1865 (emancipation), the Black woman openly sought what she had been covertly seeking during the period of slavery. She thought she would now be able to legally seek official literacy. The oppressors thought differently and acted on their beliefs. By the time of emancipation, the oppressors saw the changes that were about to come. Therefore, they enacted more laws that banned the education of slaves and free Blacks (Ihle, 1986a, 1986b; Perkins, 1983). The Black woman was disappointed once again; she was now faced with views that she was intellectually inferior and did not warrant being formally educated. There were attempts to challenge this outlook. For example, Oberlin College graduated the first Black woman with a college degree in 1862 (Perkins, 1983). These opportunities were few, unfortunately, for reasons that included poverty and geographic location. The women were either too poor or lived too far away from schools to take advantage of these few opportunities. The Black woman who sought formal education did so in spite of great obstacles put in place to discourage her. What was her motivation? Perhaps it was the promise of elevating her status using formal literacy. Faced with the double bias of race and sex (Ihle, 1986a, 1986b), the Black woman was at the mercy of the White political system. Fortunately, schooling for Black women was established in response to social pressures that campaigned on behalf of Black women and later on as a tactic to achieve hidden social agendas.

Attempts to establish education for Black girls were undertaken with an agenda that did not fully serve the students. The design of education was structured to relegate the Black girls, who would later become Black women, to even lower positions in society (i.e., the education programs were designed to educate the Black girls for their stations in life; Ihle, 1986a, 1986b). The curriculum was structured so economic and educational equality with White women would never be attained. The school curriculum was designed to engrain feelings of inferiority into the Black students. While masses of Black girls struggled to acquire any formal education that was offered (Ihle, 1986a, 1986b), there were a few girls who attained educational levels that their foremothers only dreamed about. The Black women who, against all odds, progressed through school and achieved college educations were decidedly dedicated to uplifting the race (Perkins, 1983). Many of the (few) college educated Black women chose teaching as their profession—a career that ended in marriage and perpetuated the culture of placing no value on educating Black women. The theory was that, if women of any color were educated, it would be time wasted because of the short-lived utilization of their education. Black women believed that the time spent maximizing their education would have been directed toward educating other Black people. Because "educated Black woman and marriage were not compatible" (Perkins, 1983), the social uplift of Black women faced yet another obstacle. Black women were pressured, by those who wanted to conform to White middle-class values, to fulfill their traditional roles as subservient wives and not to bother with that "education stuff."

Some educational opportunities that did flourish spawned from White northern women following the Civil War. Many White women went south out of a sense of womanhood. However, there were also those who felt a sense of boredom with the society's strictures and sought excitement from the limited means that race work offered them to put their convictions into action. Black women, who embraced such undertakings did so out of a sense of responsibility to their race (Ihle, 1986a, 1986b). Perkins (1983) believed that race uplift was the expected objective of all educated Blacks; however, the implementation of this philosophy was placed primarily on the shoulders of Black women. The idea that the Black woman had to sacrifice herself for the greater good of the race has had both positive and negative ramifications. Even Black men began to accept prevailing beliefs that the Black woman should sacrifice for and nurture the race; women were to leave the *hard stuff* to the men. We continue to see this opinion in effect today, and society's consistent subordination of women's own ideals has left a particularly negative impact on the Black woman.

Today, the Black woman is displaced from the symbol of the uplifter of the race to the position of the one in need of support. Politicians and the media would have one believe that U.S. taxpayers support all Black women and their children through social programs. The Black woman does overrepresent those who are considered illiterate, and this leads one to ask whether her struggle to become literate has been a futile attempt. Not really, it seems, because as many Black women spiral to the *bottom* of society, some few are simultaneously climbing to the *top*. Those women who are considered low literate or illiterate possess skills that, within a broader context, should enable them to be considered literate and upwardly mobile. These women are the best economists; they raise families at income levels barely appropriate for single persons. They are the best chief executive officers because they oversee the day-to-day survival of the Black family under harsh and discouraging circumstances.

Schooling for Black girls today remains unequal (National Coalition for Women and Girls in Education [NCWGE], 1997) to that experienced by White peers. She continues to be ignored, her needs are not adequately met, and her success is marginal. She often has issues that are not acknowledged in the curriculum, and she is often unable to relate to the status quo. As the years go by, perhaps with her realization that her needs are not even being considered, she loses interest and other opportunities gain her attention. Sometimes she becomes a teen mother (Lander, 1987) and, amazingly, not just once. The numbers of Black girls who have multiple births before age 20 is significant (Ferrell, 1995). Although she has a more successful school experience than her Black brothers, she does not achieve at the same level as her White sisters. Thus begins the cycle of illiteracy and poverty for Black females. The impact of this situation on the Black family is significant.

THE NEED TO MAKE BLACK WOMEN LITERATE

Lim (1996) reported that 25% of the world's population is illiterate. Women comprise 60% of this group, and Black women comprise 44% of all illiterate women (Safman, 1986). Illiteracy, therefore, is a woman's issue. Reasons that illiterate women outnumber illiterate men include reproduction issues, social position, and inadequate formal schooling (Lim, 1996; Safman, 1986). Women's reproductive roles place them at a disadvantage in the education arena. Reproductive roles not only define who women are within a species, but who they are as Black women. For example, teen pregnancy often causes young women to drop out of school. The ramifications of their position dictate unsavory outcomes for those young mothers who raise children. Later pregnancy and childrearing dictate the kind of jobs these women are able to hold. Mothering, as we would expect, then dictates career success in the lives of Black women.[2]

Women are frequently viewed as second-class citizens—what Safman (1986) called "sex-role stereotyping" (p. 5). The media, literature, and schools all portray women as second-class citizens, which helps acculturate individuals to accept the roles women can and cannot undertake. The National Coalition for Women and Girls in Education (NCWGE) (1997) proved that girls do not receive the same educational experiences as their male counterparts and helped make the case of the unequal ground that women walk on in the effort to realize their ambitions. Given the abundance of negative social forces against women in general, it is not surprising that so many Black women are illiterate. Black women are susceptible to generalized social problems; however, their problems are compounded by the racial discrimination interwoven into our society. Black women must endure the burden of womanhood as well as the burden of being Black. It is a fact that a Black woman is *more* ignored in schools than her White counterparts, she is *more* ignored by society, and she is *born* into situations that put her at risk for failure from birth. Thus, by the time a Black girl becomes a Black woman, she has endured a long and hazardous journey designed to undo her.

---

[2]Cusick (1989), Ferrell (1995), and Lander (1987).

Perhaps she was reared in poverty, perhaps she has received a second rate education, or perhaps she was physically, emotionally, or sexually abused. Her journey does not end at womanhood; she has much more to endure to make something positive out of her life experiences. The impact of her illiteracy results in economic dependence or a perpetual cycle of illiteracy and poverty (National Coalition for Women and Girls in Education, 1988). Because of her illiteracy, she is in economic jeopardy due to chronic unemployment or under-employment. She now has lower earning potential, thus dooming her to a life of poverty (Ferrell, 1995). Access to employment that would enable her to support her family is diminished and further complicated by the number of children she bears. Preoccupied with basic survival, she is unable to dream of education and its benefits (Lim, 1996).

Black female illiteracy has a perpetual effect—the *vicious cycle of illiteracy* as it is often called. The National Coalition on Women and Girls in Education (1988) confirmed that the literacy levels of children are dramatically affected by that of their parents. Illiterate women are less likely to read to their children, less likely to have literature in their home, and less likely to have literature-based interactions with their children. These reading variables as listed earlier are closely linked with the future success of children. The children of illiterate Black mothers who are illiterate are clearly born into situations that increase the likelihood that they too will grow up illiterate (Ferrell, 1995; United Nations, 1990, cited in John, 1997). Illiteracy also affects the parent–child interaction in general because illiterate mothers are unaware of and therefore unable to explore options available to their literate counterparts. These mothers and their children are often relegated to positions of social, emotional, and economic dependence. Intergenerational welfare reliance has presented debilitating issues for the illiterate Black woman and her children (John, 1997).

One of the most striking results of illiteracy is its connection with poverty. Adeseshiah (1990) believed that "there is a close connection between illiteracy and poverty at all levels . . . global, national, and subnational" (p. 3). The world's poor, however, are overrepresented by illiterate Black women. The worst aspect of poverty is not the obvious lack of material things; rather, it is the lack of *access*. Illiterate Black women and their children have limited access in society. We see rising numbers of environmentally deprived children who are being raised by Black women. The lack of access to better situations facilitates and perpetuates this deprivation. In schools today, the children of these women are more likely to be identified as having disabilities that are cognitively, behaviorally, and emotionally related. These children are in the greatest need of nurturance and enrichment. The Black woman's obligation to her dependents is critical in the cyclical process of illiteracy. Because of her limited abilities and limited access, the Black woman is subsequently unable to provide adequately for her children, who in turn are unable to provide for their children (Ferrell, 1995; Lander, 1997). Again the question begs to be asked: What is to be done?

WHAT IS TO BE DONE?

Because of the idea that literacy is integrally connected with one's ability to read, write, and generally communicate, the Black woman must attain these skills. Literacy programs, although in existence for some time, have not addressed the needs of women, or the needs of Black women specifically. Through the lens of women and literacy, and the more narrowed lens of Black women and literacy, an examination of the availability and quality of literacy programs that address the needs of the Black woman must ensue. Empowerment is derived from literacy, and Black women are surely in need of strategies to achieve power. Lim (1996) believed that "literacy constitutes an essential tool for gaining legal and socioeconomic rights" (p. 2). Once most important to the Black woman, uplift of the race, the focus now has shifted to uplift of herself and her family. Using Davis' (1988) view of literacy as a vehicle for social change, once again it has become time for advancement; it is past time for change for the Black woman.

Based on society's pyramidal structure, merely by uplifting herself, the Black woman in turn uplifts her brothers of color, White members of the working class, and, in actuality, all women who have been oppressed. Davis' (1988) position is viewed as radical because she proposes a radically different social order from that which currently exists. Literacy as a tool for empowerment affects the Black woman's ability to access and improve her position in the existing social order. Another group that must not be forgotten in this quest for literacy is those who can read and write, but are functionally illiterate in such social instruments as economics, politics, and the law. Black women must continue to place themselves in positions that challenge and improve the existing social order. No longer should they remain silent; rather they must speak out, act out, and effect change. If programs are not addressing their needs, they should move on or speak up about what is lacking.

PROGRAMS

Illiteracy is a reality that produces effects beyond the present circumstances (i.e., illiteracy of a mother creates serious issues for her children). The cyclical nature of illiteracy demands more programs that address literacy issues for an entire family. Family literacy programs, like those linked with Head Start programs, are highly populated by poor Black children; there the needs of children and their parents are met in the same site (John, 1997). "Parents learn basic skills while their children receive basic training in reading and writing" (United Nations, 1990, p. 4, cited in John, 1997). The approach has proved successful because learning together is more than gaining basic skills; it allows families to create irreversible bonds.

Programs must also be tailored to the needs of the Black women they intend to serve. Phillips, Bellorado, and Margold (1995) referred to this as the *affective* aspects of adult literacy. The Black woman comes to these programs with needs that are often greater than basic reading and writing skills. Sometimes she needs child care, moral support, and/or respect. As young children need validation and respect, so does the adult in their lives because that adult may not have received such respect at any time in her previous experience. Programs that function on the assumption that the learners need them more than they need the learners will not be successful with the Black, or any other, woman. The Black woman needs to feel welcomed, and she needs to be embraced at the literacy site. Teachers who "relate to their students via explicit discussions, curriculum and materials that reflect the cultural and class context of the learners have greater success and retention of their learners" (Phillips et al., 1985). The Black woman comes from a tradition of strong familial ties; therefore, the more she feels part of a family, the more successful she will be.

Tailoring programs to meet the explicit needs of learners involves investigation and reflection about the population the program intends to serve. An example of a program meeting population needs is the benchmark of child-care providers. A common mistake within the context of child care for the woman attending a program is as follows: The Black woman is subliminally told that, because she is Black, poor, and illiterate, she does not care who tends her children. Child care is set up without input from the mother. The mother is not given a choice of utilizing her own babysitter who she knows and trusts with her children. Her opinion is not valued, therefore she is not valued. Flexibility, experienced providers know, is key in planning and tailoring such programs. Providers cannot approach the woman with a set of rules; they must come to the woman in anticipation of establishing the rules together because the Black woman brings assets to the planning table and only she can explain what it is she *truly* needs.

Fitzsimmons (1991) explored the characteristics of Black women who persist in literacy programs. Literacy programs can utilize this information by identifying and fostering these characteristics in their students. Reasons cited for persistence in literacy programs are transportation, child care, living situation, health, and employment. Programs that address these needs are, therefore, more successful with their students. Personal characteristics that Fitzsimmons found instrumental in the persistence of the women include personal determination, positive and nonjudgmental relationships with their tutors, progress of the other students, and spiritual relationships within their support group.

Personal determination can be boosted in students by ensuring that the program is meaningful for each of them. Dean (1998) correlated earning a General Education Development (GED) diploma with personal well-being, further employment, income, and pursuit of additional education. If students can relate their personal needs to what the program has to offer, their determination tends to rise. Positive and nonjudgmental relationships with tutors/teachers as well as with peers can be fostered through communication that is supportive yet useful to the parties involved. Women could be encouraged to brainstorm solutions to problems because someone in the group may have had similar experiences. Staff must be compassionate as well as offer tough love when necessary. Witnessing the progress of other students and celebrating their achievement can be a great motivator for adult students. Women who refer to a personal relationship with God believe they are not only completing the program themselves, but are doing so in fulfillment of a compact with their creator. Programs can tap into this spiritual relationship without mixing religion with lesson planning and can foster spirituality without involving the specifics of a particular religion. Successful students in literacy also cite the support system that encourages and inspires them to persevere in their journey.

CONCLUSION

The Black woman has struggled long and hard in an effort to achieve the skills identified with literacy. Unfortunately, if it had to be judged by present statistics on formal literacy, one would be tempted to say she has failed. This is not due to her lack of will; obstacles often greater than her will have been imposed on her every step. "Life, liberty, and the pursuit of happiness," described in the U.S. constitution, was not intended to include her, thus serious consequences have ensued. The history and structure of society created a situation whereby the Black woman has been in an unrelenting uphill battle to be a recognized and dignified member of society. Davis (1988) called for radical social change; more than a decade and a half later, this change has not taken place. Complacency in the Black woman seems to have taken the place of the militancy of her sisters before her. As in any struggle, there are those who believe that the fight must continue, as well as those who feel they have fought long enough and want to give up their efforts. Perhaps those who no longer feel the need to fight have made some achievements and feel they have *arrived*. Others may see the need to continue the fight because they do not feel as if they are achieving what they want, and they need to inspire the young people coming up behind them.

Perhaps the Black woman is tired, perhaps she has given up, or perhaps neither is true. Hundreds of years after being brought to the United States, the Black woman seems to be worse off than ever. There are glimmers of hope that she will overcome, but they are simply glimmers. The needs of the Black woman differ from the needs of non-Blacks, and this difference must be addressed. Issues beyond her control impede her success, and her attempts at change are met with opposition by people who are in a position to support and encourage her advancement. The good news is that she continues to survive, and she survives the best she can given her circumstance. She continues to struggle because she believes in the promises for social equity. Illiteracy and its association with poverty can be considered a curse levied against the Black woman. What her oppressors fail to realize is the resiliency of the Black woman's spirit. She is at her strongest under pressure. Although it seems she has lost the war of achieving literacy to uplift herself and her race, she continues the battle every day. By demanding programs that address her needs, by being instrumental in creating effective curriculum, and by supporting or attending the schools that are in existence, she continues the fight for a better way of life. The Black woman continues to struggle for herself as well as her future generations just as her foremothers struggled for her and brought about change. No one knows what the future will bring; however, one should expect that continued change would take place as long as Black women are alive.

Achieving literacy as a vehicle for social change is not an easy task. As noted earlier, there are and have been Black women who have realized success. For the most part, those who have achieved have continued to feel an obligation to help their sisters and brothers. For each one that succeeds, however, there are far more who do not. Because of their choices and/or life situations, there are millions of Black women who feel they have failed themselves as well as their race. Yet, there are Black women who feel they have done themselves, and their race, and their nation well by their achievements. The figures tell us that group membership in the former is much larger than in the latter. Holding onto the belief that formal literacy is to be used as equipment in the sport of societal functioning, this Black woman who has earned a PhD (the highest accepted level of formal literacy) with honor represents the millions of her mothers and sisters who could not or have not achieved this level of formal literacy. This journey was completed and stands as testimony that Black women are alive and doing the best they can with the little this country affords them every day.

REFERENCES

Adeseshiah, M.S. (1990). *Illiteracy and poverty. Literacy lessons* (Report No. CE055129). Geneva, Switzerland: International Bureau of Education. (ERIC Document Reproduction Service No. ED321032).

Benzel, B.M. (1983). *History of the 19th century women's education: A plea for inclusion of class, race, and ethnicity* (Working Paper No. 114). Wellesley, MA: Wellesley College, Center for Research on Women.

Cusick, T. (1989). Sexism and early parenting: Cause and effect? *Peabody Journal of Education, 64*, 113-131.

Davis, A.Y. (1988). Radical perspectives on the empowerment of the Afro-American women: Lessons for the 1980s. *Harvard Law Review, 58*, 348-353.

Dean, G.J. (1998). The value of obtaining a GED in Pennsylvania. *PAACE Journal of Lifelong Learning, 7*, 73-84.

Ferrell, D. (1995). Modern day pandoras: The personal, social, and economic costs of teenage pregnancy. *Journal of Children and Poverty, 1*, 17-41.

Fitzsimmons, K. A. (1991). African-American women who persist in literacy programs: An exploratory study. *Urban Review, 23*, 231-250.

Ihle, E.L. (1986a). *Black girls and women in elementary education in the south, 1865-present. Instructional modules for educators, Module I* (Women's Educational Equity Act Program (ED)). Harrisonburg, VA: James Madison University.

Ihle, E.L. (1986b). *Black women's vocational education. History of Black women's education in the south, 1865-present. Instructional modules for educators, Module II* (Women's Educational Equity Act Program (ED)). Harrisonburg, VA: James Madison University.

Ihle, E.L. (1986c). *Black women's academic education in the south, History of Black women's education in the south, 1865-present. Instructional modules for educators, Modules III and IV* (Women's Educational Equity Act Program (ED)). Harrisonburg, VA: James Madison University.

John, S. (1997). *Family literacy as a welfare reform strategy. Family independence initiative audioconference. Family independence initiative Publication #2* (Report No. CE076780). Louisville, KY: National Center for Family Literacy. (ERIC Document Reproduction Service No. ED421618).

Lander, J.A. (1987). Black teenage pregnancy: A challenge for educators. *Journal of Negro Education, 86*, 53-63.

Lim, J.B. (1996). *Women and literacy: Definition of literacy, the causes and manifestations of illiteracy, and implications for the educator* (Report No. CE073296). Canada, Alberta: University of Alberta. (ERIC Document Reproduction Service No. ED407485).

National Coalition for Women and Girls in Education. (1988). *Women, illiteracy, and poverty: Breaking the cycle* (Clearinghouse No CE51145). Washington, DC: Author.

National Coalition for Women and Girls in Education. (1997). *Title IX at 25: Report card on gender equity* (Evaluative/Feasibility Report No. EA 028430). Washington, DC: U.S. National Women's Law Center.

Perkins, L.M. (1983). The impact of the A Cult of True Womanhood on the education of Black Women. *Journal of Social Issues, 39*, 17-28.

Phillips, K.J., Bellorado, D., & Margold, J.A. (1985). *Affective aspects of adult literacy programs: A look at the types of support systems, teacher behavior and material that characterize effective literacy programs* (Report No. CE041344). Far West Lab for Educational Research and Development. (ERIC Document Reproduction Service No. ED254758).

Safman, P.G. (1986, October 22-26). *Illiterate women: New approaches for new lives* (Report No. CE045445). Paper presented at the annual conference of the American Association for Adult and Continuing Education, Hollywood FL. (ERIC Document Reproduction Service No. ED254758).

Women, illiteracy, and employment. (1989). *Journal of Employment Counseling, 26*, 16–18.

2

Black and on Welfare: What You Don't Know About Single-Parent Women

Sandra Golden

Women should be tough, tender, laugh as much as possible, and live long lives. The struggle for equality continues unabated, and the woman warrior who is armed with wit and courage will be among the first to celebrate victory.

—Maya Angelou, (1993)

In 1979, I was a 20 year-old Black woman faced with many dilemmas (e.g., pregnant, unemployed, unemployable because of my pregnancy, separated from my husband, and, once again, living with my parents). Scared about motherhood and not sure how I would take care of myself and my child, I sought assistance from the County Department of Human Services. I thought they would lessen the burden I placed on my parents by helping me get back on my feet until I could find a job. After all, I thought, public assistance was created to help people in my situation.

I made a visit to the welfare office in my county. After leaving, I felt dehumanized and humiliated. My self-esteem had been reduced because of the caseworker's discriminatory attitude. I also felt mentally abused by the caseworker's insensitivity. It seemed the assumption was that welfare recipients were unmotivated, unskilled, uneducated or undereducated, and responsible for bringing fatherless children into the world. My caseworker never inquired about my educational or employment background, although I had completed 2 years of college course work in a secretarial program. I also had over 2 years of banking experience. Nonetheless, my caseworker automatically assumed that, by walking into the building, I possessed all the stigmas associated with public assistance and Black women. Unfortunately, our perceptions are that Black women on welfare have no interest in working and prefer staying at home, rather than obtaining employment and providing for their families.

In 1999, I conducted a study to examine whether women on welfare were affected by discriminatory practices within the welfare system. One participant, G, affirmed this idea when she stated, "People think we sit back and wait on a check." bell hooks (1993) interviewed women who depended on welfare and found that the women wanted to work. Furthermore, hooks stated that these women were acutely aware of the difference between a job and fulfilling a vocation.

Dominating systems such as welfare do not recognize Black women's social literacy skills. The welfare system recognizes academic literacy, but places little value on home, family, and community literacy. A Black single-parent female utilizes special literacy skills to negotiate within a social context that marginalizes and disenfranchises groups based on gender, race, education, and class. This chapter discusses the social literacy skills that Black women on welfare developed to function within the multiple contexts of their and their children's lives.

THE WELFARE SYSTEM

Even today, over 20 years after my encounter with the welfare system, many young Black females carry the assumed burden of being uneducated or undereducated, unskilled, and unmotivated because they receive public assistance. This assumption breeds racial and discriminatory practices that date back to the birth of U.S. public assistance in 1935. Welfare was instituted to support individuals who were affected by the Depression and World War I. The 1935 Social Security Act established two social insurance programs: one to support old-age benefits for retired workers and a second for unemployment insurance. The Social Security Act spawned federal grants such as Aid to Families With Dependent Children (AFDC). The AFDC was replaced in 1996 by the Temporary Assistance for Needy Families (TANF) block grant. Michael K. Brown (cited in Cammison, 2001), author of *Race, Money, and the American Welfare State*, argued that fiscal limitations as well as deep-seated racism shape policy governing welfare. Brown further claimed that White Americans benefited from public and private policies, but Blacks were subjected to a less desirable form, Aid to Dependent Children (ADC), and then blamed for their dependence on cash benefits.

As it did by the 1930s, the labor market discriminates against Blacks (Cammison, 2001). Daniel Patrick Moynihan's 1965 report, *The Negro Family: The Case for National Action*, officially labeled Black female-headed families as inferior, nonproductive, pathological, and dysfunctional (Dickerson, 1995). Bill Clinton's 1992 campaign promise was the "end of welfare as we know it" (O'Connor, 2002). In 1996, the Personal Responsibility and Work Opportunity Reconciliation Act (PRWORA) was passed. Paragraph 1 of the preamble to PRWORA states, "Marriage is the foundation of a successful society. . . ." The act continues to redefine the purpose of welfare as follows:

1. To provide assistance to needy families so that children can be taken care of in their own homes or in the homes of relatives;
2. To end dependence of needy parents on government benefits, by promoting job preparation, work, and marriage;
3. To prevent and reduce out of wedlock pregnancies; and
4. To encourage the formation and maintenance of two-parent families. (cited in Mink, 1998, pp. 104-193)

The law established a 5-year time limit on welfare benefits to single parents and severely restricted Food Stamp entitlements. Through the welfare reform law of 1996, individuals receiving public assistance are required to obtain employment that will ultimately enable them to become self-sufficient and no longer rely on public assistance.

REFLECTIONS FROM BLACK FEMALES

In 1999, I designed focus groups and invited 12 single-parent Black females to discuss their issues and concerns regarding the new law. The participants were specifically asked to describe how it affected both themselves and their families. The women were chosen from a group of 300 former job readiness, job placement participants enrolled in a federally sponsored program administered through an urban public school system. The women's ages ranged from 18 to 40, with three or more children, little or no education, and a limited work history. The women lived with other family members or on their own. During the planning for the focus groups, one of the women was evicted from her home and was living in a hotel with her three children. Seven women comprised the first focus group.

Among the participants, the average number of children per participant was four, with ages ranging from 16 months to 25 years of age. The youngest participant was 18 years old and the oldest participant was over 40. Based on the data from the study's demographic survey, the average household size was five. The second group had five participants and averaged three children per participant. The children's ages ranged from 19 months to 15 years old. The youngest participant was 18 years old, and the oldest age was between 30 and 39 years of age. The study's participants noted that they were not against the welfare reform law, rather they resented the discriminatory treatment from their self-sufficiency coaches (SSCs). Consensus among the group was that their SSC ignored and disrespected them. The participants also believed the disrespect was a manifestation of societal perceptions that individuals on public assistance are uneducated and lazy.

Although the participants had not achieved high academic literacy levels, they were nonetheless literate in the social contexts that made up their respective environments. More specifically, the women were acutely aware of the negative attitude exhibited by their SSC. Of the 12 participants, six had not obtained a high school diploma or General Equivalency Development diploma (GED), four had obtained high school diplomas, and two had GEDs. Although they felt their SSC did not give them the respect they deserved, they realized that defending their self-respect would result in not receiving their needed assistance. Participant D stated, ". . . SSC treats you like you are stupid." Each woman expressed that she felt her SSC had control over her financial situation (i.e., because the SSC determined whether a client received cash benefits, food stamps, child-care vouchers, and/or emergency funds for furniture and appliances). V explained that the Department of Human Services (DHS) and SSCs were impersonal and provided no support for families. The other participants agreed with her assessment.

The study's data reveal that many of the women were assigned to job readiness programs although their SSC had no knowledge of their employment background, skills, or educational background. Furthermore, the women were not assessed to determine their skill levels and place them in appropriate training programs. Some women had participated in five or more programs, yet they had not secured a job they felt would lead to self-sufficiency. M believed the SSC should show " . . . more compassion, more organization, SSC want you to get a job even if you lack skills and education. Not in sequence should be education first rather than job first." Several training programs were operating much like revolving doors, and these women were repeating programs that provided the same training.

Federally funded training programs were created to train individuals in the skills to obtain employment and, ultimately, become self-sufficient. Depending on the program's goals and objectives, some offered skills training while others focused on job readiness and job placement. The job readiness and job placement programs provided individuals with tools for obtaining a job. Examples of job readiness training included resume development, completing an application, and developing and refining interviewing skills. The program in which I worked operated in an ineffective idealism based on employment first, education second. Unfortunately, we were focused on jobs that for the most part hired females, had poor salaries, and offered little or no benefits. Target employers were fast-food restaurants, nursing homes, hotels, cleaning services, and clerical positions. My initial concern was that the women were placed in organizations that provided no on-the-job training or in positions within organizations that had no growth potential.

As a job coach and career counselor, I targeted such employers as hospitals, colleges/universities, banks, insurance companies, and the judicial system. I maintained that the organizations I targeted would allow the women to become self-sufficient because each job site offered benefits, on-the-job training, and/or tuition reimbursement. In preparation for their placement, I assessed the women's abilities, prior work experiences, work skills, and academic skills. I encouraged those without a high school education to obtain their GED, and I referred them to adult basic literacy programs or academics in the welfare-to work program.

Women on public assistance are referred to work training and placement programs without full assessment of their academic background, work history, and other factors that contribute to job placement. As indicated by D, "SSC are not prepared to direct Ohio Works First (OWF) participants because they are not trained to assess individuals." Furthermore, individuals are not provided an opportunity to choose a program or to gather information about different programs that are available. The women with whom I worked were capable, articulate individuals who knew that to be self-sufficient they needed to improve their academic and work skills. Nevertheless, their self-awareness was never incorporated into the assessment and placement processes.

Individuals who participate in job placement programs but are not successful in obtaining employment or lost their job are referred to other programs with the same objectives, as opposed to programs with a focus specific to their needs. Many welfare recipients do not receive a comprehensive assessment of their skills and abilities because of the system's urgency to move people into the workforce. Consequently, individuals are placed in programs that had a specific employment goal, but they have little or no training in work ethics or work socialization.

Hayes (2000) claimed that social structures shape both our external circumstances and our internal consciousness; being aware of these social forces allows individuals to choose to act in opposition to or in compliance with them. Although the women in the study did not have high academic literacy levels, they undoubtedly had achieved other forms of literacy based on their social contexts such as workplace, community, and home. Academic literacy, it seems, is not the only form of literacy necessary for survival. For example, the women knew that if they responded to their SSCs in a reactive or negative way and were reactive instead of proactive, the consequences could result in the loss of benefits. Consequently, they were passive and acted powerless, thus giving power to their SSC, and this power was manifested in different forms of disrespect. The women's primary goal was to visit their SSC, comply with the rules, and leave with the hope of maintaining some self-respect outside the system's doors.

The women in this study were responsible for supporting their children, therefore they developed skills to communicate with their children's teachers, with doctors, and with social and case workers. Within these social contexts, the women were clearly capable of negotiating within and navigating through their respective systems and to provide for themselves and their children. When necessary, they were equally capable of operating within the welfare system. From conversations with these women, several themes appeared regarding their issues and concerns. The most prevalent concerns were not being heard and not being considered as significant entities in the formation of their futures. These women claimed that their SSC did not relate to them as individuals because of the stereotypes and preconceived assumptions about individuals who receive public assistance.

Some of the study's participants had prior work experience and, therefore had obtained some level of workplace literacy. Hayes (2000) claimed that the nature of the women's work limits their workplace learning and ultimately results in limited formal job training opportunities. If employment opportunities fall outside normal work hours, women often have difficulty participating in related training because of child-care issues and family responsibilities. Much of the training offered to single mothers on assistance is for jobs that are stereotypically female, poorly paid, and have limited opportunities for advancement (e.g., clinical assistant or nurse's aid). Consequently, women may simply opt out of such training (Hayes, 2000). Gowen (1991) found that Black women resisted literacy programs that taught basic skills related to housekeeping jobs, food service, and/or laundry service. The women were not resistant to education, but they wanted curricula that was oriented toward a high school equivalency diploma (Hayes, 2000). Many of the women in my study stated that "education is most important" and "training and education [are] important and . . . goes hand in hand." Others felt that "employment and training on the job" are important. V stated she was concerned that ". . . those with college training have a better chance."

The women who participated in my focus groups had limited work experiences. Seven of the participants reported not having any work experience, and the remaining four reported working as a laundry service worker, nurse's assistant, and restaurant crew worker. One woman reported volunteer experience at an elementary school. The longest work history reported was 7 years as a restaurant crew worker, and the shortest work history was 4 months as a laundry service worker.

My personal experience with navigating the welfare system was discouraging. The only recognition given to me as an individual was my case number. From that point onward, I was always approached and/or recognized only by my case number. When reporting to the Human Services office, I was shuffled from one counter to another and given numerous forms to complete. Never was I asked about prior work skills or work experience, nor was I placed in a work experience activity that allowed me to use any of my skills. I was assigned to work 1 day a week at a community agency doing janitorial duties. It was not until the agency's secretary asked whether I had clerical skills that I was given a typing test, which I passed, and given an opportunity to work in an environment based on my skills.

SOURCES FOR LITERACY DEVELOPMENT

Literacies that are not recognized by the welfare system include those from the home and community. The women with whom I worked had extensive experience as home care providers for their children and other family members and/or for providing services for the elderly in their communities. Some had also gained volunteer experience in schools, community centers, or churches. Although there is little research on women's learning in the home, managing a household requires skills in time management, budgeting, conflict resolution, facilitating and creating learning environments, and home maintenance. Furthermore, single-parent females are likely to have a strong resource base of friends and community advocates. Managing all these levels of interpersonal relationships is the cornerstone for a solid career in any field.

In support of the single, working mother, Hayes (2000) argued that the work of raising children and managing a household requires considerable skills and learning. Also, she continued, the structure of the family determines how and what learning will take place in the home. For example, being a single parent and living on your own, or living in a multigenerational family structure, or contending with changes in the family structure such as a divorce has different consequences. Motherhood is another form of learning that shapes the lens that single women apply to their lives. Although society may view mothering as a natural, fulfilling, and important role for women (Hayes, 2000), it involves the ability to learn how to care for the child. The life of a single woman is complicated by the work of learning to care for a child, and Hayes reminded us that mothering does not necessarily come naturally; it requires considerable learning to be a good mother, and conceptions of what constitutes a good mother vary considerably. A woman's ability to realize her own ideal of mothering and nurturing is usually chiseled out of the contending forces that work, family relations, and social commitments create in her life.

Another important context for women's learning is the community. Historically, Black women have relied on the church for spiritual and social renewal. Today, Black women place a strong value on church involvement. The social interaction involved in church activity helps build self-confidence and a sense of belonging. It is in the church where Black women gain leadership skills through participating in the choir, women's auxiliary clubs, and usher boards. Within these organizations, they increase their social skills and build relationships with other women who are role models. Randolph (1995) believed that church opportunities provide both mother and children opportunities to engage in diverse roles. Also, church-sponsored educational programs give women and children an opportunity to improve their academic skills. Randolph suggested that religious institutions provide family support programs such as child care, recreation, and nonreligious club activities.

RECOMMENDATION

What can adult basic literacy administrators and practitioners as well as literacy and welfare-to-work programs do to recognize various literacy skills in Black, single-parent females? How can administrators and practitioners recognize a client's willingness to participate in programs that will give them self-sufficiency? I recommend that all individuals in job readiness programs undergo comprehensive assessment prior to placement. A Comprehensive Assessment Program (CAP) includes academic tests, barriers to employment inventories, learning disabilities instruments, plus vocation, career, and interest inventories. Tests should also be administered to those who exhibit learning disabilities. To accurately identify learning disabilities, more extensive expert assessment is required to pinpoint the actual disability and to begin appropriate intervention. Following the initial academic tests, individuals who attain the designated math and reading scores should be administered the Official GED Practice Test. Afterward trained, professional counselors and examiners would then conduct 1- or 1/2-hour interviews with each participant and prepare summary reports for the client and for the SSC. The reports would also include recommendations for program placement that would meet the participants' needs.

The objective of CAP is to reveal any issues that can inhibit individuals from being successful in pursuing employment, and in obtaining and retaining employment. Additionally, appropriately assigning clients ensures matching individuals with a pertinent job readiness and job placement programs. More important, CAP can help empower individuals to make internal self-improvements. In addition to program placement, it is vital to keep participants involved in the development of important goals so they become motivated and vested in their journey. Some researchers (Dickerson, Hillman, & Foster, 1995) contended that empowerment consists of

> . . . having the specific resources that are required to make, pursue, and achieve informed life choices and encompasses a process that includes (a) gaining some control over one's life by taking part with others in the development of activities and structures that allow increased involvement in mat-

ters which directly affect all involved and (b) access to power— the power to do with others rather than power to wield over others.

CONCLUSION

The welfare reform law of 1996 has some positive objectives; however, to meet those objectives and adequately serve clients, the welfare system must acknowledge and recognize the literacies of women who receive welfare benefits. Although caseworkers are overworked and have high case loads, they must be required to recognize and respect the people they serve. Furthermore, as job readiness and job placement programs are created to provide services for welfare-to-work clients, they need to implement a process that will enable them to learn about their clients' needs, experiences, and skills and to implement programs that will meet individual client needs. Dickerson (cited in Billingsley, 1990) informed us that reform must come from within the people and that successful reform cannot be based on people's weaknesses; it must be based on their strengths. Within that context, the most important component of a successful welfare-to-work program is to acknowledge the various literacies inherent within the individual and to understand often occurs outside the formal educational environment.

I began this chapter with my own personal journey within the welfare system. Since that time, I have worked in various organizations that provided on-the-job-training, educational support (e.g., college tuition waivers and reimbursement, as well as professional development activities), and financial assistance so that I could provide for my child. While on this journey, I earned four degrees (an associate, bachelor's, and two master's degrees), and I am pursuing a doctorate degree in curriculum and instruction. I chose a terminal degree in curriculum and instruction because I thought it was an ideal way to meld my Master of Education in Adult Learning and Development and my Master of Psychology and Diversity Management training and to conduct research designed to create programs that address adult needs.

I raised my child as a single parent and she is now a productive citizen who contributes to our society. I now work in adult literacy, and I am happy to contribute to the uplifting and empowerment of those individuals. I work to serve adults who are more likely marginalized because of difficult life situations. I want to create programs that celebrate and encourage success. The lesson I have learned through my personal experience and through the voices of the women in this study is: Welfare is a means to an improved quality of life, not the means to living a barely fulfilling existence. Through personal experience, I have also learned that we should take more time and care in the way we address issues that concern people. Furthermore, we should not make assumptions based on labels that are assigned to strangers. Rather, we should assess individual situations and learn from those who strive to elicit change.

REFERENCES

Angelou, M. (1993). *Wouldn't take nothing for my journey now*. New York: Random House.

Billingsley, A. (1993). *Climbing Jackob's ladder: The enduring legacy of African American families*. New York: Simon & Schuster.

Cammison, A. M. (2001). Race and welfare in United States social history [Review of the books *Race, money and the American welfare state* and *Shifting the color line: Race and the American welfare state*]. *Journal of Policy History*, 288-292.

Dickerson, B. J. (1995). Gender, poverty, culture, and economy: Theorizing female-led families. In B. J. Dickerson (Ed.), *African American single Mothers: Understanding their lives and families* (pp. 164-178). Thousand Oaks, CA: Sage.

Dickerson, B. J., Foster, J. E., & Hillman, P. L. (1995). Empowerment through the "ordinary" knowledge/scholarship/policy nexus. In B. J. Dickerson (Ed.), *African American single mothers: Understanding their lives and families* (pp. 164-178). Thousand Oaks, CA: Sage Publications.

Gowen, S. G. (1991). *The politics of workplace literacy: A case study*. New York: Teachers College Press.

Hayes, E. (2000). Social contexts. In E. Hayes & D. D. Flannery (Eds.), *Women as learners: The significance of gender in adult learning* (pp. 23-52). San Francisco: Jossey-Bass.

hooks, b. (1993). *Sisters of the yam: Black women and self-recovery*. Boston: South End Press.

O'Connor, B. (2002). Policies, principles, and polls: Bill Clinton's third way welfare politics 1992-1996. *Australian Journal of Politics and History*, *48*(3), 396-411.

Randolph, S. M. (1995). African American children in single-mother families. In B. J. Dickerson (Ed.), *African American single mothers: Understanding their lives and families* (pp. 164-178). Thousand Oaks, CA: Sage.

Sparks, B. (1999). Critical issues and dilemmas for adult literacy programs under welfare reform. In J. C. Fisher & L. G. Martin (Eds.), *New directions for adult and continuing education: The welfare-to-work challenge*. San Francisco: Jossey-Bass.

3

Unearthing Hidden Literacy: Seven Lessons I Learned in a Cotton Field

Lillie Gayle Smith

On a sweltering day in August 1963, my mother told my brother and me that he and I would not go to our aunt's field to pick cotton as we usually did. Instead she said that we would stay with her to watch "an important national event" on our new TV. Over the years, I have often recalled scenes from the March on Washington as well as words from Dr. King's "I Have a Dream" speech with pride and joy. However, it took over 40 years before I discovered and began to value the lessons I learned from the inglorious job of picking cotton during the summers of my childhood.

During the fall 2003 semester, I took a graduate class called "Black Women's Literacy." The course explored multiple definitions, theories, and constructs of literacy as they occurred in literature, research, and the lives of Black women throughout the Diaspora. The instructor, other students, and assigned readings helped me unearth how I had come to know and apply certain truths about life. Toward the end of the course, I realized, somewhat to my surprise, that one of the places that contributed much to my earliest ways of knowing was none other than a cotton field in Alabama's Black Belt. Before the "Black Women's Literacy" class, having picked cotton was something I wanted to forget, not extrapolate lessons from. I saw certainly little, if any, value in sharing it with folks at the academy, unless it was to illustrate or boast about how far I had come. Before, more than anything, having picked cotton was a memory that incensed me because it was a job my people inherited from slavery—the bitter legacy that continues to haunt all Americans, especially those who are African American. Before, having picked cotton was not an experience I would have wished to interrogate because I did not have a framework for analysis, a vehicle for validation, or a mindset receptive to discovering the positives that came from what I had perceived as a completely negative experience.

In an effort to explain how the class led me to unearth and then celebrate lessons that had lain dormant for four decades, I begin with a discussion of several theories on women's learning and how they were reflected in the "Black Women's Literacy" course, the experience conducive to my journey of "discovery." The second section focuses on the negative work history of African-American women and the positive attributes it may have engendered in them today. In the final section, I discuss the seven lessons I learned, at least to some degree, while picking cotton.

Locating my experiences within the context of women's studies proved an empowering step in my journey to reclaim and reassign those experiences. *Women's Ways of Knowing* stressed the importance of instructors confirming women as students who bring knowledge to the classroom. Recognizing women as *knowers* dictates that teachers serve in less authoritative roles and become more like coaches or allies in the learning process. In the "Black Women's Literacy" course, the professor and students, a group of diverse women, provided a safe community that respected and validated knowledge acquired beyond the walls of the academy. Unlike many educators who revel in being the sage on the stage, the professor was comfortable and sagacious enough to be the guide on the side, one who respected students as knowers as well as learners. As a result, the students poured forth their knowledge and how they had come to know.

My feelings and those voiced by my classmates mirrored Belenky, Clinchy, Goldberger, and Tarule's (1997) observation that women prefer a teacher who helps them "articulate and expand their latent knowledge" and assists them "in giving birth to their own ideas, in making their own tacit knowledge explicit and elaborating to who is, in fact, the 'midwife teacher'" (p. 217). Without a midwife teacher, one who acknowledged me as knower, I would not have disturbed my comfort with memories of repetitive, back-breaking work, which means that I would have ultimately denied myself the awakening that comes only from more fully understanding significant life experiences.

In *Women's Ways of Knowing*, Belenky and her colleagues (1997) discussed how women use their firsthand out-of-school experiences as sources of truth for knowledge that is real and valued. These scholars also explain the importance of teachers validating such experiences because women regard them as their most important learning. According to these researchers, women find concepts useful in making sense of their experiences, but they are opposed to abstractions when they "preceded the experiences or pushed them out entirely"

(p. 201). In "Black Women's Literacy," the professor and students validated what we knew and how we had come to know it, which challenged us to engage in more critical and meaningful dialogue about theories presented throughout the course, and such validation even made it easier to speak to those theories that contradicted our experiences.

All educators must constantly question their philosophies and practices and the implications they have for each student's success. Given the history of gender inequities, they must be especially vigilant as to how their classroom attitudes and activities may impede female students. Hayes, Flannery, Brooks, Tisdell, and Hugo (2000) reported that "resistance to demeaning approaches to education can be found among women at all levels of education" (p. 67). Although instructors may be oblivious to demeaning practices, many female students are acutely aware of them, often employing a number of resistance strategies consciously or unconsciously.

For example, the most striking examples of women's resistance I have observed probably occurred in a graduate course where the professor, a male, had students work problems in class. Whenever a male gave an answer, the instructor accepted it as gospel and complemented the man's accuracy or quick response. However, if a female student answered, the instructor said nothing to validate her response and would then ask a male student to confirm it. During our all-female study sessions, women complained about the instructor's gender preference, but no one approached him about it. In response, many women stopped asking questions and volunteering answers during class. Even more alarming, a large number of them, despite their maturity and graduate status, simply dropped the course. Although the women's actions first seemed self-defeating, I now see them as forms of resistance to an educational setting where they felt demeaned and devalued as learners. In contrast, the members of the "Black Women's Literacy" class stated that it had challenged, inspired, and empowered them to the extent that they wanted a follow-up course.

In addition to receiving validation and respect from the teacher, students need to respect and validate their teachers in return for optimum learning to occur. For Black women, the teacher's level of experience is especially important because it validates what the instructor has to say. According to Collins (1991), Black women regard what one has lived as a major criterion for evaluating expertise; this perspective renders personal experience more valuable than knowledge acquired through formal schooling. Although any knowledgeable professor, regardless of gender or ethnicity, could have taught "Black Women's Literacy," having an instructor who was a Black woman of the Diaspora gave greater authenticity to her voice, yielding greater validation among the students.

In addition to exploring theoretical works pertaining to how women learn, the 'Black Women's Literacy" class employed a number of literary works, which further helped me analyze my experiences. One of the novels, *Nervous Conditions* (Dangaremba, 1988), is set in Zimbabwe; it features a young heroine whose choices in life are rigidly circumscribed because she is poor, Black, and female. As captivating as the girl's journey is, the multiple literacies the older women in her life demonstrate proved more compelling to me. When and how did they learn to survive in such a racist, gendered, and class-oriented society? What kinds of literacies had they mastered to make their lives work? How did these women evaluate the success of their efforts? How did they find safe harbor in a sea littered with broken dreams? How and where did my own life as a Black female growing up in Civil Rights Era America intersect with theirs? Where are those intersecting points now? Through this novel, I developed a deeper appreciation of the complex cultural, interpersonal, and other nonacademic knowledge these women, if not all women, including contemporary ones, need in order to navigate the restrictive space and place society assigns them.

Another novel the class examined was Merle Hodge's (1970) *Crick Crack Monkey*, which highlighted similar tensions that Black girls encounter in their quest for formal literacy. Set in Trinidad, *Crick Crack Monkey* recounts the oppressive environment the young heroine must contend with in her quest for academic literacy. This book also speaks about the multiple literacies, outside of school, that Black women must acquire to survive as raced, classed, and gendered beings in a society that devalues each of these characteristics.

During our exploration of the texts, it was obvious how they paralleled some of the nonacademic survival literacies I acquired during my formative years. One of the most critical for me as a Black girl centered on learning how to navigate the delicate, restrictive space where race, gender, and class intersected in America's Jim Crow South because the message the larger society communicated to me was not what I wanted to hear or accept. Like my young sisters in the novels, I needed to find places where my dreams would be nurtured and my spirit would be fed even if it meant I had to leave the comfort of the familiar.

As I examined the research, analyzed literary works, and listened to stories that my classmates and professor shared, I began to think more deeply about those life experiences that had contributed to my current ways of knowing. Where, other than in my family or at church, had defining experiences occurred? What happened before or during my early years of formal schooling? Because Alabama did not provide kindergarten in those days, the once-popular book *All I Really Need to Know I Learned in Kindergarten* (Fulghum, 1988) offered no point of reference, so I was forced to looked beyond the classroom.

Immersed in "Black Women's Literacy," I sought to revisit and rethink those places that had contributed to the metaphysical, epistemological, and axiological foundations of my philosophy today. In something akin to an epiphany, my search led me back to ages 5 to 12 and to the cotton field where I worked for many summers. Having discovered the location, I began to excavate the lessons learned, and I decided that I needed to write about the experience for clearer understanding and greater validation. Moreover, I needed to take a risk and share my journey with others. As Brooks pointed out (cited in Hayes et al., 2000), "for subjugated groups that are only newly articulating their knowledge, the movement from inchoate, deeply private, silenced knowledge to public performance is an act of great courage," and "they are issues of power" (p. 130). Strengthened by such comments and the safe, supportive environment of the class, I chose to perform my journey and the lessons it taught through the public and private act of writing.

The notion of *going public* intrigued and motivated me because it further validated an experience I had come not only to recall, but value decades after its occurrence. Considering the possibility of sharing my discovery, I hoped that others, especially women and people of color, could likewise interrogate their experiences, even those they had forgotten or wished they had forgotten for hidden sources of comfort, clarity, and fortitude.

One of the experiences this nation would rather forget, although it continues to haunt America today, is the immoral institution of slavery. During the centuries of slavery, Black Africans were brought to this nation sometimes for the express purpose of picking cotton. Arguably no job in the annals of American history has rested lower on the menial-labor ladder than that of picking cotton. *Drudgery* and *back breaking* are two words always associated with it, and the dominant picture in many minds remains one of Black slaves laboring in plantation fields from sunup to sundown.

Although many jobs deemed difficult and undesirable have been historically limited to males, picking cotton has always been gender-equitable. Black women were forced to toil in the fields as long and hard as their men—a fact that seems to have implications for our lives today. Hayes et al. (2000) stated that, due to the interrelationships of race, gender, and identity, Black women have not been expected to adhere to the dominant culture's stereotype of femininity, and they referenced Brown-Collins and Sussewell (1986), who contended that because slave women were exploited, they developed greater independence and self-reliance than their nonslave counterparts.

To what extent and why do contemporary Black women manifest independence, self-reliance, and survival skills in response to historically negative, socially imposed roles? These and similar questions need to be investigated further because such skills impact how individuals and groups construct their identities and conduct their lives. According to the American Association of University Women, Black girls retain a high degree of self-esteem in high school, unlike their White and Hispanic counterparts who lose theirs throughout the school years. Edmonson and Nkomo (1998) asserted that Black females develop armor that is a protective buffer against racism, thus enabling them to transcend the negative messages of a racist society.

Considering the historic, negative status of Black American females, sources of their positive self-identity need to be examined for greater understanding and possible implications for females of other ethnicities who suffer low self-esteem. For example, the media and popular culture, from rap songs to magazine articles, show African-American teenage girls as heavier, yet content with their weight even when it exceeds medically established or culturally desired norms. By contrast, Euro-American girls, even thin ones, are often reported as being unhappy with their weight, and they are more likely to engage in life-threatening behaviors such as becoming anorexic, practicing bulimia, or smoking cigarettes to keep their weight down. How can these White weight-obsessed teens become more like their Black counterparts and become more independent of or resistant to the cultural messages that dictate thin at any cost?

That many African-American women continue to be engaged in hard, low-paying work is hardly news given the ways our nation has mistreated people of color as well as females. Marginalized and stigmatized in society through the triple realities of race, class, and gender, Black women have historically been stereotyped, misrepresented, or omitted in scholarly investigation, so the centrality of work to their lives is rarely examined. One book that does offer an interdisciplinary perspective is *Sister Circle: Black Women and Work* (Brown-Collins & Sussewell, 1986), which shows the panoply of Black women working in different historical and contemporary contexts. As the editor Shirley Harley (2002) pointed out in the introduction, "Work brings pain as well as joy, personal satisfaction as well as anguish, economic success as well as continued poverty, and sometimes all at the same time" (p. xvi). Following emancipation and well into the 20th century with the advent of sharecropping throughout the South, many Black women were limited to defining work, at least in part, as picking cotton. Until the "Black Women's Literacy" course, I had packed away images of me picking cotton into the recesses of my memory. However, that class somehow kept peeling away the layers, the way the fog would lift from the hollow my brother and I walked years ago to reveal a fresh world bathed in the morning dew.

The cotton field I worked belonged to my aunt who lived next door, about an eighth of a mile away. She, her husband, and the youngest of their children resided in an antebellum mansion left over from another place and time. According to tradition, the original owner, a Confederate captain, built it on the highest hill in our community so he and his family could overlook hundreds of acres and an equal number of people stolen into slavery. The mansion had approximately 6,000 square feet, two stories, and two apartments—easily the grandest and most spacious residence for miles. Twelve-foot ceilings, a 70-foot wrap-around porch, and a covered deck from the house to the well were a few of its features. To that once-palatial estate, which had grayed and become rickety over the years, my brother and I reported for work each morning.

During the late summers of my youth, 10 to 12 people picked cotton in my aunt's field, varying between six to eight adults and four to six children. Most of the grownups, all women except for two or three men, had lived through the Great Depression and the Great War (World War II) and spent all their lives enduring the strange career of Jim Crow. As such they had survived much. They were denied the right to vote and cheated out of decent wages. They lived on the lumber company's land and lost disputed bills at the company store.

Following the cultural norms, they tipped their hats and entered the back doors of White homes. If they were blessed to receive an education, they walked miles to dilapidated schools without books and blackboards.

My mother was a school teacher in the segregated schools of the South. Because we lived in the smallest of hamlets with many relatives close by, there were few things for young children to do besides play, read, learn from older family members, and watch TV. We had an abundance of the first three, but we did not have a TV to dampen our imaginations and send us faraway messages from Hollywood or New York. We did not have a TV because my mother had refused to buy one; she said she did not want my brother and me to look at White people on a black-and-white screen. At that time, the CBS Mississippi affiliate, the only station that reached our viewing area, would preempt any program that showed a Black person. In response, my mother was staging an effective boycott against the station, at least in our home. She purchased a TV set only when she learned that the civil rights movement was being sufficiently televised. Realizing the limited entertainment and educational options and knowing that my aunt's child and grandchild, both around our ages, were already working in the fields, my mother decided that my brother and I should do likewise. In retrospect, I believe she also knew that picking cotton would provide us a wealth of learning experiences.

Carol Gilligan (1982) advanced a theory about women being connected, which in essence says that a woman identifies herself based on her relationships with others. In the cotton field of my youth, I experienced and observed a spirit of community that enabled me to relate with each of its members. Elders helped everyone with tasks, shared stories, and encouraged others to deal with whatever problems life presented. The elders also took responsibility for teaching the youngsters, making sure we stayed safe, keeping us out of trouble, and sharing with us. As such this field community was characterized by caring, respect, and helping. In that kind of safe, connected place, it seemed only natural for me to feel part of the adult world as well as the children's, kin to family as well as those who were of no relation, and comfortable with those who had some formal education as well as those who had none. In some way and to some degree, I felt connected to everyone there.

My sense of being connected to a diverse human family continues to impact my life in many ways. For example, in the summer of 1998, I volunteered to teach in an English language immersion program in Warsaw, Poland. During my 5-week sojourn, there were a few days when I felt completely isolated, as if I were the only Black person on the European continent. Most of the time, however, I felt so deeply connected to my students and the other teachers that I had no doubts we were all members of the same family, regardless of color, language, or cultural differences. It is likely that I took the first steps on my journey to Poland down the rows of a cotton field.

The elders working in the cotton field acknowledged the existence and power of a higher being. Through this spiritual presence, they gained a sense of balance, a kind of peace, and an order in their lives that, at the time and under the conditions, seemed incomprehensible. Apparently guided by an unseen hand, they rested in an assurance that their lives had purpose and connections to some things much greater than the limits visible to the naked eye. Highly religious, this little band of believers prayed often, giving thanks for their meager sustenance and for making it through the trials and tribulations of their daily lives.

At times the elders sang. An observation that Robin D. G. Kelley (1993) made about Black North Carolina tobacco factory workers seems to capture the essence of their choral moments. "Singing in unison not only reinforced a sense of collective identity," but the songs—most often religious hymns—ranged from veiled protests against the daily indignities "to utopian visions of a life free of difficult wage work" (pp. 75-112).

Despite the dreary conditions of picking cotton, the people were infused with hope. They envisioned a life beyond the field and their present circumstances, so theirs was not an exhibition of despair or nihilism. They charged us, the children, to take advantage of education and to use it to make our lives better than theirs. In education, they saw possibilities for us they knew they could never have realized for themselves. They envisioned freedom they could not behold. They believed that education was a gift and did so many things to prime us for its acceptance. They motivated us to do well in school through requests to see our report cards, money for good grades, and even quizzes to test our skills in areas such as spelling and multiplication.

Because my days in the field occurred less than a decade after the Supreme Court's *Brown v. the Board of Education* ruling in 1954 and the 1955 Montgomery Bus Boycott, the hope I saw in the elders was rooted in the changes they saw as imminent through the civil rights movement, of which they would all play a part in some way. During those years, I remember that they opened their church up as the first local site for "rallies," boycotted stores in the nearby town, marched in demonstrations, and registered to vote before their neighbors did, a few marking their signatures with their X.

The elders' hope also stemmed from their taking agency in the struggle against the oppression that constituted their world. They became engaged in *infrapolitics*—a term Kelley used "to describe the daily confrontations, evasive actions and stifled thoughts that often inform organized political movements. . . . For Southern Blacks in the age of Jim Crow, politics was not separate from lived experience or the imagined world of what is possible." Bathed in infrapolitics, the adults' conversations in the field confirmed that their righteous anger against the system was much more complex than what they led the oppressor to believe. For them, saying a polite "yassir" or entering a back door was not necessarily an action without later comment or cost to the oppressor. As Kelley stated, "the appearance of silence and accommodation was not only deceiving but frequently intended to deceive." Field commentary suggested that some of their hope and esteem was rooted in a culture of resistance they created and modified in the face of Jim Crow. They may have sat on the back of the bus, but not until they "accidentally" bumped into a White passenger. They may have lost the dispute over a credit account, but they no longer shopped there or advised others not to charge anything at that store; they may have been forced to tip their hats, but they muttered a silent barrage of cuss words to accompany a feigned, culturally imposed courtesy.

Everyone has a story, but the elder workers had incredible life experiences that they were willing to share with anyone who was willing to listen. Their stories entertained, challenged, sometimes frightened, but always enthralled me. They told of jilted lovers who got blood-stained revenge, clever kin people who had duped racist Whites, and relatives up North who had secured high-paying jobs. Because one of our family cemeteries abutted the northwest corner of the field, a disproportionately high percentage of the stories centered on who had died, when, where, and under what gruesome circumstances. However, most troubling were their hushed, fragmented comments about local "boys" who returned home during the war, their minds gassed senseless while in the service. Perhaps their stories were so chilling because I had seen all of those "boys," by then old men, who sat staring on front steps or walked around houses while babbling incoherent phrases.

Axiology is the branch of philosophy that seeks to answer questions about the nature of values. As such it encompasses aesthetics, which relates to how one defines and sees beauty and nature. I find that my experiences in the cotton field contributed to my ways of recognizing and interpreting the beauty of nature. Admittedly, a cotton field does not inspire the same kind of awe as the Rocky Mountains, the Grand Canyon, or Niagara Falls, but on reflection I remember it as a place filled with examples of nature's muted majesty. Today fragments of memories flit through my mind: the coolness of sparkling dew on the morning grass, the bleeding orange and red hues of sunset, a breeze whispering on a sweaty face, the taste of ice water freezing a parched throat. I recall a cloud passing over to offer a few seconds of shade from an angry afternoon sun, the smell of honey suckle brown and morning glory, the sounds of whip-poorwills in the distance, finding a full ripe blackberry bush at the end of a row. I can still taste overripe fat figs just before they splat off the branches and onto the ground. Memory allows me to see the colors and textures of beige sand, black post oak, and red clay as well as soft fluffy white cotton set in a hard green pointed boll.

In his 1985 Atlantic Exposition Address, Booker T. Washington said "that there is as much dignity in tilling a field as in writing a poem" (Gates & Oliver, 1999). A strong work ethic was one of the lessons that I pulled from my experiences working in the field. Rising early, being on time, doing a commendable job, accepting a challenge, completing a task, and working with others are just a few of the values I learned during my early years. These habits have sustained me throughout my personal life and my career in education from first grade to teaching to graduate school.

My mother also decided that working in the field was a good way to teach me the value of a dollar. To that end, she doubled every dollar I made, let me spend some of it for whatever I chose, and made me take some to the bank to deposit it. To a little country girl, all of these sounded like important grownup activities that would allow me to make decisions about spending money. From the beginning, I set aside money for buying clothes, toys, and candy. As I grew older, I saved for school supplies, even textbooks, which all little *colored* children had to buy once we reached sixth grade. Looking back at those times, I now realize that delayed gratification, saving, and budgeting were other lessons I carried from the cotton field.

Unearthing memories of picking cotton and extrapolating lessons from the experience constitute two highlights of my graduate studies because the journey of discovery has led me to a deeper appreciation and understanding of past experiences and present perspectives. What I saw as a negative experience I now recognize as one that had a positive and profound impact on the way I view myself, others, and the world, both seen and unseen. Given the distance and difficulty of those days in the cotton field, I believe my retrieval, analysis, and subsequent reclamation of them could have occurred only through the guidance of scholarly literature and a supportive class. In short, what I rediscovered in the cotton field of my youth is yet another testimony to the power of literacies learned beyond the classroom.

REFERENCES

American Association of University Women. (1992). *The AAUW report: How schools shortchange girls*. Washington, DC: AAUW Educational Foundation.

Belenky, M. F., Clinchy, B. M., Goldberger, N. R., & Tarule, J. M. (1997). *Women's ways of knowing: The development of self, voice, and mind*. New York: Basic Books.

Brown-Collins, A. R., & Sussewell, D. R. (1986). The African-American woman's emerging selves. *Journal of Black Psychology, 13*, 1-11.

Collins, P. H. (1990). *Black feminist thought: Knowledge, consciousness, and the politics of empowerment*. New York: Routledge.

Dangaremba, T. (1988). *Nervous conditions*. New York: Seal Press.

Edmonson, E. L. J., & Nkomo, S. M. (1998). Armoring: Learning to withstand racial oppression. *Journal of Comparative Family Studies, 29*(2), 285-295.

Fulghum, R. (1988). *All I really need to know I learned in kindergarten: Uncommon thoughts on common things*. New York: Ballantine.

Gates, H. L., & Oliver, T. H. (Eds.). (1999). *The souls of Black folk*. New York: W.W. Norton.

Gilligan, C. (1982). *In a different voice: Psychology theory and women's development*. Cambridge, MA: Harvard University Press.

Hayes, E., Flannery, D. D., Brooks, A. K., Tisdell, E. J., & Hugo, J. M. (2002). *Women as learners: The significance of gender in adult learning*. San Francisco: Jossey-Bass.

Hodge, M. (1970). *Crick crack monkey*. Portsmouth, NH: Heinemann Educational Publishers.

Kelley, R. D. G. (1993, June). We are not what we seem: Rethinking Black working-class opposition in the Jim Crow South. *Journal of American History*, pp. 75-112.

4

Voices of Our Foremothers: Celebrating the Legacy of African-American Women Educators

A Personal Dedication

Sunny-Marie Birney

PART 1: LAYING THE FOREGROUND

All my life I felt I was a motherless child. I was adopted at the age of 2, and I felt I belonged nowhere. With no memories of my African-American mother, I felt out of place, alone, and without value. Similar to the unknown author of the negro spiritual *Motherless Child*, I too found myself "a long way from home." My adopted parents, two people of Euro-American descent, were wonderful people, but I always felt that a piece of me was missing. This feeling pervaded my psyche for 18 years. It was not until I went to college at the College of Wooster in Wooster, Ohio, that I began my journey home. I majored in Psychology and Black Studies, which became a time of cultural and spiritual awakening that was the catalyst for my life-long commitment to education in the African-American community. During my 4 years at Wooster, I decided I would become a teacher and assist in the educational preparation of young African-American students.

While at Wooster, I took courses about African-American women from three African-American female professors—Drs. Susan Frazier-Kouassi, Yvonne Williams, and Mary Young. These women made a lasting impression on my life. Although I had four African-American women teachers in elementary, middle, and high school who also impacted my life, it was my college professors who helped me connect my academic knowledge to a broader world and understand the dynamics of my ever-changing place within that world.

Freire (1970, 2000) referred to such phenomenon as problem-posing education:

> Problem-posing education involves a constant unveiling of reality. [It] affirms men and women as beings in the process of becoming—as unfinished, uncompleted beings in and with a likewise unfinished reality. Problem-posing education is revolutionary futurity. Hence, it is prophetic (and as such, hopeful). Hence it corresponds to the historical nature of humankind. Hence, it affirms women and men as beings who transcend themselves, who move forward and look ahead . . . an historical movement . . . a deepened consciousness of their situation leads people to apprehend that situation as an historical reality susceptible of transformation. (pp. 81, 84-86)

My professors modeled not just exemplary teaching, but also a commitment that uplifted and helped transform myself and, in turn, the African-American community. The fact that they were Black women teaching literature, psychology, and contemporary issues from a Black woman's perspective touched me. Perhaps the most important thing that I learned from my Black female teachers was that they cared about me. They cared not only about my academic work and the adjustments I was making at the collegiate level, but they were concerned overall with my mind, body, and spirit, past, present, and future.

These women teachers cared about me and held the same expectations for me as they had for their own children. In her article, "The Education of Children Whose Nightmare Come Both Day and Night," Jacqueline Jordan Irvine (1999) found that the African-American teachers in her study understood the power of caring. Irvine uncovered this caring aspect in Black teachers through an analysis of statements from students:

> Students said they liked school and performed their best when they thought that teachers cared for them. . . . Students said teachers cared when they laughed with them, trusted and respected them, and recognized them as individuals. Students defined caring teachers as those who set limits, provided structure, had high expectations, and pushed them to achieve. (p. 249)

My professors became my mothers away from home, and the academy became my "home away from home" (Gay, 2000, p. 47). Such a phenomenon is known as "other mothering"[1] and is characteristic of African-American teachers. Beauboeuf-Lafontant (2002) reported that Black teachers view "mothering as a communal responsibility" (p. 76) and an act of service. My teachers filled a void I had searched to fill all of my life. It was their presence in my life that inspired me to respond to a sacred calling to become a teacher.

It is the legacy of caring, commitment, and cultural uplifting that I celebrate in the lives of African-American women educators who came before me. I stand on the shoulders of countless visionaries knowing that I follow a path deeply rooted in a rich history of excellence, and I dedicate this chapter to those women who made it possible for me to envision a dream—a dream inspired by our Creator, a dream to build schools throughout the African Diaspora.

PART 2: THE ART OF SERVICE

Education as the Practice of Freedom (hooks, 1994) and *Teaching as a Sacred Calling* (Irvine, 1999)

Carter G. Woodson (1933, 1977) defined *service* in terms of the responsibilities of the public servant within the African-American community, "The real servant of the people, then, will give more attention to those to be served . . ." (p. 131). Woodson continues:

> The servant of the people is down among them, living as they live, doing what they do and enjoying what they enjoy. He may be a little better informed than some other members of the group; it may be that he has had some experience that they have not had, but in spite of this advantage he should have more humility than those whom he serves, for we are told, "Whosoever is greatest among you, let him be your servant." (p. 131)

In the prior passages, Woodson described the role of servant as did Jesus when explaining to his disciples that the greatest is the one who is the servant. Such beliefs are the very elements that distinguish true teaching as an art of service. Although a teacher "has had some experience that they [the students] have not had" (p. 131), she must present information in such a way that students can verbally express themselves and become intrinsically empowered, resulting in a cocreative, reciprocal partnership between student and teacher. Such collabora-

---

[1]Beauboeuf-Lafontant (2002), Irving (1999), and Case (1997).

tion is beneficial to both teacher and student. Freire (1970, 2000) illustrated this point by saying:

> . . . [O]nly through communication can human life hold meaning. The teacher's thinking is authenticated only by the authenticity of the students' thinking. The teacher cannot think for her students, nor can she impose her thought on them. Authentic thinking, thinking that is concerned about *reality,* does not take place in the ivory tower isolation, but only in communication. (p. 77)

Freire named this form of education *liberation education*—an education for the practice of freedom. "Liberation education consists of acts of cognition, not transferals of information. It is a learning situation in which the cognizable object intermediates the cognitive actors-teacher on the one hand and students on the other" (p. 79).

In the same light as Freire, bell hooks (1994) in her book, *Teaching to Transgress,* described the true essence of education as being a "practice of freedom" and a "sacred vocation," in that it invokes a collective relationship between learners and educators. She asserted this notion in the following passage:

> To educate as the practice of freedom is a way of teaching that anyone can learn. That learning process comes easiest to those of us who also believe that there is an aspect of our vocation that is sacred; who believe that our work is not merely to share information but to share in the intellectual and spiritual growth of our students. To teach in a manner that respects and cares for the souls of our students is essential if we are to provide the necessary conditions where learning can most deeply and intimately begin. (p. 13)

hooks further stated:

> . . . learning is where paradise can be created. The classroom, with all its limitations, remains a location of possibility. In the field of possibility we have the opportunity to labor for freedom, . . . an openness of mind and heart that allow us to face reality even as we collectively imagine ways to move beyond boundaries, to transgress. This is education as the practice of freedom. (p. 207)

On every level, reflecting on my own educational experiences, I can identify with the assertions made by Freire and hooks. The African-American women teachers and professors who I had—in elementary, middle, high school, and in colleges—exhibited a profound understanding that education was less about the regurgitation of information and had much more to do with how I was able to expand my mind and heart. They also displayed a true commitment to education as a sacred vocation. My choir teacher, Mrs. Jessie Reeder, for instance, was especially cognizant of her work as being a calling. Because she taught music, Mrs. Reeder had the flexibility to incorporate Church music into her curriculum. She introduced her students to an array of musical traditions such as Gospel, Spirituals, and traditional sacred music, which we sang in Latin, Italian, and Greek. At least two thirds of the songs we performed during our concerts were songs that spoke to the goodness and righteousness of God.

On my graduation from high school, this same teacher sent me on my way with a book bag depicting four African women, and I use it to this day! Mrs. Reeder instilled in me the understanding that music education was more than the songs she taught and the musical theory behind the songs. She was able to connect with me, one African-American sister to another, and she is forever etched in my heart for the creative art of service she provided.

PART 3: THE FOREMOTHERS: CARRYING THE TORCH

Emma Wilson, Lucy Laney, and Mary McLeod Bethune

African-American women throughout U.S. history have impacted the lives of Black children and adults by establishing independent schools, church-affiliated Sabbath schools, and/or teaching in schools supported by Black and White philanthropic groups.[2] Additionally, Black women formed clubs such as the National Federation of Afro-American Women and the Phillis Wheatley Association to address the educational needs of the African-American community. Black women particularly advocated formal education for Black women (Lerner, 1972, 1994).

The legacy of Black educational excellence and determination that passed down through foremothers such as Mary Church Terrell, Marie Becraft, Anna Julia Cooper, Catherine Ferguson, and Elizabeth Wright serve as a reminder for me that nothing is impossible. The most significant fact that I found during my research on these educators was the relationship between teachers such as Emma Wilson, Lucy Laney, and Mary McLeod Bethune. This connection solidifies the prophetic sacredness of the educational process that Freire (1970, 2000), hooks (1994), and Irvine (1999) documented in their writings. The relationship among these women is an example of womanist pedagogy (Beauboeuf-Lafontant, 2002), friendship, mentorship, and sisterhood.

A womanist pedagogy embodies three principles: (a) oppression is an interlocking system, (b) individual empowerment combined with collective action is the key to lasting social transformation, and (c) the concept of humanism—the notion that liberation is for self and all human beings.

---

[2]Lerner (1994, 1972), Halasa (1989), Giddings (1984), Collins and Tamarkin (1990), and Salley (1993).

Emma Wilson was the founder of the Mayesville Industrial Institute in Mayesville, South Carolina, in 1882. This educator is a symbol of the womanist tradition. Her institute, like many of the Sabbath schools, provided academic, cultural, and spiritual studies for its pupils. It was this Institute that the 7-year-old Mary McLeod attended for her elementary school. Later, after graduating from the Moody Bible College in 1895, Mary moved back to Mayesville and accepted an assistantship with her former teacher, Emma Wilson, at the Mayesville Industrial Institute.

The following year, 1896, Mary obtained a full-time teaching position at the Haines Institute in Augusta, Georgia, founded by Lucy Laney. While teaching at Haines, a vision to build her own school became clearer in Mary's mind. In 1904, she opened the doors to her own school, The Daytona Normal and Industrial Institute for Negro Girls. She would later go on to start Bethune-Cookman College, a Historically Black College, develop grassroot community-based educational facilities, and serve as Director of the National Youth Administration in President Franklin D. Roosevelt's cabinet.

The pedagogy implemented by Bethune, the educational foremothers, and many contemporary African-American women educators is described by Beauboeuf-Lafontant (2002) as a womansist philosophy. My foremothers, the African-American teachers and professors whom I have had throughout my educational journey have incorporated these three characteristics summarized by Beauboeuf-Lafontant (2002). It was not just the facts that they wanted their students to remember, but rather the facts applied within a broader context to transform and change societal systems and world institutions. For these women, academic literacy was seen as the means to the end, not an end in itself. The foremothers were concerned with the mind, body, and spirit; thus, the education they coconstructed with their students emphasized multiple literacies. In the introduction of *Literacy: The Word and the World*, authored by Paulo Freire, Giroux (1987) described literacy modalities as the Freireian Model of Emancipatory Literacy:

> Literacy is a dialectic relationship between human beings and the world, on the one hand, and language and transformative agency on the other. Within this perspective, literacy is not approached as merely a technical skill to be acquired, but as a necessary foundation for cultural action for freedom, a central aspect of what it means to be a self and socially constituted agent. Literacy is fundamental to aggressively constructing one's voice as part of a wider project of possibility and empowerment. (p. 7)

The foremothers, as with such contemporary African-American women educators as Marva Collins (Collins & Tamarkin, 1990) and Lorraine Monroe (1991), were mindful that the education their students received was one that encompassed academic, cultural, community, critical, and informational literacies. They understood that the students would need to be equipped with factual knowledge coupled with critical thinking skills to assist them in navigating and transforming negative social conditions.

PART 4: INSTILLING THE VISION AND PASSING THE TORCH

My Personal Dedication

In concluding this chapter, I look back and evaluate just how monumental the contributions of African-American female educators, both past and present, have been to me as a Black woman, a doctoral student, and a professional educator. I have been deeply moved by the life experiences of my Black teachers and professors. The legacy of academic excellence is one that I cherish for myself as a student and one on which I secure my feet when I teach (i.e., sharing, caring, and nurturing relationships). My Black teachers have truly been the Black mother I never knew. These Black women saw in me something I was not able to see or appreciate. I am no longer a motherless child. I am part of a collective group of women who historically have mothered countless millions! The power brought forth by knowing, interacting, and studying about the contributions and the work of Black women while studying with Black women is a miraculous experience! Seeds have been deposited within my spirit that I, in turn, am able to deposit in the lives of people I encounter through teaching.

Although I have not been in the traditional classroom for 3 years, I have touched the lives of people (children and adults) in ways I never imagined possible. On resigning from my position as a sixth-grade teacher in Lorain, Ohio, I started an educational consulting business, Yetu Shule Multicultural Enterprises. By developing this business, I am able to continue my life work as an educator by lecturing, tutoring, and developing educational programs for nonprofit, community-based organizations. The principles of Yetu Shule (Kiswahili for Our School) are based on the notion that education should serve to liberate, uplift, and build strong individuals, families, organizations, and communities through individualized tutoring, workshops, training seminars, educational programming, and curriculum development . . . incorporating a holistic, cultural, and spiritual approach . . . customized to meet the needs of each client. I use concepts such as *liberation, individualization*, and *holistic education* to ground my business philosophy because I found them missing from the public school system.

Furthermore, as a consultant, I am able to educate my daughter at home. Home schooling affords me the opportunity to be the mother to her I did not have and to instill in her a vision of educational excellence that she too can pass on. Home schooling provides my daughter numerous occasions to transcend traditional ways of knowing, thinking, and learning. She is free to tap into her powerful and creative mind, body, and spirit, and to make cultural connections often neglected in public schools. My daughter and I cocreate her educational skills and goals. We have a partnership that embodies the womanist pedagogy (Beauboeuf-Latontant, 2002), an Emancipatory Literacy (Giroux, cited in Freire

& Macedo, 1987), and a philosophy from Freire (1970, 2000) that reflects the belief that teaching and learning are a sacred process (hooks, 1994).

Finally, by creating Yetu Shule and providing home schooling for my daughter, I am able to continue to develop my vision of building community-based learning facilities throughout the Pan-African world. I am using similar foundational principles in my consulting work as I do in my home with my daughter. To assume a task as extensive as mine, one must be supported by a history of excellence such as the legacy of African-American women educators described in this chapter. It is to them that I dedicate my life's work as a teacher. I am eternally grateful for the example they have shown me, and I am determined to pass this torch of community service to my daughter and others whom I encounter through my educational activities.

REFERENCES

Beauboeuf-Lafontant, T. (2002). A womanist experience of caring: Understanding the pedagogy of exemplary black women teachers. *The Urban Review*, *34*(1), 71-85.

Collins, M., & Tamarkin, C. (1990). *The Marva Collins' way*. New York: Putnam.

Freire, P. (1970/2000). *The pedagogy of the oppressed*. New York: Continuum.

Freire, P., & Macedo, D. (1987). *Literacy: Reading the word and the world*. MA: Bergin & Garvey.

Gay, G. (2000). *Culturally responsive teaching*. New York: Teachers College Press.

Giroux, H. (1987). Introduction. In P. Freire & D. Macedo, *Literacy: Reading the word and the world*. MA: Bergin & Garvey.

Halasa, M. (1989). *Mary McLeod Bethune*. Danbury, CT: Grolier.

hooks, b. (1994). *Teaching to transgress*. New York: Routledge.

Irvine, J. J. (1999). The education of children whose nightmares come both by day and nights. *Journal of Negro Education, 68*(3), 244-253.

Lerner, G. (1972). *Black women in White America*. New York: Vintage Books.

Lerner, G. (1994). Early community work of black club women. In D. G. Neiman (Ed.), *Church and community among black southerners 1865-1900*. New York: Garland.

Salley, C. (1993). *The Black 100: A ranking of the most influential African-Americans, past and present*. New York: Citadel.

Monroe, L. (1991). *Nothing's impossible: Leadership lessons from inside and outside the classroom*. New York: Perseus Books Group.

Woodson, C. G. (1933, 1977). *The mis-education of the negro*. New York: AMS Press.

5

Lessons From Down Under: Reflections on Meanings of Literacy and Knowledge From an African-American Female Growing Up in Rural Alabama

Bessie House-Soremekun

The desire for literacy has characterized the culture of African Americans since their arrival here under the myriad brutalities of slavery.

—Dyson (1973, p. 31)

Reflecting on meanings of literacy and knowledge forces a coming to terms with different racial/ethnic communities and differential access to learning and to the varied forms of literacy within the United States. Levels of access to literacy impact how groups have developed from an educational standpoint and, more important, in terms of how the early skill acquisition has prevented some groups from exerting power or influence on society as a whole.

This chapter examines the development of several forms of literacy in rural Alabama during the years immediately following the civil rights movement.

The prevailing thesis centers on the relationship among race, knowledge, and power. A fundamental premise is that African Americans' early access to literacy was affected and shaped by historical factors interwoven with the development of the slaveocracy in the southern states. Predominant among these factors were strategies used by the slave owners to discourage Africans from acquiring reading and writing skills. Literacy was also impacted by written and unwritten rules of behavior mediated on the formal and informal realms of Southern Society, as well as by oral and written modes of communication. For African Americans, the oral tradition was and remains today the preferred mode of communicating and transmitting cultural traditions from one generation to another. Dr. Michael Eric Dyson (2003) has argued,

> . . . A big problem that black slaves confronted was how do you survive having your own literacy and the forms of intellectual life that it nurtured–attacked, even outlawed, for God's sake, by the state? The oral tradition became a powerful way for black folk to preserve dangerous memories of their beauty and intelligence in a hostile white world that thought of them as beasts and morons. It's a hell of a hard thing to have textual variation, or to encourage different interpretations, when white supremacy is winnowing your thoughts and banishing your body from the precincts of cultural appreciation. (p. 27)

Here the complex links between knowledge and knowing are examined, as well as the contests over power that emerged from this phenomenon after the Montgomery Bus Boycotts and the Freedom Marches of the 1950s and 1960s.

Historical and Political Context

> The Montgomery Bus Boycott of 1955-56 marks a watershed in the modern era of America's Civil Rights years. For twelve and a half months, black residents of Alabama's state capital walked, carpooled and rode in taxis and hearses temporarily converted into buses rather than ride in the back of segregated Jim Crow buses. (Carson, Barrow, Bill, Harding, & Hine, 1991, p. 49)

The civil rights movement was born in the state of Alabama during the 1950s. Contextually, the lifestyles of all Alabamians and Americans were affected for decades to come by the Montgomery Bus Boycotts of 1955-1956 (Carson et al., 1996). The boycotts were precipitated by Rosa Parks' refusal to give up her seat to a White man who got onto the bus.

Numerous events of the civil rights era, the language it embodied, the politics of its broader implications, Rosa Parks becoming the Mother of the modern civil rights movement rhetoric, and the information that gave meaning to the struggle served as symbols for possibilities yet to come. Few Alabamians had TV at this time; the TVs that did exist transmitted scenes in black and white rather than in color. The televised portrayal of life in "black and white" mirrored the polarized relationships that existed at this time between the Black and White communities. Most homes, however, had radios, and in this context the spoken word reigned supreme.

It is important to recognize the role that the Black Church and religious leaders played in articulating and helping African Americans interpret the rules of their engagement with the White community. Sometimes those rules were written, but more often they were unwritten. Dr. Martin Luther King, Jr., through the use of both his written and oral modes of communication, evoked powerful imagery regarding the contours of possibility in a changing America. With his brilliant oratorical skills and impassioned pleas, he demonstrated that, in some cases, the spoken word was more powerful than the written word. An example of his brilliant oratory is a speech that he wrote and delivered on December 5, 1955, at the Holt Street Baptist Church, in Montgomery, Alabama. In opening the speech, he referred to the Negroes' struggle for equality in this country and then moved on to discuss the courageous actions of Rosa Parks. He stated:

> For many years now Negroes in Montgomery and so many other areas have been inflicted with the paralysis of crippling fear on buses in our community. On so many occasions, Negroes have been intimidated and humiliated and oppressed because of the sheer fact that they were Negroes. . . . Just the other day, just last Thursday to be exact, one of the finest citizens in Montgomery—not just one of the finest Negro citizens, . . . was taken from a bus and carried to jail and arrested. . . . You know my friends there comes a time when people get tired of being trampled over by the iron feet of oppression. There comes a time my friends when people get tired of being flung across the abyss of humiliation where they experience the bleakness of nagging despair. There comes a time when people get tired of being pushed out of the glittering sunlight of life's July and left standing amidst the piercing chill of an Alpine November. (King, 1991, p. 5)

The end result of the despair and suffering that the movement sought to banish was fundamental change that occurred under the umbrella of the Civil Rights Act of 1964 and the Voting Rights Act of 1965. The Civil Rights Act was the foundation for the establishment of Affirmative Action legislation. Affirmative Action sought to open the employment arena for hiring more minorities, women, and disabled. The ultimate goal was to "provide a level playing field" for all Americans.

KNOWLEDGE AND KNOWING

I am a product of the rural South, having grown up in the small city of Lanett, Alabama. My earliest recollections are that the city lay on the Georgia state line next to another small city known as West Point, Georgia. Both areas were small in terms of sheer size and population. Only a small number of people lived in both areas. The city of Lanett had a post office, a city hall, police and fire departments, and a few commercial businesses. Many African Americans in my hometown were devoutly religious, and this was something about which they were proud. I grew up in the Methodist Church, therefore part of my literacy was interwoven with learning to recite the Apostles and the Nicene Creeds and to read and understand the Bible. My religious training helped me know and understand God as the creator. The training also helped me understand issues regarding morality and what a morally constituted life should be. I learned to sing numerous Methodist hymns. In fact I know many of these hymns by heart because I sang them so many times. I was a member of the church's youth choir, and my mother was the pianist.

I grew up in the 1960s and 1970s. Because I was in elementary school during much of the 1960s, I was too young to understand the meanings, methodology, or goals of the civil rights movement. My extended family was much larger than the standard nuclear family. In other words, my extended family included my father, mother, grandmother, aunt, uncle, brothers, sister, and cousins. We ate together, lived together, studied together, and became, for all intent and purposes, one functioning family unit. Lines of strict blood lineage were often blurred as my aunt treated me as if she were my mother, and we treated our cousins as if they were our brothers and sisters.

It was a middle-class family where education was highly valued. My mother, grandmother, and uncle were all school teachers and my father served in the military. All had gone to college and placed an emphasis on the "learned professions." Books and newspapers were readily available, and all of us were encouraged to perform well in school. Standard English was the preferred mode of expression. Within such an environment, I developed an early interest in books and writing. I also became an avid reader who excelled academically in school.

I have a vivid recollection of my first-grade teacher, Mrs. Annie P. Sykes, who still lives in Lanett. Many of the things I learned in her class remain with me even today. She stressed the basic building blocks of learning. She made us learn our alphabet and insisted that we sound out our vowels. We learned the three Rs—reading, writing, and arithmetic. In her class, we learned that letters make words and words make sentences, sentences form paragraphs and paragraphs make essays. When I was in the fourth grade, my teacher recommended to the principal and my parents that I be skipped to a higher grade because of my academic performance. My mother refused the offer because she had also skipped a grade when she was in school and believed that students should stay with their peer group. By remaining in a similar age group, my mother believed that a child's intellectual and emotional development would proceed at an appropriate pace.

FORMAL AND INFORMAL LITERACY

Formal literacy was important to all members of my family. *Formal literacy* refers to the various types of knowledge and knowing that is acquired through formal educational modes and activities (e.g., attending school and reading texts). Formal literacy was problematic to African Americans at this time for many reasons. First, during the civil rights era, America operated under the legal premise that validated the idea of "separate but equal." In Alabama, many of our politicians were adamantly opposed to integrating our schools. I remember seeing Governor George Wallace on TV standing in a door on the University of Alabama campus and preventing Black students from entering the school. During the civil rights era, Wallace was a well-known segregationist and racist. Many other White Supremists in neighboring states served in similar roles and shared similar ideologies. Lester Maddox in Georgia, Jesse Helms in North Carolina, and Strom Thurmond in South Carolina were among the most noted. When the legal foundation for the "separate but equal" philosophy was overturned in the courts, it took many years to bring Black schools up to the level of their White counterpart institutions.

I attended an all-Black school for the first 6 years of my education; our school integrated when I moved to the seventh grade. Our Black elementary school teachers were brilliant and capable. Nevertheless, our textbooks and written materials were largely inferior to those in White schools. Sometimes several pages of important textual material would be missing, and our books were almost always outdated versions rather than newly revised editions. Moreover, there was little African-American and far less African history included in the curriculum. It was not until I was an adult that I learned about the salient contributions that African Americans made in enhancing the development of this country. Other ethnic and cultural groups were also omitted from the texts. During the time I was in elementary and junior high school, I never read a book authored by a Black man or a Black woman. At that time, Black women were "rendered voiceless" in written textual matter. With regard to the exclusion of Black women's voices, Patricia Hill Collins (2000) wrote:

> The shadow obscuring the Black woman's intellectual tradition is neither accidental nor benign. Suppressing the knowledge produced by any oppressed group makes it easier for dominant groups to rule because the seeming absence of an independent consciousness in the oppressed can be

taken to mean that subordinate groups willingly collaborate in their own victimization. Maintaining the invisibility of Black women and our ideas is critical in structuring patterned relations of race, gender, and class inequality that pervade the entire social structure. (p. 3)

The lack of written text materials about and by people of color had a negative impact on the self-esteem and attitudes of African-American people. To some degree, we were rendered invisible and marginal in a society that valued Whiteness. Our voices were neither heard nor considered worthy of inclusion.

The oral realm of African-American discourse served as a balm to the hostile written materials that surfaced in book stores and academic life. As stated earlier, African-American culture has survived through the oral traditions that have served in many vital functions. Many African Americans who were born in the South were direct descendants of slaves brought from Africa. The native Africans brought with them remnants of African culture, including storytelling and oral discourse. My family continued to pass the storytelling tradition from one generation to the next. My grandmother, Bessie, for whom I am named, was a great storyteller. During the course of her lifetime, I had hundreds of conversations with her. She died a few months before her 104th birthday.

My grandmother and I discussed many topics, including religion, philosophy, the nature of human existence, politics, health issues, and economics. She told me what it was like growing up in the late 1800s. I was fortunate to have had the opportunity to know well an individual who lived for more than a century. Grandma Bessie talked to me about her life history and took me as far back as she could to our family's beginnings. She told me about World War I, World War II, and the Vietnam War. She was a remarkably brilliant and articulate woman even at her advanced age. I was delighted to know she had attended a teacher's college for Black people in the late 1880s. Teaching was her vocation, and in this capacity she taught our family most of the things she knew. I now know that everything I needed to know about succeeding in life I learned from my grandmother Bessie. This literacy was a form of knowing that I inherited.

One of the greatest stories she ever told me that is still etched in my memory today is about her father, the late Samuel Phillips. Samuel was a slave on the Phillips' Plantation in Dadeville, Alabama. Because his skin color was dark, he ended up being a field hand. He had to perform arduous work in the fields of the plantation during the daytime when the sun was hot. Field work was quite different from the light housework performed by slaves who worked inside the plantation houses. Often the house slaves had lighter skin color and, in some cases, were the illegitimate offspring of the plantation master and his female slaves. Many slave women were sexually abused by their masters and had no recourse from their sexual advances.

My great grandfather told my grandmother that pigs were given food in a big trough in the yard. After the pigs had finished eating, the plantation owners poured food for the field slaves into the same trough from which the animals had eaten. The field slaves were given no utensils and had to eat with their hands. They also were not provided any shoes to wear. After the Emancipation Proclamation was signed and the slaves were set free, the first thing my great grandfather did was buy himself a knife and a fork. He had obviously watched many times from outside the windows of the big house as the Whites ate their meals at the dinner table. The purchase of the knife and fork represented a great deal to this former slave. For him, it was a way to elevate himself to the "higher levels of humanity" from which he had been denied as a slave. He understood that this form of literacy was necessary for his advancement in society.

This and many other stories helped shape my worldview when I was a young girl growing up in rural Alabama. The love and nurturing that we received in my household and from other Black folk in my community helped provide a cushion against the harshness of the outside world. It was within this context that I made a decision, during my fourth-grade year in school, that I wanted to obtain the highest degree awarded in academia (i.e., the PhD). Although I had no idea about how long it would take to acquire this degree, I knew I would attain it one day. I also knew that it would secure my place as part of the legacy that was my family's quest for formal literacy.

EXPLICATING THE RACE RULES

Various rules of the *race game* overshadowed my upbringing in the rural south. Although some of the rules were written down, in many instances they were not. Some of the written or formal rules of the game were clearly explicated in a body of legislation, passed in the late 19th and early 20th centuries, known as "Jim Crow laws." Jim Crow institutionalized "separate but equal," meaning Blacks were forced to use separate restrooms and were not allowed to eat in public dining establishments. They were forced to sit on the back of the buses and had to attend separate and inferior schools. The South's exclusionary practices negatively impacted the self-esteem of African Americans all over this country. The message I interpreted from such forms of inequality was that Black people were unequal to Whites and had minimal value. What a profound message for an African-American girl growing up in rural Alabama! Such was the reality for individuals growing up in the 1960s and 1970s and witnessing civil rights efforts that would eventually change a culture.

Eventually I realized that knowledge meant power. As Southern Blacks became more aware of the stakes in the political struggle, they realized they could no longer postpone the inevitable confrontation with the establishment. Freedom marches, speeches, freedom rides, and countless sit-ins were all part of a process in which knowledge, political change, and the quest for a new social order were inexorably interwoven.

Many unwritten rules still beset us. As a young girl, I noted that Whites in our community always insisted that Blacks address them as Mr. and Mrs., but Whites never addressed Blacks with these same salutations. As I grew up and went to high school, I often accompanied my grandmother Bessie to the grocery store, the drug store, and the homes of some of the White people for whom she worked. After she reached the age of 65, she stopped teaching and began to do domestic work for some of the wealthy Whites in our neighborhood. She would wash and iron their clothes, neatly fold them, and place them in a basket, and she would always refer to them as "Mr. Frank," "Mrs. Lois," or "Mrs. Gladys." I never heard a White person in my town call my grandmother Mrs. Fannings. They always called her "Bessie."

I was very angry when Whites called my grandmother by her first name. After we said goodbye to the individuals for whom she worked, I often asked my grandmother why they did this, why they never addressed her as Mrs. Fannings, especially because my grandmother was much older than they. Whites not only denied her equal respect, but they disrespected her age as well. I remember clearly that my anger boiled over one day when I came home from college and I took my grandmother to Hood's Pharmacy to get her prescription filled. Behind the counter stood a White teenaged student. When my grandmother's order was filled, the young girl said, "Bessie, your prescription is ready." I then answered, "Her name is Mrs. Fannings." When we got outside, I immediately turned to my grandmother and said, "Mama Bessie, why do you allow the White people here to call you by your first name and you always refer to them as 'Mr.' and 'Mrs.'?" She turned to me and said in a mild tone, "That's all right honey. That's how they were raised. That's what they are used to." My grandmother made sure that I understood this form of literacy was part of the unwritten rules in the segregated south of my country.

Although I did not understand the broader implications of many southern acts that were perpetrated on us by Whites at the time, as an adult the meanings are becoming more clear. By not addressing Blacks with formal titles, Whites once again elevated themselves to a higher ranking of humanity. For them we were faceless and, to some extent, nameless nonentities whom they encountered from time to time. Sometimes we were "auntie," "hey you," or "boy." Whatever the case, all of these names represented disrespect for the person being addressed.

There was also something more fundamental in these encounters. The use of formal titles and salutations binds individuals, in a literary sense, to the formal realm. The use of formal titles puts distance between speakers engaged in a verbal exchange. The use of first names and nicknames are part of an informal realm where there is familiarity and less distance between the individuals involved. Hence, by their actions, Whites were putting distance between the Black persons and themselves, but not putting distance between themselves and the Black persons in this dual exchange. One reason that I use my title—for example, Mrs. House-Soremekun or Dr. House-Soremekun—is a direct result of the way Blacks were treated in the South. It is my way of getting respect for my grandmother after her death because she was never given any, by Whites, during her lifetime.

My quest for knowledge and formal literacy has continued through the years and has taken some interesting and unusual routes. I graduated with honors from Lanett High School in 1974. I then attended Huntingdon College in Montgomery, Alabama, where I pursued my undergraduate degree in English. I graduated Magna Cum Laude from this institution in 1978. Language, either oral or written, embodies many meanings and sends many messages. Because I earned good grades in school from the first grade and beyond, Whites in my community would always tell me that "I was a credit to my race." I found it rather interesting that they never said that I was a credit to the "human race." In essence, my contributions were being linked to my racial group rather than to the broader society. This was one way Whites kept a distance between Blacks and themselves, and thereby reiterated their power over us. Also when I graduated with honors from Huntingdon College, several of my professors wrote letters of recommendation for me. My history professor wrote that "I was the ablest Black student to ever have attended Huntingdon College." Although this was certainly a strong endorsement of my academic skills and abilities, I once again was racially categorized. He could have said, "I was one of the ablest students to ever have attended Huntingdon College." Here again formal literacy was underscored by the unspoken rules of White power in the lives of Blacks. Attaining a high degree of formal literacy still did not enhance my chances of being seen as an equal.

My continued quest for literacy ultimately led me to become an exchange student at the University of Tubingen in West Germany. I also conducted my dissertation research in Nairobi, Kenya. I received my PhD in International Studies from the University of Denver in 1988. From there I joined the Kent State University faculty in the Department of Political Science in 1989. Since that time, I have taught courses in African Politics, Women and Political Development, World Politics, Entrepreneurship, Human Rights, and Third World Development. I have also published three books, numerous scholarly articles, and book chapters. In this way, I have been involved in the production and distribution of knowledge that has impacted the lives of many people, particularly people of color.

REFERENCES

Carson, C., Barrow, D., Bill, B., Harding, V., & Hine, D. C. (Eds.). (1991a). *Eyes on the prize: Civil rights reader.* New York: Penguin.

Carson, C., Barrow, D., Bill, B., Harding, V., & Hine, D.C. (Eds.). (1991). A letter from the Women's Political Council to the Mayor of Montgomery,

Alabama. In C. Carson et al. (Eds.), *The eyes on the prize: Civil rights reader* (p. 44). New York: Penguin.

Collins, P. H. (2000). *Black feminist thought: Knowledge, consciousness, and the politics of empowerment* (2nd ed.). New York: Routledge.

Dyson, M. E. (1993). *Reflecting Black: African American cultural criticism*. Minneapolis: University of Minnesota Press.

Dyson, M. E. (2003). *Open mike: Reflections on philosophy, race, sex, culture, and religion*. New York: Basic Civitas Books.

King, M. L., Jr. (1991). Speech by Martin Luther King, Jr., at Holt Street Baptist Church. In C. Carson et al. (Eds.), *Eyes on the prize: Civil rights reader* (p. 49). New York: Penguin Books.

Section II

6

Transformative College Literacy of Literate Black Women Peer Counselors

Robin Wisniewski

I think [being a literate Black woman] means to be independent, not to be dependent on anybody to provide for you because you can do things for yourself. Knowledge is power, so if you're literate you can make your own way. It's freedom. You can do whatever you want to do. It doesn't limit. The possibilities open up. (Lauryn, first-semester peer counselor, senior biology/premedicine major, Fall 2002)

[Being a literate Black woman means] that I can speak and what I have to say will be heard because I know what I am talking about. If I don't know about a subject, I want to find out more. If I literally don't know about something I can't talk about it. I can't voice an opinion let alone defend it or be for it because I don't know anything about it. If you're ignorant of everything that's going on and you have no idea and you're just walking around, then how can you say, we need change, or we need this and that? No. You need to be educated so you can be this influence so you can help others. So you can go out and not be somebody's quota. So you can go out and be able to stand and be who you are and also be a great influence. (Vania, third-semester peer counselor, senior accounting major, Fall 2002)

THE PEER COUNSELING PROGRAM

In 1997, my professional charge was to provide literacy support for college students with disabilities, from low-income backgrounds, and in the first generation in their family to attend college. In the university learning center where I worked, the literacy services were to be an addition to the existing math tutoring, writing tutoring, and content area study groups. The services both supplemented and complemented the existing writing and math tutoring as well as study groups. In the large midwestern, predominantly White university, my vision for the program was to create a staff who embraced a collaborative, peer learning environment. Traditional college literacy programs had been based on administrative tasks, mechanistic teaching, and basic skills development. The new program would embrace a counseling perspective rather than a traditional perspective. The program philosophy would embrace a counseling perspective rather than draw from that of traditional college literacy programs based on administrative tasks, mechanistic teaching, and basic skills development.

A counseling perspective in college literacy programs encompasses basic counseling skills in addition to techniques that address self-paced instruction, emotional factors surrounding conflicts, and reading skills (Johnson & Carpenter, 2000). Armed with both a peer assistance vision and a college reading program counseling philosophy, I hired the first four peer counselors in the spring of 1998. Through a process of sorting and synthesizing views on the peer counseling role, the first four peer counselors generated the following belief statements about the peer counseling program:

> As members of the peer counseling team, we believe that academic peer counseling is the process of setting goals and objectives, implementing new strategies, and providing resources through listening, encouraging, collaborating, and empathizing. We believe that the environment we create is comfortable and educational and provides students with focus and individualized attention. We believe that students are individuals full of potential and who possess a diverse set of strengths. Students are important and talented; therefore, they are also teachers.

The peer counselors' statements summarized their beliefs about how peer counseling was defined, how the environment felt, and how students were perceived. Within their belief statement, they addressed the idea of implementing new strategies. The idea of implementing new strategies became a core feature of peer counselor education, thereby validating these strategies in course content that were proved effective college literacy programs (Allgood, Risko, Alverez, & Fairbanks, 2000; Nist & Simpson, 2000).

During the eight semesters that followed, the number of peer counselors grew from 4 to 15. Individually, they assisted between 80 and 100 students per semester with implementing new strategies in the areas of studying, textbook reading, notetaking, organization, time management, test taking, test anxiety, motivation, self-confidence, stress, career exploration, and other college adjustment and success issues. In light of students with disabilities being one of the three primary populations the peer counselors served, peer counselors generated an understanding of mobility impairments as well as the diagnosis and treatment of disorders such as brain injury, learning disabilities, anxiety, and attention deficit hyperactivity disorder (ADHD).

When the number of peer counselors grew, the peer counseling group interviewed and selected prospective peer counselors. Original applicants to the peer counseling position in 1998 were psychology majors, but as the semesters progressed, the majors represented a wider variance and included people with such content areas of math, speech, early childhood education, art history, science, accounting, computer information systems, integrated social studies, economics, art education, communication, biological sciences, human resources, and integrated language arts. The variability allowed discussions among the peer counselors that included the literacy process in many content areas.

Regarding the literacy nature of the peer counseling program, I had a *transformational agenda*. My goal was to note a marked change in perspective in individual peer counselors, the students with whom they met, and the program's curriculum leadership. Theoretically, the transformative agenda resides within the notion of democratic leadership, where my leadership responsibilities were to facilitate authority within the program that was shared among the staff. Both the peer counselors and I had a responsibility to contribute to our own literacy learning and the literacy learning of the university students with whom we met.

MY TRANSFORMATIVE JOURNEY

My transformative journey began with the awareness of my own expectation for change in myself. However, I held a limited view of self-change that involved the addition of new knowledge to my thinking, rather than a new understanding of myself as I leaned from interacting with others. Over a 4-year period from 1998 to 2002, my theoretical orientation in college literacy emerged from the single perspective of adding new knowledge, to using strategies to gain understanding, and finally to a perspective of the liberation of thought. The liberation of thought involved helping others discover themselves as they learned, rather than the class material they were to understand for a class. This empancipatory view led to the invitation of Lauryn and Vania, two Black female peer counselors, into my journey of transformative learning and a chapter in this book.

In transformative leadership, the leader can help others transform with self-understanding of transformation. The limited view of self-change that involved adding new knowledge to my thinking was born out of my identification with the branch of psychology having to do with processing new information into memory. Atkinson and Shiffrin (1968) proposed a model of processing new information into memory that involved three parts: information being received through the senses, information being transferred into short-term memory, and information being solidified into long-term memory. Since this model's introduction in 1968, alternative views of memory have refined Atkinson and Shiffrin's model to include different ways to process memory into long-term memory (Craik & Lockhart, 1972), an integration of auditory and visuospatial information for processing into long-term memory (Baddely, 1990), and ways to get information into long-term memory while focusing on how to remember the information (Morris, Bransford, & Franks, 1977). When focusing on how to remember the information is applied to college literacy, a student can use a graphic organizer, discuss text content, and relate topic examples while considering how to retrieve information for a test.

Another explanation of knowledge gaining that has informed college literacy practice is the knowledge construction described by Piaget (1976). Referred to as *schema* by Bartlett (1932), Piaget described the process of schema reconstruction where learners construct new knowledge through their own questioning and reflection. Rather than information processing, schema theory focuses on integrating new information with information already in someone's mind.

The perspective of gaining new information as described in the information-processing model and schema theory informed my understanding of the need to assist students with their college reading in terms of what they understand, process, and recall. I discovered that I was the agent in the peer counselors' construction of the meaning, thus adding a social layer to literacy learning. In the view of Vygotsky (1978), two minds are better than one in the learning process. Bruner (1986), the leader in the theory of discovery learning, referred the guidance by one of the learners in social learning who was more skilled as *scaffolding*. In college literacy practice, both learners make gains through discussing the meaning of the text. The peer counselors, as the more experienced literacy learners than their peers, assessed students' interest and background knowledge, modeled strategies to scaffold students' growth (e.g., questioning, paraphrasing), and used materials for interaction with text (e.g., graphic organizers).

bell hooks captured the college literacy context I was beginning to create with learning together as an essential activity. hooks (1994) wrote: "Making the classroom a democratic setting where everyone feels responsibility to contribute is the central goal of transformative pedagogy" (p. 39). I considered the college learning center as the classroom for peer counselors. The conference room in the learning center contained a table where we met for class and weekly meetings, and an open room with 10 tables and three private cubicles where the peer counselors worked individually with students and confidentially conversed with their colleagues. Through project-based assignments in the class meetings as well as through their sessions with students, the peer counselors were responsi-

ble for sharing, questioning, and doing work. The context allowed the fundamental attribute of collaboration to take place where "thinking is distributed
among the members of the group [and] the group shares cognitive responsibility
for the task at hand" (Bruffee, 1999).

It was not until the first 2 years practicing the knowledge gaining and social
nature of knowledge gaining that I began to articulate the concept of *transformation* with a focus on identity development and culture and marginality issues.
College literacy transformation is both personal and social. Henderson's (1999)
description of a *democratic curriculum leadership* role, where transformation is
central, also upholds "an inquiry-based, growth-oriented understanding that
emphasizes the connection between democracy and education" (p. 4). bell
hooks (1994) laid the foundation of responsibility of the transformative, democratic leader:

> With education as the practice of freedom, students aren't the only ones
> who are asked to share, to confess. Engaged pedagogy does not seek simply
> to empower students. Any classroom that employs a holistic model of
> learning will also be a place where teachers grow, and are empowered by
> the process. The empowerment cannot happen if we refuse to be vulnerable
> while encouraging students to take risks. (p. 21)

With transformative pedagogy as my focus as an educator in a democratic college literacy setting, I had a responsibility to share, question, and work toward
personal and social liberation through my own vulnerability and through my
encouragement of others. As a White woman developing as a democratic curriculum leader, I became aware of an internal conflict. The researchers and the-
orists on whom I drew were White male, as evidenced in the 14 names I cited
previously in my explanation of information processing, schema theory, and
social learning. As a result, I identified with the need to place *women's* experience as central to college literacy discourse.

Yet this placement as women's experience as central to transformative
practice created an assumption of *Whiteness* as central to literacy learning. A
specific need for Black women's experiences to be central in research is emphasized by Collins (1990):

> Because elite white men and their representatives control structures of
> knowledge validation, white male interests pervade the thematic content of
> traditional scholarship. As a result, Black women's experiences . . . have
> been routinely distorted in or excluded from traditional academic discourse.
> (p. 291)

Just as Collins exposed the elite White male as dominant in scholarship, my
value of *women's* knowledge construction was in danger of forming the central

force of Whiteness, just as Yancy (2000) noted in his critique of the feminist movement. With my value of *women's* learning, I situated Black women as "an invisible group on the sidelines that easily can be combined with other groups [in] a convenient fiction that conceals their power and importance" (Etter-Lewis, 1993, p. xvii). Included in a transformative agenda, wrote Joe Kincheloe (1999), is the exposure of "educational processes that privilege the privileged" (p. 81). In transformative college literacy, I expose the privilege of a White woman in a peer counseling program to present transformations that follow Collins' (1998, 2000) Afrocentric and feminist ways of knowing.

Anne Brooks (2000) defined *transformative learning* as leading to ". . . some type of fundamental change in the learner's sense of themselves, their worldviews, their understandings of their pasts, and their orientation to the future" (p. 140). I experienced a fundamental change as I changed from the view of gaining knowledge to the view of gaining knowledge socially, through questioning my own identity and views, and bringing otherness to the forefront of literacy learning.

As a White democratic curriculum leader in a college literacy peer-based program, my central question became: "In what ways do Black women peer counselors 'transform?'" This chapter now turns toward a specific understanding of Lauryn's and Vania's perception of the conditions within the transformative context as well as their marked changes during their peer counseling role in the predominantly White college program.

LAURYN'S AND VANIA'S TRANSFORMATIVE CONTEXT

John Mezirow (1978, 1994), an early theorist in transformative learning, highlighted two conditions of transformation: critical reflection as an examination of an individual worldview out of a disorienting dilemma, and the reorganization of a frame of reference. Studies of transformation in adult women have grown over the past decade, and researchers have since added to and reorganized Mezirow's conditions, identifying relationships and individual identification in a particular *context* for transformative learning in women.[1] Despite the growing number of studies and the expansion of Mezirow's conditions, Black women are excluded, or visible only in a fraction of transformation studies. Anne Brooks cites a portion of studies[2] in her review of transformation research that point toward a familial relationship and an individual identification as protection from racism. I encountered these two areas of familial interaction and indi-

---

[1]The Group for Collaborative Inquiry (1993), Pope (1996), Scott (1997), and Sveinunggaard (1993).

[2]Edmondson Bell and Nkomo (1998), Pope (1996), and Turner (1997).

vidual identity as themes in Lauryn's and Vania's view of college literacy in their role of peer counselor in the program.

Familial Interaction

Lauryn and Vania were from distinctly different backgrounds. Lauryn was from an urban setting where she "went to a predominantly African American High school. It was 99.9 percent." Vania was from a rural setting where she "came from a predominantly White school. Most of the people that were Black in my school were my relatives." I asked about their perspective of inclusiveness in different environments—namely, the peer counseling group. The word *family* was interwoven in their narratives about the peer counseling program, and they related their integration into the peer counseling family to environments where they had also experienced an inherent feeling of family.

Lauryn compared the peer counseling program to the familial nature of her high school: "[in high school] we know each other. It was more comfortable. Not that I got along or was in love with everybody. . . ." Peer counseling was familiar to her. She described the ways the program was familiar and related to the familial nature of her high school:

> [The Peer Counseling program is] more like the culture of a family setting in high school. There's no separation. There's not anybody who I don't get along with at all. If I judge anything, or if anybody judges anything, I don't think it's on the basis of race. It's more like, "I might not like this about you," or "I might like this about you."

I wondered how the predominantly White peer counseling program created a family environment when compared with Lauryn's majority status in her high school. Lauryn replied with a description of the characteristics of the peer counselors:

> The people who come into this program are people who are open-minded, people who probably generally get along with a lot of people anyway, who probably care about people or who have those types of supportive personalities. Like in my major, it's more of a diverse group of people, more randomly chosen. These people chose this thing because those are the types of people that they were. . . . They choose peer counseling because they get something from helping other people. They like to help other people. They want to see people succeed . . . kind of support personality types. They like to build people up. They like to see people do their best. They were probably chosen because they have that type of personality. Not academic achievement, because they're intelligent in certain areas, so they have something to contribute to be able to help.

I found Lauryn's perspectives of the peer counselors' characteristics to be evident in her description of the beginning of the semester, when she related her feeling about her first day as a peer counselor as "horrible." After talking with other peer counselors and "hearing things that they do," she felt more confident and comfortable in the second week of work.

Vania's statements of family included the "diverse church" in her hometown and the university scholars program for academically strong college students from disadvantaged backgrounds. Vania described her transition from feeling isolated to being included in her transfer from a regional campus of the university to the scholars program and the peer counseling group. Then she compared the organizations to the inclusiveness in her church:

> This year alone has been the biggest change. I was from a regional campus. I was going home every weekend because I didn't know a single person up here. To me it was just a big college atmosphere . . . [where I] need to go back home, need to be where I'm familiar. But with [the scholars program] it's been a whole other experience. They've really taken me on as a family. They've always looked out for me. And even in [peer counseling], the different people that I've [found to be] really, really truly been genuine to me. . . . It's been a complete turn around for me because I gained a lot of friends and people I respect. I've been appreciative of that . . . a lot has changed from the time I've been to high school to here. I come from a very loving church, and we consider ourselves a big family so I look for that when I go places and it's not always there. And my first years here it definitely wasn't here . . . this is probably the semester where I connected with a lot of people. In peer counseling here . . . now it's like it's this big group and now we're all close and I like that.

Throughout our discussion about the influences that the peer counselors have had on her, Vania noted specific individuals and their influence. In her written narrative for this study, she added a sentence about a particular peer counselor: "The friendships I have built meant so much to me. Lynn, I especially want to thank you for making me feel welcome."

Individual Identity

Although Lauryn and Vania identified the peer counseling group as having familial interaction, their oral narratives revealed strong feelings about their individual identities. They identified stereotypical or racist incidents in their classes with White male majors in Accounting and Biology/Premedicine, and they affirmed their desire to be seen as individuals rather than through the race lens.

Lauryn related the individuality she felt in peer counseling to the views of how she felt in her major, where she had experienced "blatant racism." Lauryn explained reactions in her major coursework as "outright condescensions" and attributed the peer racism to having been "raised in different environments" and not having exposure to different people. Because of this, she said, "There are people who don't know how to react to me as a Black woman." She told me how she felt "singled out" in one of her classes:

> I'm in a class right now . . . there was this one girl I would talk to. I'm the only Black person in the class so it's like maybe 30 people. Everybody is really comfortable to talk with one another and they'll joke with one another, even people that they didn't know before the course. And then with me it's like they won't say anything because it's almost a fear like "how is she going to react? Is she going to get angry if I joke a certain way?" . . . I'm not exactly sure what it is. It's just the impression that I get because I know there are stereotypes so they don't know how far they can go with me or what they can say so I don't say it's anything like rude, or "I hate you," or "I dislike you." Just like, "I'm not familiar with your culture. I don't know what to say to you."

In the peer counseling program, she felt like an individual where she "didn't feel like I was a race . . . I didn't feel like I was singled out" such as in her major where "there are instances where I feel like a race, like a Black person." She described herself as open-minded and "nonconformative to general beliefs." In addition to her insights about race, faith was a fundamental aspect of her individuality:

> God is just the center of everything. Just like prayer. I know it's been God that has brought me this far in my school because there [have] been times when I have been very discouraged and I know that there [were] times when people prayed for me and just seen things turn around immediately. So I just know that God is the center of all of this. I just believe that all things are possible through God. It's not separable. God is the center of all my success.

Like Lauryn, Vania related her individuality to the stereotypical views she noticed: "Most people think, 'oh [I] either come from a single parent home, or a broken home, or live in the ghetto,' or different things like that." She described the salient features of her faith and personality and talked about how she would prefer to be viewed:

> The first thing I want people to think . . . [is that] I am a Godly young lady, and that's first. It's not about, "okay, Vania's this African American or this Black or whatever you want to call it. This is who she is." . . . I don't really worry about being a Black person.

Vania looks for people's first impressions of her to consist of her faith as central to her character. When she starts a new group activity, respect becomes most important as she "tries to get a feel for the group." The respect others gain from her comes through knowing her opinion is valuable:

> Even though it might not necessarily be the right opinion or the opinion they were looking for, it's my opinion. I'm not a person to go along with the group. I say according to how I feel. and how what I believe to be right or what I believe to be the moral or the right thing, or however you want to perceive it.

Vania attributed the respect for her opinion in the peer counseling program to both the atmosphere in the project as well as her personality and contributions to the peer counseling group:

> I think I bring in the funny side and the reality side of things. With the group, we have a lot of, between psychology, sociology, and education atmosphere I bring in the basic, basic. I come from a business background. Here it is, here's how it goes. Simple as that. Don't make it more complicated. That's just always been me. I just learned that even growing up. I'm straight forward, I tell you the honest truth. You can always count on my honesty. My word is my word. So, as the group, I joke around, but you know you can always count on me.

The themes of the familial interaction and individual identity were salient in Lauryn's and Vania's narratives. They viewed peer counseling as a family-type environment and compared it to other contexts where they felt comfortable and individual. Research on women's development refers to the notion of individuality as a "developmental challenge" (Brooks, 2000, p. 148). Edmondson Bell and Nkoma (1998) believed that a Black woman's focus on individual identity is a protection against racism and apparent social standards. Vania and Lauryn recognized the racism and stereotypes, contrasted the separateness to either race implications or familial group affiliation, and stated how they would prefer to be perceived by others.

LAURYN'S AND VANIA'S LITERACY TRANSFORMATIONS

Surprised by the themes I found in Lauryn's and Vania's conditions of transformation in the college literacy context, I also expected to be surprised by their actual literacy transformations. My assumption had been that Lauryn and Vania would experience a transformation from the belief that literacy was about learning content to a belief that literacy was about the integration of strategies and content. Their move from content-focused to domain-specific reading strategies was evident throughout this research. In their last narrative, I noticed one emerging perspective that differed from my original assumption: Their transformation included a move beyond that of multiple literacies to empowerment. Lauryn's and Vania's answers to the opening question of the last interview open this chapter. Based on the advice from the editor of *Readers of the Quilt: Essays on Being Black, Female and Literate*, the question I posed to the two Black women was, "What does it mean to be a Black, literate woman?" Their answers included reflections about the issues of power, freedom, individuality, and social justice.

As Lauryn and Vania explained how they encouraged and motivated their students, they showed that their transformation was not only from a single to multiple literacy stance in terms of content area reading. They articulated how they managed an extension of themselves into a role of empowering their students as literate college learners. I choose specific quotes from Lauryn and Vania's responses to represent this transformation from learning *from* text to learning *with* text and using strategies to become empowered through knowledge construction.

In Lauryn's first interview with me, she reflected on her peer counselor role as "contributing" to helping students learn specific subject material: "When I came into [peer counseling] I was trying to help everybody with their specific subjects and I felt bad that I didn't know everything about psychology or [other subjects]." Lauryn felt the need to help in subjects with which she had experience—namely, the biological sciences. Vania also chose to focus on her area of expertise, accounting and business courses, ". . . just hoping to be able to help students in different studies that I was comfortable in doing."

In the interviews I conducted and in their second writing sample, Lauryn and Vania articulated changes in their perception of their roles as peer counselors. Lauryn described the change from singular focus on content to the integration of strategies within the content area: "I found out that my job was not to master every subject at [the university], but to use strategies with [the subjects.]" Strategies she used included concept cards, mapping, and notetaking techniques. The integration of strategies with the content area demonstrated Lauryn's attention to her students' individuality. She described her students' variant ways of studying:

> One student is very methodical, plans everything out bit-by-bit, and the other one is less, not less organized but just different in the way they keep track of things. One likes to write things out and the other likes to keep things mentally, but she's still organized. Just like differences in the environment they study in. One likes a quiet environment; she likes to go to the library. And one likes the television or [other] distractions. Silence is a distraction to her. Her mind wanders. Background noise helps her to stay focused in some kind of way.

Rather than focusing on specific study tools and individual study differences, Lauryn conveyed a preference for conversing with her students as a study strategy because it "helps [students] understand what they read or put it into their own words . . . having them explain it back to me, by helping them form their thoughts and make sure everything is clear in their mind." Also, focusing on the individual student while integrating study strategies with content, Vania described her change from a single view of learning text information to the integration of study strategies and content:

> [Meeting with students] changed me because I was able to be more open to learning new ways, learning and teaching. Because the first semester, I was like, "whoa." I really felt like I wasn't seeing my students' progress at all because I wasn't, to me, showing them enough. I wasn't pulling out what they can do. Then by learning the new strategies and implementing [them] in different ways and learning about different disabilities and how, "okay, you may be able to do it this way but that person can't. What's the next way you can go about it?"

Lauryn's and Vania's work with students became more student-centered over the course of their peer counseling journey. In her second interview, I asked Lauryn about the successes in her sessions. Lauryn targeted caring as central to the rapport she needed to work well with her students:

> I know that they can tell that I care. It's just like a good feeling for me to see them happy or excited about their grades. Like the one girl coming out of the biology building, "oh, guess what I did! I got a B!" It's just nice to see that. I'm so happy for them and I think they can tell. People can tell how you feel about them, can sense how they feel about them. I'm glad I had the students I had.

Vania shared that she individually assesses students and meets their needs while focusing on the whole person:

> It starts with finding out where they are. It starts with background knowledge, basically. You do that usually within the first two sessions, finding out their study habits. How are their grades in school? Do they like to read? Even if they don't like to read, do they read? . . . To try to get them to that step to where they're reading even though they may not enjoy it, it's very necessary that they read and understand, so we possibly read together. Or they read something and bring in questions. . . . But the asking questions, getting familiar, and understanding is just the start of it. [They] need to get aware of what's going on because it's going to influence you whether you're going to be part of it or you're not.

The focus on students as both individuals and whole persons naturally extended Lauryn's and Vania's beliefs about literacy into their sessions. With their belief that literacy involves power, knowledge, freedom, and social justice, Lauryn and Vania empowered their students through encouraging and motivating them. Lauryn encouraged her students to be confident in their learning. She commented on how her self-perception influenced giving her students voice to question:

> I am somewhat of a nonconformist and I think that that helps them because I don't look at them, [and] say, "this is where you are and according to the rule book, according to statistics you have a 10 percent chance of doing this. It doesn't matter what other people say. It's possible. You can do it." And I think that's an encouragement to them, too. They see that they can do. They're not buying into what people tell them or what society tells them, or what teachers have told them or parents. They see the evidence in their lives against what other people say to them. They say, "well, you said this and that wasn't true." So they see what else might not be true.

As far as Vania was concerned, her students were individuals, and it was her responsibility to understand them as students, thinkers, and people. She connected with them and, as she became more experienced, increased her awareness that she was giving her students a voice. They were becoming empowered as learners. She provided an example supporting her belief of encouraging her students to talk to their professors:

> [The professor] is really stand-offish, he's really like, "I'm just here because I'm the [company] executive . . . I'm this, I'm all that . . ." and he can't really teach the students . . . these are freshmen coming in, and a good portion of them probably want to be here, and I'm not saying all of them are here for valid reasons, but if a student is coming up to you wanting help and just asking questions and you don't have time for them, I think that's very wrong. By reading and getting knowledgeable, you're able to go in there in the classroom and answer questions, know what you're talking about, be very knowledgable about the subject matter, be able to defend and also bring something to the classroom. You're not just going there as another student, another freshman who really doesn't want to be here, here because their parents told them they have to come to college because that's the next thing in life to do, no. You're going in there so that professor can see, "no, I'm not just another student. I'm here. I'm working hard. I'm dong my best and I'm going to succeed. . . ." That's what I tried to help my students be able to do.

Although Lauryn and Vania were peer counselors for a different length of time, they began their peer counseling position expecting their job to focus on helping students learn their coursework. Then they gained experience and integrated strategies with content to learn together with the text. Finally, they encouraged, motivated, and gave their students voice. With differences in background, major, and experience with peer counseling, both Lauryn's and Vania's literacy beliefs developed, and they extended these ideas in their literacy work with their peers. They viewed their students as individuals and whole persons, and they revealed their passion for giving students voice, encouragement, and motivation, ultimately empowering them as college literacy learners.

MY REFLECTIONS

In the first half of this chapter, I described the college literacy peer-based program conditions as well as my own transformation in my theoretical perspectives and practice as the leader of the peer counseling program. To carry out my transformative agenda as an educator, I provided a context for authentic inquiry learning with the goal of facilitating a fundamental change in college literacy perspective and practice among my counselors. Lauryn and Vania shared their perceptions of the college literacy transformative context, relating conditions of familial interaction and individual identity within a peer counseling culture.

For college literacy practitioners, the conditions of a transformative agenda coupled with Lauryn's and Vania's perceptions of the contexts assists in building college literacy environments that are deliberative, inquiry-based, and collaborative. With a fundamental belief that the knowledge of the group was greater than the separate parts, I was working on my skill to assist peer counselors in the discovery of their interests, awareness of their practice, and to facilitate their personal and social liberation. In college literacy programs, we need to not only acknowledge a democratic philosophy, but also engage in the practice of leading a democratic curriculum. Democratic curriculum leadership is comprised of inquiry that is deliberative and multiperspective, includes the exposure of biases, and the necessary effort to create our own transformation as educators.

The second half of the chapter carried the themes I encountered from Lauryn's and Vania's narratives regarding transformative conditions as well as the specific college literacy transformation that occurred during their peer counseling experiences. As a researcher, my investigation of Black women's experiences as central to transformation reflects hook's (1994) contention that ". . . one's experience is recognized as central and significant" to the learning journey (p. 37). Lauryn's and Vania's oral and written narratives provided a vehicle for relating their change in perspective and practice as peer counselors.

Placing Black women as central to the exploration of transformative college literacy contributes to a number of studies about women's literacy transformation and exposes the assumption of Whiteness as central and normal. Alvermann (2001) warned that we are "destined to presume a neutral model of literacy teaching and learning, one free of biases and power relations" when we design research studies that "reinforce notions of the inevitability of certain groups of people and literacy practices being positioned as more (or less) powerful than other groups" (p. 285). The investigation of Black women as peer counselors continues to erase neutral literacy research and teaching. By interpreting Black women's perspectives, rather than simply inserting their transformations into a White group, Black women become central to theorizing college literacy transformation.

When I began the role of leading a college literacy program in 1998, I could not imagine the power that would emerge from a purposeful, collaborative, inquiry-based democratic curriculum perspective. My cognitive theoretical perspective was transformed into a cognitive and social constructivist standpoint, and ultimately to emancipatory leadership. When I labeled myself as a democratic curriculum leader in college literacy, my critical questioning turned toward the realization of individual identity and social justice related to the peer counselors and myself. Lauryn and Vania taught me that, in a democratic, inquiry-based context, they developed their personal identities within a family unit. Consequently, these conditions allowed them to transform their college literacy beliefs from the isolation of content into student empowerment. Additionally, their transformation taught me that my educational ideal was not only to assist peer counselors in strategic, cognitive-based college literacy, but to expose the perpetual cycle of oppression by focusing on the liberation of individual and shared voices.

REFERENCES

Allgood, V. P., Risko, V. J., Alvarez, M. C., & Fairbanks, M. M. (2000). Factors that influence study. In R. A. Flippo & D. C. Caverly (Eds.), *Handbook of college reading and study strategy research* (pp. 201-220). Mahwah, NJ: Erlbaum.

Alvermann, D. E. (2001). Reading gender and positionality into the nine case studies: A feminist poststructuralist perspective. In E. S. Moje & D. G. O'Brien (Eds.), *Constructions of literacy: Studies of teaching and learning in secondary schools* (pp. 263-285). Mahwah, NJ: Erlbaum.

Atkinson, R. C., & Shiffrin, R. M. (1968). Human memory: A proposed system and its control processes. In K. W. Spence & J. T. Spence (Eds.), *The psychology of learning and motivation: Vol. 2. Advances in research and theory*. New York: Academic Press.

Baddeley, A. (1990). *Human memory: Theory and practice*. Needham Heights, MA: Allyn & Bacon.

Bartlett, F. C. (1932). *Remembering: A study in experimental and social psychology*. Cambridge, England: Cambridge University Press.

Brooks, A.K. (2000). Transformation. In E. Hayes & D. D. Flannery (Eds.), *Women as learners: The significance of gender in adult learning* (pp. 139-154). San Francisco: Jossey-Bass.

Bruffee, K.A. (1999). *Collaborative learning: Higher education, interdependence, and the authority of knowledge* (2nd ed.). Baltimore, MD: Johns Hopkins University Press.

Bruner, J. (1986). *Actual minds, possible worlds*. Cambridge, MA: Harvard University Press.

Collins, P. H. (1990). *Black feminist thought: Knowledge, consciousness, and the politics of empowerment*. Boston: Unwin Hyman.

Collins, P. H. (1998). Toward an Afrocentric feminist epistemology. In S. Kemp & J. Squires (Eds.), *Feminisms* (pp. 198-205). New York: Oxford University Press.

Collins, P. H. (2000). *Black feminist thought: Knowledge, consciousness, and the politics of* empowerment (rev. ed.). New York: Routledge.

Craik, F. I. M., & Lockhart, R. S. (1972). Levels of processing: A framework for memory research. *Journal of Verbal Learning and Verbal Behavior, 11*, 671-684.

Edmondson Bell, E. L. J., & Nkomo, S. M. (1998). Armoring: Learning to withstand racial oppression. *Journal of Comparative Family Studies, 29*(2), 285-295.

Etter-Lewis, G. (1993). *My soul is my own: Oral narratives of African American women in the professions*. New York: Routledge.

Henderson, J. G. (1999). The journey of democratic curriculum leadership: An overview. In J. G. Henderson & K. R. Kesson (Eds.), *Understanding democratic curriculum leadership* (pp. 1-22). New York: Teachers College Press.

hooks, b. (1994). *Teaching to transgress: Education as the practice of freedom*. New York: Routeledge.

Johnson, L.L., & Carpenter, K. (2000). College reading programs. In R. A. Flippo & D. C. Caverly (Eds.), *Handbook of college reading and study strategy research* (pp. 321-364). Mahwah, NJ: Erlbaum.

Kincheloe, J. J. (1999). Critical democracy in education. In J. G. Henderson & K. R. Kesson (Eds.), *Understanding democratic curriculum leadership* (pp. 70-83). New York: Teachers College Press.

Mezirow, J. (1978). *Education for perspective transformation: Women's re-entry programs in community colleges*. New York: Teachers College Press.

Mezirow, J. (1994). Understanding transformation theory. *Adult Education Quarterly, 44*(4), 222-232.

Morris, C.D., Bransford, J. D., & Franks, J. J. (1977). Levels of processing versus transfer appropriate processing. *Journal of Verbal Learning and Verbal Behavior, 16*, 519-533.

Nist, M.L., & Simpson, S. L. (2000). An update of strategic learning: It's more than textbook reading strategies. *Journal of Adolescent and Adult Literacy, 43*(6), 528-539.

Piaget, J. (1976). *The psychology of intelligence.* Totowa, NJ: Littlefield, Adams.

Pope, S.M. (1996). *Wanting to be something more: Transformations in ethnically diverse working-class women through the process of education.* Santa Barbara, CA: Fielding Institute.

Scott, S.M. (1997). *The grieving soul in the transformation process: New directions for adult and continuing education* (pp. 41-50). San Francisco: Jossey-Bass.

Sveinunggaard, K. (1993). Transformative learning in adulthood: A socio-contextual perspective. In D. Flannery (Ed.), *Proceedings of the 35th Adult Education Research Conference* (pp. 275-280). University Park: Pennsylvania State University Press.

The Group for Collaborative Inquiry. (1994). A model for transformative learning: Individual development and social action. In R. Brockett & C. Kasworm (Eds.), *Proceedings of the 35th Adult Education Research Conference* (pp. 169-174). Knoxville: University of Tennessee Press.

Turner, C.W. (1997). Clinical applications of the Stone Center theoretical approach to minority women. In J. Jordan (Ed.), *Women's growth in diversity: More writings from the Stone Center.* New York: Guilford.

Vygotsky, L. S. (1978). *Mind in society.* Cambridge, MA: Harvard University Press.

Yancy, G. (2000). Feminism and the subtext of Whiteness: Black women's experiences as a site of identity formation and contestation of Whiteness. *Western Journal of Black Studies, 24*(3), 156.

7

Black Women/
Black Literature

Christina McVay
Joanne Kilgour Dowdy

I conducted this interview as a way to document Christina McVay's thoughts and philosophy regarding teaching Black women in the Pan-African Studies department. We believe that the book is better served by including the experiences of those have gained from the study of Black women and Black literature, regardless of ethnic background. Christina McVay is one of many White instructors who have sung the praises of Black oral and written language throughout her teaching and writing career.

Joanne: So tell me a little bit about yourself.

Chris: I was born and raised right here in Portage County, went to under-graduate school here (Kent State University), in fact. I came here in 1969. I was right in time for the shootings, which is a whole other conversation. I majored in German and Russian, went to graduate school in German at Ohio State, got a Fulbright, went to Germany for a year. I came back and got married, which was a mistake. I am basically a single person, so it lasted 3 years. . . . I came back here to do some graduate work in the English Department and was working on a dissertation on race in Faulkner and Conrad when I was invited to teach English in the Pan-African Department. That totally drew me away from the dissertation, and so here I am. Teaching Black literature, mostly, and other non-Western, non-White, minority, ethnic, whatever you want to call it, that's what I'm doing. And this is what I *like* doing.

Joanne: What are some of the classes that you teach?

Chris: I teach *Oral and Written Discourses*, which is about Black English as a language, *The Legacy of Slavery in Literature*, *Pan-African Women's Literature*, *African-American Masterpieces*, *Black Autobiography*, and a few more I'm not thinking of right now. When we revised the curriculum a few years ago, it was great because I had free rein to create some classes. That was nice. And it was nice to be trusted like that, too. . . . I just stumbled into this department! That's been the story of my life, you know? John Lennon said in one of his songs, *Beautiful Boy*, "Life is what happens to you while you're busy making other plans." Boy, is that the truth. I said that in class one day and then asked, "Oh, you guys know who John Lennon was?" "Yeah, wasn't he one of the Temptations?" Okay, right time period. But, yeah, the best things that have happened to me, I just fell into them. You know how I ended up in Pan-African, really? I was working on my dissertation in the English Department and teaching freshman English as a grad student, and I stopped in at a bar where my brother was tending bar. It was payday. I sat down at the bar and Tom said, "You want a draft?" and I said, "No, it's payday, I'll have a real beer," and the guy next to me, a Black man, laughed, and said, "You must work at the University," you know, because we get paid on the 25th. I said, "Yeah, I'm in the English Department," and he said, "Oh, so am I." There were no Black people in the English Department in the mid-1980s. I said, "You are not in the English Department. I have never seen you." And he laughed and told me he was Wiley Smith. He was the coordinator for what we call the Communications Skills and Arts Division, and he started telling me what he does over here. I ended up having a couple of beers with him, but I told him that it kind of aggravated me that there is a freshman English program over there in Pan-African because I never got any Black students in my class, so if I do Black literature, it's White me standing in front of a White classroom, and it's like we're talking about some alien universe. Wiley said, "Well, if everybody in the English Department felt like you, we'd be okay. We could dispense with our classes, but we can't." And he invited me to come over and said when they got an opening, if I wanted, he could arrange for me to come teach over there. So I came over, I think it was not even a week later. I stopped by, and we sat and talked for a long time. He was a really great guy. So that's how I ended up teaching here: I stopped at a bar to have a beer and say hi to my brother.

Joanne: You have been awarded for teaching excellence, right?

Chris: I've gotten actually a few awards. In the December issue of *Ohio Magazine*, I was on their list of the 100 best teachers in the state. They have a quote from an anonymous student. Students frequently say that they come away from my class with a new and different perspective on things. And that's nice to know—that I make them think.

Joanne: Tell me how you came to be involved with Black Women and Literacy in the Pan-African Studies Department.

Chris: You know, I never really thought specifically about being involved with Black Women and Literacy in the Pan-African Department until I saw the question you e-mailed me this morning. I mean, I do it, but I think of myself as a literature person, and yet of course obviously language fascinates me. I majored in German and Russian after all. For a while, I was trying to learn Arabic on my own. I was trying to learn Greek on my own. I did not get very far with either one of those, but language is interesting to me. And it's the fact that I grew up in a pretty tidy, White, disciplined environment and was led to believe that there are rules you have to follow, and that language is a pretty fixed thing. And when I got into college and realized, you know, that's not the way it is at all. You can be so creative, and one of the communities that has the greatest oral dexterity is the Black community. I believe that comes from that long oral tradition from Africa right through slavery and Jim Crow in this country. One of the things that I consider most challenging about being in the Pan-African Department, and most rewarding, too, is getting young Blacks to realize that they *like* language, by and large. Because they have been through this school system, which convinces so many that they hate English. They think they hate it. And they do, at least the way it's been presented to them. So getting them to look at it in a fresh perspective is really a rewarding thing. I really enjoy that. And then, boy, the language that comes, the creativity, the flow, because they've got it. They've grown up with it. And part of the trick is getting them to feel comfortable enough to forget that I'm an English teacher, because that makes them self-conscious.

Joanne: Tell me some of the things you do to get Blacks comfortable with the written English word and to explore their "excellence" because of this legacy that they have inherited.

Chris: Well, one of the assignments that seems to really break things wide open is to write a slang dictionary, but they have to do it like the real dictionary. They've got to tell me what part of speech this is, give a definition. The other choice is to write a dialogue in slang or Black English or whatever you choose to call it, and then write a translation of it in so-called "proper" English, which I prefer calling consensus English. And they seem to relax and have fun with it. But I have to first get across to them that they can be real, that they can be themselves. And the only way I know to do that really is to do it from the first day of class. I just be me. I don't know how to be pretentious. Thank goodness. I can't put a finger on how to do it, but they have to be comfortable with me. And that might just be a gift I have. I think most of my students are. I'm sure there are exceptions, but most of my students are.

Joanne: Tell me some instances with black women on this journey you call making them comfortable, making them see that you are unpretentious, so that they can get to the writing.

Chris: Probably one of the best relationships I've had with any student is with Chandra P. Do you know Chandra? She came here as a STARS student and was in my freshman English class that very first summer. She didn't particularly stand out from the other students in the group. She was an honor's student, and she took my freshman English Honors colloquium immediately after that summer. During that first year, they read *A Raisin in the Sun*, which I sometimes get tired of, but it's a classic. I asked them to write a personal, subjective response to something in that play, and boy, she zeroed in on the line where Walter has messed up big time, right? And Beneatha's mad at him—everybody is mad at him. He lost that money, and Beneatha is giving him a really hard time. Momma turns says, "You know, the time to love a man is not when he's doin' good and he's on top of the world. It's really easy to love him then. The time he needs love is when he's down." Chandra focused in on that and wrote an essay about how that was a lesson she needed to learn and apply because she tended to really get down on the Black men in her life. It was a very good reflective paper. She came into my office for something, and we sat there and talked about the state of Black men. That has become a real interest of hers. Later, she and I went to Memphis a couple of times because she was making a video about Ida B. Wells for her senior honor's thesis project and I was her advisor. Ida B. Wells started her anti-lynching campaign because of three men, one of whom was very good friends with Wells and her family, who were lynched in 1892 in Memphis, so Chandra wanted to film in Memphis. She and I went down there, and we did some interviews, but she was still connecting that to this focus on Black men and being supportive of Black men rather than critical because everybody is so quick to get down on Black men. She incorporated that into this film, that whole point of supporting Black men today. She went from the lynchings of those men, and Ida B. Wells speaking out, to Black men on this campus. It was the first film she made, and the transition from 1892 to today is not as smooth as I would have liked, but it was good nonetheless.

Joanne: I wanted you to talk a little bit about you as a White woman, older than your students, creating an environment where Black females are writing and reading, joining you in this journey of celebration of the English language. What are your thoughts, comments, reactions?

Chris: You know, with students in virtually all my classes in Pan-African, it takes maybe 2 weeks before somebody in the class will say, "Miss McVay, what are you doing over here anyway? Why are you teaching this class?" And my response is usually along these lines: "Okay, you noticed I'm not Black. I know how to read literature, and I know a lot about language. I can help you learn how to read literature. I can help you see what the language is doing. I can teach you how to talk about language and literature. But I can't bring the Blackness to what we're doing. That's your job." And in fact, I learn from my students. I'm never going to pretend to be an expert on Blackness. And they appreciate that. They get to be a co-teacher, you know? So, that works. I throw readings at them where the language is used in such an interesting way, such a fascinating way, that you really do have to celebrate it. I mean, Zora Neale Hurston. Some of her stories, you know? Look at what she's doing here. This is fun, this is brilliant—I don't know many people who can do this; well, I do know some people who are as creative with language, but I sure didn't grow up with them.

My father appreciated that creativity, and I think he taught me to appreciate language. My dad used to read to us, and he would do voices and act out stories. He just loved words. In fact, if my mom asked me to set the table or take out the trash or something and I whined, my dad would say, "Yours is not to wonder why, yours is but to do or die." I thought those were my dad's words. I did not know that that was Tennyson in "Charge of the Light Brigade" until, I don't know, high school or college, so that's the kind of guy my dad was. He was a truck driver, for Pete's sake, and he was quoting poetry at us all the time. So I did grow up with that, although in school it was very strait-laced when it came to language. Very, very proper. But it's not hard to loosen up.

Joanne: That's because the Black students are special.

Chris: Because they've got this tradition, this background. And an English classroom full of White students, I hate to say it, but it is just so deadly dull. They are bored. Really. That is my experience. But once you can flip that switch and make Black students understand they can celebrate their own language. . . . Of course, some people will say, "But then they might think they can write papers using that language." No, they don't. They know there is a time and a place. That's not a problem. And I'll move them back and forth between the Black English and the consensus English that is expected in an academic environment. I'll go back and forth. So we can draw comparisons. And that makes it palatable. For example, the use of an abstract term on the one hand, whereas over here you can have fun using metaphor.

Joanne: Give me some more suggestions for teachers who want to make a comfortable environment for their Black female students, so that they can celebrate the English language the way you do.

Chris: You know, Joanne, this is exactly why I have a problem with education people. They want you to be able to put it into a formula, a model. I don't know how to do that. I don't know if you can do that. I think you're either born with it or you're not. Some people can't make anybody comfortable around them. God forbid, wouldn't that be terrible? If people just can't be comfortable around you? We know people like that. And I feel sorry for them. And the harder they try, the worse it gets. I don't have an answer to that. It's not good to pretend you know things you don't, for Pete's sake. If you don't know, just say, "I don't know." There is nothing wrong with teachers saying, "I don't know. Help me." But I know teachers who will play all kinds of mind games and go through all kinds of intellectual calisthenics to avoid saying or even looking like maybe they don't know. That's probably the big one in the classroom. Maybe the way you carry yourself. I sit in class. There are some days when I'm doing a lot at the board and I might stand, but for the most part, I sit. But I'm not even really sure if that makes a difference. I do share some personal things about myself. I try not to dwell on them. I don't want to take the whole class period talking about me, but you know, I'll talk about my son and I'll talk about the boring school I went to and hated when I was in high school and how I first got interested in Black America, which was at that boring school. My parents sent me to a Catholic girls' boarding school out in the middle of the woods in Pennsylvania. It was actually a convent. There were 700 nuns there and 150 schoolgirls. And it was the 1960s. The world was very, very interesting, and I wanted to be out there. I'm not even Catholic. My parents thought I needed discipline. And the other girls there were there *by choice*, which boggled my mind. How could anybody want to be in a place like this? So that immediately put up a wall between me and them. I mean, I was not unfriendly, but I couldn't get close to them. We were too different. You want to be here; I don't; that's just too big a divide. The second year I was there, a Black girl from Shaker Heights showed up who also did not want to be there, so we immediately became best friends. Nothing else mattered. That's what pulled us together. And she had an older brother and sister who were at Fisk, and they were sending her Eldridge Cleaver, *The Autobiography of Malcolm X*, you know, a lot of Black power literature. So there's Alice and I, sitting in our room with the door locked in this convent in the middle of the woods in Pennsylvania. That is where I became radicalized. That gave me a real jump on most of the White people I knew. You know? We had nothing to do. We read a lot of books. We really read a lot. And sometimes, I think that I'm sorry that when I came to Kent State as an undergraduate, I never took any courses in the Black Studies program. I was very, very interested in race in America, and I already had a fairly decent background. But I never came and took a class here. Why didn't I? Because, and I should have known better, but without thinking I guess I thought that that's for Black kids. That was what everybody—that is, what all the White people—thought. That's what I thought. I was certainly very supportive of the program. But it never occurred to me to take a class. I was here [at Kent State] as an undergraduate from 1969 to 1974. But then, you know, looking back, I think, no, it's a good thing that I went ahead and just floundered around. Couldn't make up my mind about what I wanted to be when I grew up, you know, but I majored in German and Russian. I learned a lot. Then I also got a master's in Comparative Literature, which at that time was essentially European Literature, but I know a lot now about what Westerners have considered the best literature they had to offer and the best culture, and that gives me some authority to say "Guess what? Toni Morrison is just as good. James Baldwin is just as good as any of the German or Russian classics you want to refer to, so I can get down and dirty with you." That European background actually serves me well. I pretty much taught myself Black literature, Black culture, starting back at the villa, reading, with Alice. But when I started teaching Freshman English in PAS in the mid-1980s, I really did my homework in Black Literature. I knew enough about literature, I could do that. . . .

Joanne: Let's back up. You were saying that the students say . . . ?

Chris: Black students have been told by teachers, by the whole school system, frequently by their own parents, that Black English is bad, improper. But as an English teacher I start pointing out things that you can see in this language, things that you can communicate in this language, its succinctness and beauty. Sometimes I have to work pretty hard to undo what they've been told and convince them that Black English is a legitimate language. (You just shouldn't use in your college papers.) Then I frequently get comments from students like, "Oh, it's so nice to hear somebody say that" or "I never thought about it like that." That is rewarding, and that's what education is about. . . . That reminds me of another young Black woman who graduated, and she is e-mailing me now. She had taken my "Oral and Written Discourses" class, and she is getting fed up with her father, who tells her not to use Black English. She was an Education major. She keeps telling me about these arguments that she and her father are having, and—I don't know—maybe she wants me to have lunch with him and straighten him out. But what was your question again?

Joanne: When you teach black literature to Black women, what are some of the lights that go on?

Chris: What are some of the lights that go on in my head or in theirs?

Joanne: Both.

Chris: Oh, in my own head, my favorite writers, by and large, are Black women. I've always believed that you learn more about, at least in my experience, I have learned more about right and wrong and how you treat people and how to be a good person from reading literature. Much more so than by going to Sunday School and church and all of that, which you had to do in my family. So to me literature is not just an academic thing. It really is not. It's a life thing. The Black literature that I have read and most particularly the Black women writers, like Morrison, Hurston, both Margaret and Alice Walker, have made me a different person from who I was 20 years ago. Part of that, I'm sure, is just age. But there are values that I was taught as I was growing up that I've rejected now. Like our western focus on the individual. I'm much more of a community person. And I've learned to respect our elders instead of worshipping youth, to respect our past and tradition instead of being obsessed with the future and the idea of progress. Then there's the idea that we inherit the sins of our fathers—20 years ago, I would have kicked and screamed and argued against that. Now I'm a firm believer. I came to reject the spiritual upbringing I had had. I frequently tell students that if I had been brought up in a Black church, I would probably still be a Christian, because of the passion. I went to a Catholic girls' boarding school, but I was brought up in a very dry, dry Protestant church, prim, proper, you had to be quiet all the time. There was no passion, that was a no-no. And how absurd, you know? I'm still not a Christian, but I have a spirituality now that I have learned. It is in part actually from Black students, primarily females, and from Black literature, primarily females. So, for me, it's a life thing. It's definitely had an impact on my personal life. And now that I sit here and say this, I think probably more lights have gone off for me than for my students. I suppose I'm really doing this teaching for myself—for very selfish reasons, clearly. Yeah. Okay. But students, Black women of all ages, will sometimes say, "Oh, so *that's* where that comes from. I thought it was my family, but it's a Black thing." They're making connections between what we read in this piece of literature and their own experiences. It's very important that they see that what they thought was an isolated thing is actually something that has made them and members of their family part of a community. So it's important that they see themselves in what we're reading.

Joanne: So you told me how you came to be involved with Black women and literacy and literature. So what does this mean to you in the context of your life journey, having been involved with this for 20-something years? What does it mean to you in your book of life?

Chris: Oh, everything. Everything. As I just said, it has changed me as a person. It has changed my values, or maybe helped me see clearer many of the values that I live by. I wouldn't want to be doing anything else. And I feel I am living, doing something I enjoy, that I consider valuable and important and rewarding. How many people in the history of the world have been able to pay their bills, to make a living, doing something that they really, really enjoy? Every morning I know I'm going to do something all day long that I enjoy. God, that puts me in a very exclusive club.

Joanne: Any other thoughts or feelings about this thing called teaching in Pan-African Studies, working with Black women?

Chris: You know, actually, I have been thinking for years that I really need to reconnect with Alice from the Villa because she lived in Shaker Heights, and a couple of her friends were undergrads at Kent at the same time I was, and they were involved in the bus boycott and the demand for Black history classes and all that. They were politically very active on campus. Who wasn't back then? Alice and I lost touch some time in the 1970s. I have ideas about how I could find her. I don't know why I don't do it. I think she'd be stunned that I'm teaching in this department now. But I think I'm afraid that she's changed too much. And I guess that I'm just afraid to know what she's become. What if she's a rich, beautiful Black woman who isn't particularly interested in Black culture anymore? Wouldn't that be a weird irony? Yeah, that's what I'm afraid of. But then if I'm wrong, what am I missing out on? So, I really should look her up.

Joanne: Think of all those great classes . . . the Black voice.

Chris: Yeah, boy.

Joanne: There's a book for you to write.

Chris: I've thought about that several times. That is a book. That is a picture, isn't it?

Joanne: Write it like you're telling me.

Chris: Yeah, and I know my parents did not send me to the Villa for that reason, you know?

Joanne: All the more reason.

Chris: Right. It's funny how things work out. It would be a good story. But I need time.

Joanne: I just want to say thank you a million.

Chris: Absolutely. Thank you.

8

Teachers as Leaders in Urban Education: Testimonies of Transformation

Joan T. Wynne

The stories people tell have a way of taking care of them. If stories come to you, care for them. And learn to give them away where they are needed. Sometimes a person needs a story more than food to stay alive.

—Barry Lopez, Crow and Weasel

I began writing this piece because I wanted to tell the story of the dramatic changes I had witnessed in 13 teachers who were participating in an Urban Teacher Leadership (UTL) program. Not only had those teachers' changes been dramatic, but they were also quick in coming. After just one semester in the program, they spoke about transformations so compelling that, like the ancient mariner, I talked about these remarkable teachers and their testimonies of change to all who would listen. So I thought the UTL story was about them. However, when I asked my late friend and mentor, Dr. Alonzo A. Crim, to read their story, he asked, "But what is it that these teachers and the program taught you? What did you learn?"

Reflecting on Dr. Crim's question, I began to see more clearly that the teachers' stories of transformation and mine were intricately intertwined. Throughout our journey together, lessons unfolded for all of us. The most important lesson, I think, emerged one day when the teachers and I were in my office practicing for a panel discussion to be given at a national conference, an opportunity to describe our experiences in a new UTL Master of Science Degree Program. While practicing, one of the panelists, a teacher of African descent, Yolanda,[1] said to us, "I don't want to tell that part of my story because I hate to admit that I once felt that way about my students." She was referring to some unconscious racist notions that she had held prior to her participation in our program, notions about the incapacities of children of color who live in poverty—notions that I, too, as a young teacher had once absorbed. Remembering her words, in a moment, crystallized for me what this program was really about. I had thought, when helping to design the program (a program that was the brain child of Lisa Delpit), that its major focus was developing teachers as leaders. Although advocacy of urban children and their families was the theme undergirding all the components of the program, during the initial creating process, what seemed paramount to me was facilitating the development of leadership skills for teachers. Over a year into the program, however, after listening to these teachers and reflecting on their experiences, I now realize that reckoning with the ravages of racism has been the central focus in the lives of the participants as well as mine—and the most important impact of the program.

As the story of that impact unfolds, like Yolanda, I have an admission. Although I have spent much of my life confronting racist attitudes, I know that being White I am riddled with racism. I have breathed in the disease that seems endemic in the U.S. culture. Thus, none of my comments on society's addiction to racism or the UTL participants' struggle to unravel it, in any way, reflects an assumption on my part that I am free of such unconscious attitudes or acts— only that I am on a journey of unlearning racism. So when I challenge educational institutions and society at large on their racist policies and belief systems, and when I tell of the journey of these teachers to shift their way of thinking, I am also attempting to uncover that racism buried in my own psyche—to constantly undo my own miseducation about children of color forced to live in poverty by a culture who devalues them.

Part of Yolanda's story as well as the other 13 UTL teachers' testimonies, only 1 of whom is White, may be more fully understood if they are put in the context of the consequences of the miseducation of and about urban children who live in poverty, especially children of African descent—a miseducation that impacted all 13 of the program's first cohort. The other part of their stories involves the power of education that liberates.

---

[1] Yolanda is a fictitious name.

RACISM AND MISEDUCATION

From my experiences in and out of the classroom these last 30 years, from others' research and mine, and from conversations with scholars of African descent, I have learned that the miseducation *of* urban children of color typically comes from the miseducation of adults and society at large *about* those children and their families—a miseducation rooted in racism. It is rooted there because U.S. culture has been built on a history, traditions, epistemologies, politics, and economics steeped in hegemonic thought. Those aspects of mainstream culture were part of the investigations of UTL teachers in the first semester of the program. They began such explorations in an orientation retreat cofacilitated by Dr. Alonzo Crim as well as during their first two courses, one team-taught by Dr. Asa Hilliard and me, "The Psychology of the Inner-City Child," and the other team-taught by Dr. Lisa Delpit and me, "Creating Excellence in Urban Education." During this same semester, the cohort further explored those issues while attending two professional conferences held at the university that dealt specifically with teaching children of African descent. After these early experiences, the teachers reported, during evaluation sessions, significant shifts in their thinking about their students, the parents of those students, and the communities where their students lived.

Those shifts that the cohort continued to make throughout the program constantly reminded me of the gravity of the impact of our biased notions about the performance of urban children of the poor. Years ago Jean-Paul Sartre (1963) best captured that impact when he spoke of his European history and what he called "that super-European monstrosity, North America":

> It seems that we are the enemies of mankind; the elite shows itself in its true colours—it is nothing more than a gang. Our precious sets of values begin to moult; on closer scrutiny you won't see one that isn't stained with blood. (Schwartz & Disch, 1970, p. 618)

When hearing the UTL teachers talk about previous attitudes they had held about the children they taught, the children outside the circle of the "elite," I began to understand again the full weight of Sartre's assertion that "we are the enemy." Our larger, hegemonic society, "super-European monstrosity" had effectively seduced itself and these teachers of color into thinking that students of their same ethnicity, who happened to be poor, were intellectually limited, unmotivated to learn, and academically crippled by uncaring parents. At the end of the first year of the program, when reading evaluation forms written by this first cohort, I continued to recognize the level of the seduction through their words of change:

- "I have learned that urban children can succeed just like any other child in any other setting."

- "I learned that urban children have a lot of strengths. Their environment should not be used to hold them back. They are intelligent beings. Their environment does not indicate what they can do."
- "I have a new conversation about what our urban children can achieve—a conversation I would not have had before."
- "My philosophy has changed since the program. I now believe teaching is a service. I have a mission to nurture my students academically and emotionally. I want to connect them to the world."[2]

Before reading these admissions of change, I had witnessed with the cohort what I had seen previously during my own experiences as a new teacher and with other urban teachers—"internalized oppression"—believing the distorted messages about one's own group" (Tatum, 1997, p. 6). Because of the dominant culture's "stained values," our history, and continued practices of oppression, even teachers of African descent often absorb faulty notions about people of color. These distortions permeate the society. Consequently, teachers, both Black and White, of the urban poor often act out of an unconscious assumption that those students, their parents, and their communities bring no real value to the educational experience. Like many in society (and myself when a first-year teacher), most of the UTL teachers came to the program assuming that if their students of color failed to achieve academically, then the students, their parents, and their "dysfunctional " communities were responsible, not the schools and not the teachers. During the cohort's candidate interviews, as well as during their Orientation Retreat for the program, the teachers consistently complained about lack of parental support for their students' education.

Until my experiences with the UTL program and my work with a co-reform effort, I do not think I fully realized the complexities and heavy weight of the impact of internalized oppression. Previously, while teaching at Morehouse College, the only all-male historically Black college in the nation, and Howard

---

[2]Questions on evaluation form: "What do you think are your strengths as a teacher/leader? What have been your greatest points of growth as a result of this program? Name one or two particularly memorable experiences in the program. Where have you grown as a leader? Name at least one specific leadership role that you have taken as a result of this program. Name two or three instructional strategies that you have used in your classroom since beginning the program. How has your educational philosophy changed since the program began? What specific things about urban children have you learned because of the program? What specific things about leadership have you learned because of the program? What changes, if any, have you made in your professional life as a result of the program? What changes, if any, have you made in your personal life as a result of the program? What, if anything, are you doing differently at your school as a result of something you've learned in the program? What has changed about you as a scholar? What would you like to change about the Urban Teacher Leadership Program?

High School, a Black high school, I had worked alongside many professors and teachers of African descent who had resisted assuming the societal stereotypes about their ethnic brothers and sisters. Thus, I had not fully understood the capacity of racist notions to infect the minds of so many of its victims. First in the co-reform effort and then in the UTL program, however, I began to see how pervasive and insidious are the distortions of power and privilege among oppressed people.

In a recent conversation with Yolanda, more evidence of the depth of the grip of past internalized oppression unfolded. During the initial year, she along with the first cohort had gone through a process of developing a personal leadership profile. Her leadership skills, as well as the others, were individually assessed by their supervisors at their schools and several of their peers and then sent to a professional firm to be analyzed, where their strengths were identified and suggestions for growth were offered. During the year, the cohort was asked to select a mentor at the school who would periodically assess the growth of a specific leadership skill chosen by the participant to develop. After the first 15 months of the program, during an individual evaluation session with two of the professors, each cohort member reported her profile progress. It was during that session that Yolanda revealed the distorted messages about her capacity to achieve—messages that she had absorbed during her growing-up years in a public school. She said,

> While I attended school, an integrated school, I got the message that being Black, I would never do as well as the White students. I mean I always thought, "You're Black, so White students will always do better than you." I took that with me into my classroom with my students . . . and I almost dropped out my first semester of this program because I felt I didn't have what it takes to compete with the White students that were in one of my classes. Here I was in this majority White university wondering what I was doing at this place. If it hadn't been for you and Dr. Hilliard, I would have dropped out. But now I feel I can do anything. And, now, that I've been inducted into an honor society—well.

On that same day, another teacher confessed that before enrolling in the UTL program, she did not set high enough standards for her students. "I just felt sorry for those children who were raggedy. I didn't think they could do very much. But now in my classroom, they are learning twice as much as they were—before I didn't understand how smart they really are."

These courageous confessions persuaded me that refusing to address the distortions of internalized oppression with teachers of urban children of color jeopardizes every player in the classroom. The teacher loses sight of her own power to teach all children, and she unconsciously sends messages to her students that they are unteachable. The cohort's admissions of their vulnerability due to racism's clasp may suggest that every White teacher, before she puts another foot in an urban classroom with children of color, needs to hear Yolanda's story as well as all the others' stories. They need to hear them because those stories indicate a new imperative in preservice and inservice education: a long and honest dialogue that allows us as White teachers to confront the consequences of society's denial of the reality of oppression. The damage we do because of that denial is at times unthinkable! Through denial, we protect institutionalized racism, allowing it to continue to grow in our society like a cancer. Thus, we become partners in creating and sustaining internalized oppression, damaging teachers of color like Yolanda, and, then, the children they teach by blaming all of them for the failures of the schools that so poorly serve them.

Because the UTL teachers were honest enough to confide their changes and were open enough to change, they taught me how unconscious I had been of the most significant root cause of the ills of urban education. I have spent decades in urban schools facilitating staff development about diversifying instructional strategies. For years I have taught urban faculties collaborative learning models. I have even facilitated diversity trainings. Yet until these teachers shared their testimonies of change, I had not understood how stupidly I had "followed the wrong god home." I had spent much of my professional life asking teachers to change their teaching strategies, when this was only the tip of the iceberg. Paradigms of oppression, and all their disguises, not just bad pedagogy, lurk underneath the surface, blocking our hopes for building effective learning communities. It is those negative belief systems that disrupt the academic growth of our urban children of the poor, corroding every fiber of our school systems. It is those belief systems that I now realize I should have been confronting first within educational circles all those years, not cooperative learning, diversity training, or varying instructional strategies. All of those issues may indeed need to be raised, but examining attitudes about students and their parents needs to happen first. The experiences of the UTL program have persuaded me that dramatic shifts in thinking about how to teach more effectively by varying instruction seem to happen more quickly after first addressing erroneous belief systems about the intellectual capacity of children and parents living in poverty. Teachers need a safe space to take an honest look at the consequences of those attitudes on these communities, on themselves as professionals, and on the systems that are supposed to serve the students, parents, and teachers in communities besieged by poverty.

As a result of these cohort stories, I am clearer about what those systems lack because I now better understand the profundity of the lessons I thought I had learned years ago from some of the masters I have studied. I thought I had learned from Alonzo Crim (1991) about the importance of a "community of believers." I thought I had learned from Lisa Delpit (1997a, 1997b, 1998) about the brilliance of all children, especially those "economically disenfranchised children of color." I thought I had learned from Asa Hilliard (1997a, 1997b, 1998, 1999) the imperative of teachers being in caring relationships with their students. From all three I thought I had learned how important it was to acknowledge the gifts that children of the poor bring to the classroom. Yet until my experience with the UTL teachers, I had talked in educational circles most often about other things—about more effective methods to teach reading, writing, and even science.

Ladson-Billings et al. (2000) validated this need for another kind of conversation, as well. While discussing a school restructuring effort, she said: " . . . even when there is wide support for change, without confronting the underlying beliefs of teachers about the educability of particular groups of students, that change is likely to be subverted" (p. xiii).

In the UTL program, however, by continuously participating in a different dialogue, by exploring underlying beliefs, I was witnessing the speedy changes this cohort made in their professional and intellectual lives as a result of examining erroneous societal assumptions about families of color who live in poverty. I heard these teachers speak about the powerful effect of learning that their own cultural history was rich in valuable lessons to be lived and taught. I listened as they talked in and out of the classroom about the profound significance of their discovery of an African worldview, of how that new knowledge had impacted their making sense of their own experiences and those of their students. I watched their faces as they revealed their surprise at how they had unconsciously *bought into* the dominant culture's false research, stereotyping their Black male students as somehow antisocial and unteachable. I understood when one of the cohorts, Rachelle, confessed to me in my office one day: "Yes, the teachers at my school and I have often explained away a students' behavior by describing him as 'that bad-ass boy.'" We were all beginning to understand how easy it is to fall back on society's determination to negatively label these children and, thereby, to write them off—to do what Ladson-Billings et al. (2000) insisted that "far too often, teachers do." They "demonstrate a belief that it is more important to control and manage African American learners (particularly males) rather than teach them" (p. x).

Developing an understanding of the consequences of those kinds of beliefs and learning the significance of integrating cultural histories and values into instruction seemed to impact the practices of all, including our only White cohort member. While visiting her classroom one day, I observed her using an African-centered affirmation with her mathematics class—a class composed of only African males. She began the class with every student reciting a libation, which she had learned from one of her UTL colleagues of African descent. She was using the practice as a way to explore the consequences of establishing a cooperative learning environment on academic achievement for students who were struggling with mathematics. Rather than trying to control the students' behavior as they loudly chanted the affirmation together, she pushed them to discuss the implications of the chant for their working together to achieve academic excellence. Her strategy stands in stark contrast to those teachers described by Ladson-Billings who want only to "manage African-American learners." I am convinced that her life story was dramatically changed by her deep connection to her African-American teacher cohort and their willingness to support her growth while they grew.

Because of witnessing these teachers' unusual capacity to so quickly shatter their belief systems, coupled with my previous experience researching a co-reform effort that was struggling with racism, I began to believe that all dialogue about educational change should begin with a discussion about "the pain of racism, the necessity for constant surveillance lest it slip into our souls." The experiences of these courageous 13 caused me to wonder whether, by my being in another conversation for so many years, I had forgotten the need for that "constant surveillance." Had I allowed it to "slip deeper into" my soul, the souls of the teachers I taught, and the children they taught? Because of my White privilege, had I too seldom addressed the torment that mothers of color face each time they are "confronted with racism's ugly face," especially those mothers of children in urban schools?

As I watched the UTL 13 shed the trappings of their miseducation about these Black mothers and their children, I was reminded again how seldom White educators address the accepted values of the culture that Sartre suggested are "stained with blood." Through the cohort's grappling with historical lies embedded in school curriculum that they and I had often unwittingly taught, I became more aware that the "how" to teach was not all that needed to change; more important, it was the "what" we teach that had to change. I had not known enough or maybe been brave enough to talk to large faculties about changing the "what" we were teaching children. Over the years, I had talked about infusing diverse cultural histories, art, literature, and so on into mainstream curriculum, but I had never challenged the lies or the values we teach. I most often stayed safe by teaching others "how" to teach. Yet as Freire and Macedo (1987) indicated, "There is no such thing as a neutral education." We either enculturate our youth by teaching within a context that sustains the present hierarchal epistemologies or we teach within a context of transformation.

The limited and often dangerous perspective of teaching only the mainstream cultural values has created distortions about the integrity of other cultures. Thus, society at large ignores or, worse, condemns any philosophy that is inconsistent with Eurocentric values. Because such messages from the media bombard our every waking hour, many teachers cannot escape the misrepresentations about children and parents in poor neighborhoods of color. When teachers assume no value can come from these communities of color, they typically expect little from those students, teach less instead of more, and, therefore, get less together, she pushed them to discuss the implications of the chant for their working together (Rokeach, 1968). Many teachers, both African American and Anglo, have absorbed these false notions, yet I have met other African-American teachers who have not. Regardless, the power of our culture's miseducation about the capacity of these students to achieve is so pervasive that it threatens the quality of their education and, ultimately, their lives.

That miseducation due to faulty belief systems threatens mainstream children as well (Delpit, 1997a, 1997b). It threatens them on a number of levels. Intellectually, it distorts their worldview, keeping them from grappling with the fact that they are only 18% of the earth's population. Its notions of superiority limit these children's ability to understand and learn from the wisdom of other cultures. As Rokeach (1968) found in his research in 1960, it hinders their problem-solving skills. But the largest threat is to their sense of moral integrity. For, like James Weldon Johnson, I believe that dealing with racism "involves the saving of black America's body and white America's soul" (Schwartz & Disch, 1970).

EDUCATION THAT LIBERATES

"Saving bodies and souls" is the other side of the 13 teachers' story—the power of education when it liberates. From the dramatic testimonies of transformation that these 13 offered while still participating in the UTL program, the possibility for education to unshackle the mind from monocultural intellectual traps and myopic visions of one-dimensional children becomes clear. As the program progressed, the teachers' unconscious negative attitudes and belief systems of hopelessness for their students unraveled. From their comments in class and the transcripts of their recorded program evaluations, we learned that these teachers were beginning to:

- see not only the problems, but also the blessings of the child's home culture;
- understand the value of connecting that culture to what the student was expected to learn in school;
- see beauty in other dialects and languages—not just in standard English;
- appreciate the need to value the language the child spoke at home to help the child develop a proficiency in the standard dialect;
- understand the alienation of parents from the school;
- look at the parents and their communities as possessing wisdom that could inform the schools; and
- develop a "discipline of hope." (Student surveys)

These new insights, spoken and written about by the teacher/leaders, may need consistent reinforcement within a support network because, as Pauline Lipman (1988) suggested: "In popular culture, African American inner-city neighborhoods are demonized as pathological, dysfunctional, and violent. . . . These images obscure the real strengths of supportive African American communities, families, and institutions." Being constantly bombarded by those images, within and outside the schools, our teacher/leaders may slip in and out of their new consciousness. However, if we are successful in sustaining the support network we are developing with them, their insights may be long-lived and replicated throughout their schools and districts.

THE URBAN TEACHER LEADERSHIP
MASTER OF SCIENCE DEGREE

In our country's culture, teachers are more often than not discouraged, discredited, and/or disrespected by all levels of society. Politicians scorn them, legislators make laws to constrain them, the media scoffs them, parents and administrators blame them, and students often resist them. Many times I have heard undergraduate students ask preservice teachers, "Why do you want to be *just* a teacher?" In designing the UTL program, we wanted to encourage teachers to see that they are much more than a "just," and that they do not have to leave the classroom and become administrators to be seen as worthy. Nor did we want them to assume that they had to leave the classroom to assert their influence beyond the classroom. We wanted to foster the understanding that a career in the classroom is a profound privilege, a sacred trust, and, as Asa Hilliard (1999) said, "the most important profession."

This understanding was affirmed by Karla,[3] one of the members of our first cohort. After 1 year into the program, our department chair visited one of the UTL classes and asked the cohort to share any particular insights they might have gained as a result of their participation in the program. Karla responded, saying that one of her colleagues at her elementary school had asked her whether pursuing this degree was going to get her out of the classroom. She told her colleague, "No, it makes me want to stay in the classroom; working with my kids is the most important thing I do."

The growth in their professional pride was part of their journey toward development as leaders. For them, as for many teachers challenging negative notions about themselves and their students, it became both a personal and public journey. Encouraging this cohort to take such a journey inside and outside their classroom became an important component in the UTL program. Many in the cohort were willing to address the issue for themselves, but because of their feelings of isolation within the school environment, they were at first reticent to share their ideas with their colleagues. The reasons for this seem evident. Teachers are typically left out of the loop of leadership in their schools, and all too often, if given leadership roles, they lack the skills that will lead to their success as leaders. Historically, education has excluded from its leadership the professional force whose experience and insights could inform and enrich its deci-

---

[3]Karla is a fictitious name.

sion-making process. An even bigger reality for this cohort were the results of investigations of scholars like Delpit (1998), which indicated that many schools have effectively shut out the voices of teachers, parents, and students of color.

As we designed the UTL program, besides being conscious of the necessity to initiate a dialogue with the cohort on such imposed silences, we also wanted to help develop the skills they would need to work within site-based management models and other school reform efforts that were increasing in the schools. In those systems, teachers are expected to collaborate with other teachers on issues of instruction and curriculum, present innovative pedagogy to colleagues, help define budgets, and serve on schoolwide and community councils, committees, and boards. They are asked to share instructional expertise across districts; collaborate with community and foundation leaders in finding resources for their classrooms and schools; become more intimately involved at local universities in the preparation of preservice teachers; and organize diverse groups affiliated with schools in the larger community to encourage a bigger investment in the accomplishment of school goals set for student achievement.

We recognized that to adequately perform in those new roles, teachers need more opportunities for formal training in leadership skills and in principles of action research. They need encouragement to shift from their perception of isolation into recognition of themselves as active participants in a larger context. In developing this sense of the whole, they need support so that their contribution as professionals can grow beyond the walls of the classroom. They need encouragement to see themselves as professionals and leaders, especially if they are to deal with the debilitating impact of racist attitudes toward children and parents in urban schools.

Others outside of educational reform also have seen the necessity to change the way we think about who becomes leaders, who is included in the circles of power—an issue crucial to understanding the impact of racist epistemologies. Peter Block (1996), a business consultant, warned:

> Our task is to create organizations that work, especially in a world where everything constantly seems up in the air. We know that fundamental change is required. We keep talking about cultural change, but this will not be enough if we stay focused on changing attitudes and skills. No question that beliefs and attitudes need to change, but unless there is also a shift in governance, namely, how we distribute power, and privilege, and the control of money, the efforts will be more cosmetic than enduring. (p. xix)

One of the program's primary functions was to encourage the UTL teachers to see themselves as teachers and leaders, not one or the other. We believed that as teachers they would empower their students to achieve academic excellence, and through each teacher's success in the classroom, she would then as a leader influence her colleagues by sharing her best practices to revolutionize individual schools so that every child at every school academically flies.

Earlier, during their selection interviews, these teachers never mentioned the responsibility of faculties and schools to change to create more effective learning environments for their students. The teachers in these sessions seemed convinced that the children and their parents must change if the children were to achieve any modicum of academic success. There was an overwhelming collective conviction that if parents did not get involved in the children's education, the children would never succeed.

Surprisingly, after only one semester into the program, these teachers began to change their assumptions and modify their instructional practices. After continuous exposure in the program to research that indicated a high level of achievement for all students was not only possible, but was occurring in schools in different parts of the country who served students from similar backgrounds as theirs (Sizemore, 1982), the teachers began to expect and demand more from their students. In their program journals, the teachers began documenting their changes in beliefs about their students, the parents of their students, and the capacity of teachers to more effectively teach their students. All of these changes signified a tremendous leap in deconstructing the racist assumptions of the society in which they live.

Another characteristic of racism, the notion of *elitism*, at times reared its ugly head. One of the teachers, Alice,[4] admitted in a conference after her first semester in the program that:

> Frankly, I felt that I was better than these kids. I really hate to admit this, but before this program, I felt like I was above my students. Now, though, I don't believe in student failure. It goes back to me being a better educator. Now that I've been educated about urban children, I really do believe that all children can learn. And for the first time I really believe that my job is important. And now I want to become more intellectual, not in a stuffy sense, but in the sense of really knowing what I'm supposed to know to be a great teacher.

Her admission of believing that she "was better than these kids" spoke to the often unconscious negative attitudes held about children of color living in poverty.

Alice's sudden realization that her "job is important" suggested her need to combat the overall lack of status that the profession holds in the larger society. Her newfound professional pride insinuates the consequences of teachers absorbing the dominant culture's attitudes toward economically disenfranchised people of color. Regardless of the teacher's ethnicity, for many of them their sense of power seems to get distorted. No matter how vigorously they initially blame the students, parents, or communities for their students' academic failures, the teachers, on some level, are aware that they are not meeting the learn-

---

[4]Alice is a fictitious name.

ing needs of those children. Because of that awareness, they tend to assume that teachers are powerless to produce results for urban children. Thus, for many teachers, getting out of the classroom seems the only avenue to power and importance.

Another teacher/leader's comments spoke again to the proclivity to blame the students and their parents for academic failure. After just one semester into the program, she said, in a session where she was evaluating her participation in the program, that:

> I used to constantly attack parents for not being involved in their children's education. But now I see them in a whole different light. I used to think it was the child's fault for not learning, but now I understand that they have different styles of learning. That even though I may be African American just like my students, still their home culture is different from mine and I need to understand that. Meanings are different, you know, according to cultural differences and socioeconomic status. I'm trying now to bring more of the students' culture into my lessons. I'm also surprised at how much I know now. . . . Before I only had opinions, but now I have research based knowledge. . . . I can talk more intelligently to other teachers now about what we need to do to make it better for our kids, because I know more now. I can talk from a base of real knowledge. I understand the need for research to problem solve. I mean solutions need to come from research.

Her growing confidence as a spokesperson for her newly formed philosophies, as indicated in this assessment session, became apparent as well when she, in the beginning of the school year, gave a presentation to the faculty at her new school about more effective instructional strategies to teach writing. This is quite an accomplishment for a teacher who had never addressed her faculty at her previous school.

In a later interview at the end of the first year of the program, the same teacher said that because of the program she had expanded her instructional strategies to include cooperative learning and culturally responsive pedagogy. In addition, during this interview, she said she no longer blamed parents for the children's failure to achieve; she looked to herself to find the strategy to allow each child to succeed. The negative notions about parents and their inability to parent well if they are poor seemed ubiquitous in the beginning of the program with all 13 teachers.

In her journal, another teacher/leader, Christine,[5] spoke of changing her attitudes about students and parents:

> I've gotten rid of my hopelessness about the children. I've changed my 29-year philosophy of teaching and children. I'm much more connected to my

---

[5]Christine is a fictitious name.

students. I feel more like the students are mine. If someone hurts my students, it's like they are my own. I've changed my attitude about parents. I
don't blame them anymore.

These teachers were beginning to challenge their assumptions about the
students, parents, and communities where their schools were housed.
Unconsciously these teachers, although they were African, had bought into the
Eurocentric worldview, "I think, therefore I am." One ramification of that view
in our educational systems is a belief that children can learn well without being
connected to their teachers. It is a belief that does not work for most urban children of color living in poverty. The African-centered worldview suggests that
relationship is at the heart of everything, and that the African child learns best
when she feels connected to her teacher (Nobles, 1995). Christine's realization
that her children responded better to what she was trying to teach when they felt
a kinship with her came after her study of African culture and the psychology of
the inner-city child. During these graduate experiences, she altered the way she
related to her students in her classroom and noted the difference in their academic performance.

SIGNIFICANT CHANGES FOR THE TEACHER LEADERS

I think it is important to recognize that these teachers were making dramatic
changes in their classrooms and schools while teaching a full load during the
day, 5 days a week, attending classes at the university, writing research papers,
giving professional presentations at local, state, and national conferences, and
taking care of their families. In this cohort, only one participant lived without
children and/or a spouse.

Repeatedly, the 13 teachers seemed to unravel the severe impact that
unconscious racism wreaked on the lives of their students and on the impotence
of their schools to educate those students. All of the teachers taught in urban
schools where the majority of their students of color suffered low academic
achievement. I never dreamt that the transformations in belief systems and
classroom practices could happen so quickly, but indeed they did.

I knew the magic that Crim, Delpit, and Hilliard had worked on my thinking was formidable, but I had come to them after years of attempting to question
my beliefs and after having been influenced by many other thinkers of African
descent. These UTL teachers had come with previously unchallenged racist
notions about children of color who lived in poverty and, as many said to me,
either ignorant of the qualities of their own African culture or with unconscious
notions of the inferiority of that culture. So how is it that in such a short time so
much could shift? For it was not just their words that told us they had changed,
but also watching them in their classrooms with their children. We observed

them modify their instructional strategies to include collaborative learning; writing circles for children, including kindergartners; literature honoring the child's culture; and more hands-on experiential learning tasks. We saw them begin to respect their children's gifts by giving them decision-making power in the classroom—one first-grade teacher created an advisory board of two parents and two students each semester to help with curricular and disciplinary decisions. We began to see them demand high performance from their students instead of giving up on their students' ability to achieve at optimal levels.

We heard the cohort talk to each other about how they were being more creative about engaging the parents in the learning process of their children, and we heard one teacher say, "Even if I don't get the parents involved like I want them to, I know it's my business to teach their children how to read and write and compute. I'll try to include the parents, but if I'm unsuccessful, I'll just move on because I'm responsible for my students' achievement." That was a mouthful for a teacher who had come into the program blaming parents for her students' inability to learn what she thought she was teaching.

In addition, while observing these teachers make presentations to their faculties, we heard them try to answer questions of resistant teachers. We heard them answer with confidence about the promise of their students, quoting research they had read and ideas they had learned from their teacher/leader mentors.

The evaluations submitted by the teachers, conversations in the college classroom, and the observations in their classrooms demonstrated that these teachers were becoming more effective instructors; more fluent in their writing and more aware of their need to continue to grow as writers; able researchers; bold leaders in their schools; and professionals who wanted to engage others in positive dialogue about important issues impacting the education of our urban children.

SIGNIFICANT CHANGES FOR ME

Although I learned many important lessons from this cohort of remarkable teachers, the most important one, I believe, is this: Until we confront the racist practices and philosophies that hinder many urban children's academic progress, those children will rarely "fly" in our institutions. Seeing these 13 struggle to break away from negative notions about their students suggests to me that if we want to reform our schools, we must collectively address negative belief systems. Because the profession in K–12 schools is comprised of at least 80% White females, that confrontation should be initiated by them. As I noted elsewhere (Wynne, 2000), we cannot keep waiting for people of African descent to voice it.

Too often I have seen them get nowhere when they raise the issue with White audiences. Yet when they raise it among themselves, it is powerful; and I have seen it in this program transform lives. If only we White educators could hold such conversations with each other and get out of denial, we might make some serious headway in dismantling institutionalized racism. However, it seems that our attachment to White power and privilege prevents us from "confronting racism's ugly face."

Confronting power and privilege is part of the challenge of any educator groomed for leadership. Although the results of many research studies suggest that if we are to raise the level of academic achievement of our children we need to empower their teachers as leaders,[6] few have tackled the issue of changing negative belief systems about urban communities as they try to empower teachers. In addition, too few school reform studies look at this issue. The Carnegie Forum on Education (1986) reported that, "without teacher support any reforms will be short lived," and successful reform "lies in creating a new profession . . . of well-educated teachers prepared to assume new powers and responsibilities to redesign schools for the future" (p. 2). Nevertheless, since the initial implementation of the UTL program as well as my experiences with a K–8 co-reform effort, I am beginning to believe that until White educators confront racism head on, the Carnegie Commission's call to redesign schools will be as Kozol (1975) suggested—"just moving around the same old furniture within the house of poverty," with nothing significantly happening to force schools to effectively educate children of color, especially those who live in urban settings.

Another significant lesson for me happened while watching masters like Crim, Delpit, and Hilliard facilitate the dialogue about these tough issues. Their ability to hold without rancor these discussions about the results of oppression kept me on a learning curve. Growing up in the south, in a segregated society, seeing the abuses that segregation wrought on the entire culture kept me angry at my ancestors, White neighbors, and colleagues most of my life. Seeing these three educators who have dedicated their lives to serving children and teachers, especially those of African descent, deliver without anger instruction that holds the promise to counteract the abuses of racism forced me to look again at my unwillingness to move beyond acrimony and blame. These three master teachers weaved a tapestry of truths so splendidly that often the cohort and I sat in awe. Some scholars might wince at the mention in a research study of expressions of naked admiration like these as well as at the telling of the soulful examinations brought forth by this program. Yet for me those experiences and outcomes are essential to the story of our research. Kozol (1975) suggested "that discipleship like this may be, in the last event, the only thing that can empower a person to live by his beliefs." Being surrounded by denial and psychic numbing about the devastation that my culture is wreaking through racism, I occa-

---

[6]Pellicer and Anderson (1995), Lieberman (1992), and C.S. Anderson (1982).

sionally need a certain reverence for those masters from another ethnicity to carry me forward so that I do not "slip imperceptibly backwards into deadness" into that abyss of denial (Turner, 1975, p. 147).

QUESTIONS AND CONCLUSIONS

After sifting through my research data, I still have several questions. What does it mean for these Black women, these teacher/leaders, to be literate in this new way? Often their individual responses in journals, classes, and evaluation interviews suggested that, as a result of studying their rich and ancient cultural history, they had each grown personally as women of color. They talked about the influence of this history not only on their students in the classroom, but also on their children and families at home. They talked about their growth as writers, leaders, and teachers using culturally responsive pedagogy. In reaching for a broader literacy, will they now be able to take on the mantle of powerful Black women professionals in a racist society and transform those places in society where they interact? Will that literacy continue to advance them? Will that literacy encourage them to mentor other Black women and/or teachers riddled with the same insecurities that they initially possessed?

A question for all teacher educators is why, in such a short time, have these teachers, who came to us rife with confusions about urban children of the poor and their parents and unconscious of their negative beliefs about them, significantly changed not only their attitudes but also their behaviors? My hunch is that one of the most powerful factors is the opportunity to study with urban gurus like Crim, Delpit, and Hilliard. Yet because 12 of these 13 are teachers of African descent, did their ethnicity allow them to open sooner to the teachings of these masters. Could it happen as quickly if 12 of the 13 had been White teachers? Without intimate contact in cohorts such as these with teachers of color, will White teachers be able to transform as quickly? Those questions were aroused again after a recent conversation with a colleague who is working with another urban education program at the university. In that conversation, she complained that she often still feels as if she is "banging her head against a brick wall" because several of her students after a year in that program are continuing to blame parents for the schools' failure to teach children. Most of her cohorts are White. How much does their Whiteness prevent them from shifting into new ways of thinking about urban children of color living in poverty?

In living these questions, I have a growing concern that no teacher leadership program can be successful raising the level of academic achievement of urban children of color until it opens up the discourse about racism in the classrooms, the schools, and in society. I have learned from these exceptional UTL teachers how powerful that dialogue can be in shifting attitudes, behavior, and instructional strategies.

The impact of the program on exposing the distortions of mainstream culture seems significant to me. Hearing members of the second cohort, who later entered the program and who are all teachers of African descent, slip into some of the same parroting of mainstream rhetoric about urban children of the poor and their families reminded me again of the need for and the power of the program's attempts to examine racist discourse. In addition, after having read Lipman's (1998) research on the restructuring of two schools in the south, I am more convinced of the imperative for serious conversation about belief systems if any positive change is going to happen in urban schools, especially where White people are in control. In Lipman's study, all the elements of school reform supported by White educators involved in engineering reform efforts were part of the change efforts of the two schools—elements such as teacher empowerment, shared governance, collaboration, professional development, and more time for reflection. Yet while involved in those strategies, many teachers at these two schools "unwittingly reproduced, perhaps even intensified, the marginalization of African American students" (p. 296). Lipman suggested that a major cause for this result was the lack of any sustained conversations about belief systems steeped in race, class, and power inequities. Our program dealt, quite deliberately, with those attitudes and beliefs.

When left unchallenged, those negative belief systems subject the dominant culture not only to erroneous notions about its superiority to other humans, but also its assumptions of power over the natural world. Many scientists suggest those notions have caused irrevocable damage to the earth's resources and the species' life support system. We continue to dump toxic waste into our streams, rivers, oceans, soil, and air, and we strip the land of oxygen-producing trees and forests because we assume an entitlement to all the riches of the earth to meet our unquestioned demands for luxury while one half of the world's population goes hungry. If the scientists are correct about the magnitude of the planetary damage, then failing to address the faulty assumptions of superiority, power, and privilege that racism begets becomes criminal negligence against the ability of future generations to recognize the perils of the planet, and thus their ability to steward the earth toward survival.

Choosing words like *racism* and *planetary survival* may seem too dramatic for some. Using words like *diversity*, *multiculturalism*, and so on over the last decade or two, however, has produced little change that I can observe in epistemologies that continue to intellectually suffocate children and teachers across the country and protect the power and privilege of the elite. Our euphemisms do not lead to real change in schools, in our society, and in the world. Moreover, they contribute to the telling of lies by reducing the lie to pabulum. John Mann, said that "The term 'inequality' suggests a kind of passive accident. . . . It is a gentler word than racism or exploitation. . . . It is an easier word than oppression. . . . Precisely for these reasons it is a useless word" (cited Kozol, 1975, p. 116).

Joao Coutinho (1970), an African- and Native-American scholar said, "There is no neutral education. Education is either for domestication or for freedom." I would add that education either supports or denounces racism. When we refuse to address racism, we give consent to it. No one seems to say it any clearer than Jonathan Kozol (1975) when he admonished those of us in the dominant culture that, "It is not good enough . . . to feel compassion for the victims of the very system that sustains our privileged position. We must be able to disown and disavow that privileged position. If we cannot we are not ethical men and women, and do not lead lives worth living" (p. 6).

The program's attempt to address racism seems to have caused significant repercussions in the personal and professional lives of the teacher/leaders and me. Of course the real test for our UTL program will be what happens to the children in these 13 teachers' classrooms. If within 3 to 5 years of the end of their program we are able to witness student transformations similar to their teachers, with raised levels of academic achievement and social consciousness for these students, we will have much more to say about developing teachers as leaders.

To participate in this journey with these teachers was a gift of watching them "enter the fire of the world, and stand there shining" (Oliver, 1992, p. 2). As I continue to grapple with the "savage inequalities" in our public schools and in our society, I need the stories of these UTL teachers "more than food to stay alive."

REFERENCES

Anderson, C.S. (1982). The search for school climate: A review of the research. *Review of Educational Research, 52*(3), 368-420.

Blick, P. (1996). Stewardship: Choosing service over self-interest. San Francisco: Barrett-Koehler.

Carnegie Forum on Education and the Economy. (1986). New York: Carnegie Foundation.

Coutinho, J. (1970). Preface to Paulo Freire's article, "Cultural Action for Freedom," published in pamphlet form by the *Harvard Educational Review* and the Center for the Study of Development and Social Change.

Crim, A.A. (1991). *Educating all god's children. In Reflections: Personal essays by 33 distinguished educators.* Bloomington: Phi Delta Kappa Educational Foundation.

Delpit, L. (1997). *Other people's children.* New York: The New Press.

Delpit, L. (1997). Ten factors essential to success in urban classrooms. Unpublished speech, UACC Town Meeting, Atlanta, GA.

Delpit, L. (1999). A letter to my daughter on the occasion of considering racism in the United States. In *Racism explained to my daughter.* New York: The New Press.

Diversity trainers' handbook. (1995). Washington, DC: Multicultural Institute.

Freire, P., & Macedo, D. (1987). *Literacy: Reading the word and the world.* South Hadley, MA: Bergin & Garvey.

Hilliard, A.G. (1991). Do we have the will to educate all children? *Educational Leadership*, *49*(1), 31-36.

Hilliard, A.G. (1997a*). SBA: The reawakening of the African mind*. Gainesville, FL: Makare.

Hilliard, A.G. (1997b, Spring). The structure of valid staff development. *Journal of Staff Development,* Spring, *18*(2).

Hilliard, A.G. (1997c). *Tapping the genius and touching the spirit: A human approach to the rescue of our children*. The ninth annual Benjamin E. Mays Lecture, Atlanta, GA.

Hilliard, A.G. (1999). *The spirit of the African child*. Unpublished speech at the Urban Atlanta Coalition Compact Town Meeting, Atlanta, GA.

Hilliard, A.G. (1998). Characteristics of effective teachers. Conversation about his research.

Kozol, J. (1975). *The night is dark and I am far from home*. Boston: Houghton-Mifflin.

Ladson-Billings, G., Pollard D.S., & Ajirotutu, C.S. (Eds.). (2000). *African-centered schooling in theory and practice*. Westport, CT: Bergin & Garvey.

Lieberman, A. (1992). School/university collaboration: A view from the inside. *Phi Delta Kappan*, *74*, 147-155.

Lipman, P. (1998). *Race, class and power in school restructuring*. Albany: State University of New York Press.

Nobles, W. (1995). *African psychology: Toward its reclamation, re-ascension and revitalization*. San Francisco: Institute for Advanced Study of Black Family Life and Culture.

Oliver, M. (1992). *House of light*. Boston: Beacon.

Pellicer, O., & Anderson, L.W. (1995). *Handbook for teacher leaders*. Thousand Oaks, CA: Corwin.

Rokeach, M. (1968). *Beliefs, attitudes, and values: A theory of organization and change*. San Francisco: Jossey-Bass.

Sartre, J. (1963). Preface to *The wretched of the earth*. New York: Grove. (Reprinted in Schwartz, B., & Disch, R. (1970). *White racism: Its history, pathology and practice*. New York: Dell Publishing).

Schwartz, B., & Disch, R. (1970). *White racism: Its history, pathology and practice*. New York: Dell Publishing.

Sizemore, B. (1982). *An abashing anomaly: The high achieving predominately black elementary schools*. Pittsburgh, PA : University of Pittsburgh Press.

Tatum, B.D. (1997). *Why are all the Black kids sitting together in the cafeteria? and other conversations about race*. New York: Basic Books.

Wynne, J. (2000). The elephant in the classroom: Racism in school reform. *ERIC,* 1/2000; and *Resources in Education*, May 2000. EdJustice website, February 2000.

Section III

9

Storytelling

Wanda J. Franklin
Joanne Kilgour Dowdy

Storytelling is an important function in life for all people because they help create a foundation on which we build an understanding of the world as well as
provide a filter through which we experience life. When children come to
school, they bring with them the stories that their communities value. If teachers
pay attention to these stories, they can learn valuable information about the
level of creativity and complexity of thinking that the storyteller is able to produce (Champion, 2003). Storytelling practices can then be used as vehicles for
teaching students reading and writing skills because students use "storying"
structures to organize, comprehend, and produce language and meaning.
Experienced teachers can enhance the way students use community knowledge
through the art of stories and, therefore, enrich the learners' experiences at
school (Delpit, 2002).

Reading about the origins of storytelling is an illuminating journey. In various texts, storytelling is linked to the origins of human life and African civilization. Many authors identify Africans as the first storytellers (Jones, 1967;
Prahlad, 1998). Discovering more accomplishments by Africans is an inspira-
tion for proud descendants of African Americans. However, it is frustrating to
know that the facts about Africa and its contributions to all civilizations are
often buried under mainstream ideas and Eurocentric cultural analyses (Jones,

1967; Prahlad, 1998). A skewed approach to world history is not unusual in academic circles, so it takes an arduous excavation by determined students to unearth certain important treasures from the African legacy.

THE TIMELESS NATURE OF STORIES

As we, the authors, read stories recorded and written by Black storytellers, we found a community of like minds and themes among them. Some stories were old friends who brought back pleasant memories from childhood, and other stories were new acquaintances that represented a future of pleasure in our lives. We found stories that Wanda's family had told. Wanda's memory of one story is:

> My father was the 10th of thirteen children. One story he frequently told described the interaction between his sisters, brothers, and him. My Aunt Lillian and Cousin Sol, to his dismay, told the story to us as young children. The aunts claimed that father was a spoiled child. He would wait until everyone was seated at the table, ready to eat, and then start crying. "I want some gravy," he would sob. My aunt would have to leave her food and return to the kitchen to make gravy for him. He would have hot gravy for his biscuits, but she would have cold food. I found great pleasure in this story because it could make my father squirm in his seat almost 60 years later. I also enjoyed the fact that it gave me a glimpse of my father's childhood persona.

Many times when Wanda did research on storytelling and came across a familiar tale, she would ask, "How did the storytellers know that story?" Wanda believed that she and her family were the only ones who knew the story. It was also interesting to Wanda to note the subtle differences in stories that she recognized. For example, the story of "Tongue Brought Me Here" was one that Wanda's father and pastors told when she was a young girl. As she recalled, the setting of the story was different from what was published in one of the books. In one publication, the story was in an African jungle; in another book, it was set in an American forest. One storyteller used *mouth* whereas Wanda's father used *tongue* to describe the events. In another telling, the character's *skull* was talking, yet the other story depicted the narrator as a bodiless head with eyes that opened and closed and facial expressions that changed as the story unfolded. In all cases, the essence of the story remained the same (i.e., the theme was a cautionary tale about the consequences of talking too much).

As Wanda's father told the story:

> A young man was walking in the woods late at night and hunting with a few of his friends. The friends left him behind in the woods. As he tried to catch up with them, he came upon a skull in the fork of the road. The young

man looked closer. The skull spoke: "Tongue brought me here; tongue will bring you here too." The lad was shocked that the skull talked and ran off to meet his friends. He told them that he had found a talking skull. His friends did not believe him. They told him that he was just seeing and hearing things. So he relented. The next night, he came upon the skull again. He cursed the skull and said, "You made me look like a fool. I told my friends about you and they did not believe me." The skull answered: "Tongue brought me here; tongue will bring you here too."

This time, the young man ran to find his friends and brought them back to the spot where he spoke with the skull. He commanded the skull: "Talk!!" The skull did not answer. He shouted to the skull: "Talk!" The skull remained still and silent. His friends began to laugh and walk away. They told him that the skull did not talk. The boy, desperate to be believed, made a deal with his friends. He said that, if the skull did not talk, they could kill him on the spot. He then pleaded with the skull to talk. He kicked it, hit it, and cursed it, but it still would not talk.

His friends killed him on the spot. As soon as he was dead and his friends had left, the skull turned to him and said: "Tongue brought me here, and I told you tongue would bring you here too."

Wanda's childhood pastor told the story differently:

Several young men were returning from the seasonal hunt. As they made their way to the village, one of the young men saw a head hanging from a tree. All the young men stopped to marvel at the site of a man's head swaying in the wind. The sun was going down fast, so the hunters hurried to get home before dark. All but one hunter left the scene. He stood there questioning the circumstances surrounding the fate of the man whose head was in the tree. He spoke out loud: "I wonder how he got in such a mess?" The head's eyes opened and he answered. "My mouth brought me here. Talking will bring you here, too."

The young man was awestruck. He couldn't believe his ears! He ran as fast as he could to reach the other hunters. As he ran into the village, he retold the events of that evening to everyone. He told about how the hanging head opened his eyes and spoke to him. No one believed him. The elders ordered the men of the village to follow him back to the hanging head. The young man's instructions were to find the talking head. If the head talked to the young hunter, the elder would make him a ruler of the village. If the head did not talk to the young man, the men of the village were to kill him for lying and to hang his head next to the skull in the tree. The men returned to the tree the next evening. The young man begged the head to talk. The head remained silent.

The men of the village laughed at the young man. They stoned him to death, cut off his head, and hung it in the tree. As soon as all the men left, the first head turned to the young man's head, opened his eyes, smiled, and said, "My mouth brought me here. I told you talking would bring you here too."

STORYTELLING AS A LIGHT OF HOPE

Storytelling is the oldest art that humans know and use daily. Its purpose has changed over the centuries, but it still fulfills basic societal and individual needs. Telling tales provides a means to communicate and express feelings to others. *Storying* is self-nurturing and articulates human hope, fears, and dreams (Greene, 1996; McCance, McKenna, & Boore, 2001). In the story *Mary Lou Thorton: My Family*, the narrator, Mrs. Thornton, tells about her family's migration from Kentucky to Ohio. She describes each member of her family, their birth order, and how 7 out of 13 children died as babies. The story demonstrates how much she enjoyed her childhood and valued her family. It also speaks to the pride she feels for her parents:

> As a family, we'd entertain ourselves at home. We sang. We would all dress up and entertain our parents in the evening by having plays. I'd read to my parents and tell them about whatever books I had read. They would just enjoy listening to it. My mother had about a fourth grade education, and father had about a fifth grade. But he was a whiz when it came to math. But they taught themselves to read the paper, and the Bible, and they did it quite well. (McCance, McKenna, & Boore, 2001, p. 101)

The purpose of a story is to describe how people make sense of the events of their lives, experiences, and actions. Joanne's story about how she came to understand her life journey demonstrates the way in which perspective can be achieved through the process of telling a story. Joanne explained to Wanda:

> I remember going to a doctor about a problem I was having with my back. During the conversation, where he was getting some background information about my health history, I began to talk about my sister's imminent death. My recounting of the history of my sister's illness and the short time the doctors told me that she had left with us, led the doctor to ask questions about my health history. He also asked about the coping strategies I had used to deal with certain traumatic events in my life. While the doctor worked on my spine adjustment, I was able to put my sister's illness and my physical symptoms into perspective. It was then easy for me to understand how my body's symptoms represented the level of stress that I was experiencing. I could see that my body was reacting to the news of my sister's illness and coping with the inevitable fact that she would die. My nervous condition and tight muscles were a symptom of my mental distress.

The constructs involved in the division of stories are culture, social interaction, race, and class. Every story that we tell or hear has a purpose and helps keep our lives knitted together.

> Stories show how human actors do things in the world, how their actions
> shape events and instigate responses in other actors, thus changing the world
> (and often the actors themselves) in some way. Stories also reveal the way
> events and other actors act upon others, shaping possibilities and the way
> we view ourselves and our world. (Mattingly & Lawlor, 2000, pp. 4-14)

It is clear from the prior story that I told about my visit to a doctor recently, and the story that Mrs. Thornton told, that we are all storytellers who are acted on and are actors in the drama of stories. We are always using a beginning, middle, and ending in our retelling of events. These are boundaries of passage, not points in time. Through these time units, a story imposes order and meaning on the life events and interpretation of the storyteller (Banks-Wallace, 2002).

STORYTELLING AS A CONDUIT OF CULTURE AND HISTORY

Community of Culture

The process of storytelling follows culturally specific rules (Banks-Wallace, 2002). Culture, tradition, and the worldview of the storyteller determine a story's themes (Jones, 1967). However, themes are woven together and produce a collective worldview within a specific population. Storytellers are motivated by a need for coherence with other persons' stories; therefore, individual stories interconnect with others into larger stories that progress toward a community's narrative. Together the small stories join and create a collective meaning. The communal meaning imparts an understanding of the culture for all who are involved. This understanding is what researchers seek to embrace when they join a new community of storytellers.

A paper written by two authors with similar backgrounds in Black culture, academic orientation, and interest in African literacy practice creates a community that also generates a story about storying. Another important theme in our paper/story is that Wanda is a nurse and a teacher, Joanne is a teacher and performer, and both writers regard storying as a path to healing and building healthy communities. The stories that we choose to include in this chapter are ways of sharing with a wider community, and we see ourselves making a contribution to a smaller community of Black, female writers and readers. Our written story revolves around ways to bring positive life choices into a person's life. Our African heritage, passed down through an oral history from Caribbean and African-American ancestors, makes it possible to tell each other stories that resonate in the choices we make for creating this chapter. The readers of the chapter and the two writers then form a community of literacy students and serve each other in the ritual of revealing meaning in the context of the story that is created through this exercise.

Wanda relates the story of her family's cultural system:

> My family had a collective emphasis on survival. Whether it was financial, physical, psychological, or emotional survival, we all knew what our ideal for living should be. My father would tell my sister and me about the survival of his grandmother. She lived to be over 115 years old, and some said she was over 120 years old when she died. The issue was that she survived. She was a slave. She had three daughters that she raised by herself in horrific post- Civil War Mississippi. She slept under houses, share cropped, and bore unmentionable atrocities. She lived through the Civil War, Jim Crow, Klu Klux Klan, World War I, the Great Depression, and World War II. Nonetheless, she never had a negative word to say about anyone.
>
> In her sixties she lost her eyesight. Because she had such a positive attitude, God restored her sight when she was one hundred years old. The story my father and family tell of this foremother emphasizes how God repays us when we "live right." My grandmother not only survived, but thrived. The grandchildren were often reminded that grandmother endured these hardships and that we had to find it within ourselves to endure whatever we were going through. We were encouraged to use her story as a resource for motivation and inspiration.

Culture and Customs

Cultural beliefs are the bases for stories. A culture's superstitions, ideas about appropriate behavior, and cautionary lessons for children are contained in stories.[1]

Mothers traditionally use stories to teach children about life and nature, who they are, and from where they came. The practice of storytelling creates a record of African-American customs and culture. Many African-American stories are related to the church and religious customs, while other stories are related to lessons and traditions (Jones, 1967; Prahlad, 1998). Among the many functions that stories perform, they also teach and entertain.

Wanda tells a story about how she was taught about safety issues while being entertained:

> My mother told a story about how she found out about violence toward women and girls. When she was young, she was told not to go into the corn field when the cornstalks were moving. In the rural south, there were paths and wagon trails that crossed large cornfields and wooded areas. Many times my mother, aunt, and their best friend would walk to town, church,

---

[1]Banks-Wallace (1999, 2002), Emden (1998), and Polkinghorne (1998).

school or play along these pathways. One summer, they noticed that some cornstalks were moving when the wind was not blowing. It frightened the young girls. They looked to see what was happening, and saw a group of males, old and young, standing in the middle of the cornfield. One of the men the girls knew. He was an old widower. My mother knew he would try to "do things" to girls. The girls realized that they were looking at a bunch of men waiting on a group of girls to sexually assault the girls. The young ladies ran home as fast as they could. They told my grandmother what they saw, and she told them, "never go into the cornfield when the cornstalks are moving."

Spirituality Themes

Based on discussions with six researchers who documented Black American experiences on academic life, hypertension, domestic violence, breast cancer, and end-of-life treatments, it is clear that spirituality was important to the people interviewed.[2] Responses included phrases such as: "God was in control," "Prayer and faith helped them to make it," "Having a good relationship with God" was important, and "Living a godly and moral life was an obligation." Similar references to spirituality and religion are also found in both old and contemporary stories told by Black women.

Themes of spirituality and mistrust among patients have also been documented by Dr. Parham, Assistant Vice Chancellor, Counseling and Health Services and Director of the Counseling Center at the University of California, Irvine, and Dr. Joseph White, Professor Emeritus at the University of California. Dr. White recounted a story from his childhood to illustrate a point about communicating with minority students. Dr. White recalled that he and his brother were required to regularly attend church services. He reported that his brother got the "Holy Ghost" and "spake in tongues." Whenever he wanted to irritate his brother, Dr. White would tell the story and repeat the phrase "spake in tongues" to make his point and deliberately use Black vernacular speech. The theme of the story was that sibling rivalry never dies. By telling this joke about his brother to Black students, using the speech code of his Black family, Dr. White added humor and cultural flavor to the presentation. He also demonstrated to his audience that he could tell a culturally specific story that would help him communicate successfully with minority students and open the window on that culture so that outsiders could get a glimpse of the values upheld in his Black community.

---

[2]Phillips, Cohen, and Tarzian (2001), Ashing-Giwa and Gantz (1997), Abrums (2000), Lannin, Mathews, Mitchell, Swanson, Swanson, and Edwards (1998), Dupree (2000), and Waters (2000).

In his speech to professionals in the health field, Dr. Parham noted the importance of spirituality to Black clients and illustrated how it permeated the Black worldview. He contended that Black people are fundamentally spiritual folk, and that the Black community believes that spirituality is the life force of their people. The psychologist alerted White counselors to the fact that one barrier to successful therapeutic relationships between White counselors and Black clients was based on cultural mistrust. If the Black client does not trust you, insisted Dr. Parham, a therapeutic relationship cannot develop.

African Americans are a spiritual group that appreciates communalism over individualism. The Black community, researchers have found, tends to place more emphasis on the collective experience.[3] Nevertheless, some African-American individuals feel they are outsiders and need to tell their individual story that challenges the group's worldview and Black mainstream culture. To understand the individual within a larger cultural context, storytelling can serve a specific client's needs. Stories told by individuals within a specific community are a means of demonstrating personal choice within a larger cultural narrative.[4]

Humor in Storytelling

African-American stories, either in the oral or text tradition, have been handed down from generation to generation and from Africa to the United States. One element that can be consistently traced throughout African-American story-telling is humor. Humor was used to emphasize the contradictions, ironies, and sarcasms that African Americans face while living in the United States. Humor was also used by Black Americans as a covert way to criticize White mainstream society (Prahlad, 1998).

Wanda remembers a story her father told:

> . . . a young boy stayed out playing past his allotted time. When he got home, his mother asked him why he was late again. He told her that he saw a lion walking down the street, and he had to stay and watch him. The boy's mother said "There ain't no lions around here. Show me." The boy took his mother outside to show her what he saw. Sure enough, the boy pointed to what he thought was a lion. (Someone had cut out a figure of a St. Bernard dog that resembled the shape of a lion and displayed it in their yard). His mother became angry and sent him to his room to pray and ask God to forgive him for telling a lie. She told him that he was not to come out of his room until he heard from God. The boy went to his room and

---

[3]Banks-Wallace (1999, 2002), Emden (1998), and Polkinghorne (1998).
[4]Banks-Wallace (1998), Emden (1998), and Polkinghorne (1998).

returned five minutes later. His mother asked him why he had returned from his room so soon. The boy replied: "God said it was okay. He thought it was a lion too."

Tales of Struggle

There are two primary divisions of African-American storytelling. The first division is based on the history of Africans in the United States. Within this division are subsets of themes about slave against master, horrors of slavery, oppression, and religion (Jones, 1967; Prahlad, 1998). Stories within the slavery division contain ideas about how slaves sometimes lose, a slave's evasion or endurance of punishment, creative ways to deal with White people, survival of the slaves, and the struggle for freedom (Jones, 1967; Prahlad, 1998). Trickster characters and animal stories are also included in the slave story division (Jones, 1967).

Virginia Hamilton (1985) told a story within the slave category called *The Talking Cooter* about a slave called Jim who had a wish to be free:

> He imagined that one day an animal would speak and tell him the secret of how to become free. One day, Jim meets a cooter, or a mud turtle. He threw a rock at the turtle and struck him. The turtle spoke and asked to be friends with Jim and played the fiddle for him. Jim thought that, if his slave master were to hear the turtle talk and play the fiddle, he would get his freedom. (p. 151)

Religion, the other division of documented stories, also played an important role in African-American storytelling. Many older African Americans identified with the suffering of Christ, the stories of Moses and the Israelites, and other biblical characters (Jones, 1967; Prahlad, 1998). The church was the center for social and religious life in the community among Blacks. Religious experiences such as shouting, getting the Holy Ghost, and testifying are themes found in these African-American stories. Tales of the supernatural (e.g., ghosts, the return of the dead, and haunted houses) can also be found in this division (Jones, 1967) of tales.

The late Dr. Martin Luther King, Jr., like many Black preachers, used biblical stories in his sermons to illustrate points. In his sermon entitled "The Three Dimensions of a Complete Life," he used the story of the Good Samaritan from Luke 10 to examine a challenging time in his life and to challenge others to examine their commitment to the civil rights movement:

> They were just like me. I was gong out to my father's house in Atlanta the other day. He lives about three or four miles from me, and you go out there

by going down Simpson Road. And then when I come back later that night—and brother, I can tell you, Simpson Road is a winding road. And a fellow [was] standing out there trying to flag me down. And I felt that he needed some help; I knew he needed help. [*Laughter*] But I didn't know it. I'll be honest with you, I kept going. [*Laughter*] I wasn't going to take the risk. (*That's right*). I say to you this morning that the first question that the priest asked was the first question that I asked on that Jericho Road of Atlanta known as Simpson Road. The first question that the Levite asked was "If I stop to help this man, what will happen to me?" (*That's right*) But the good Samaritan come by and he reversed the question. Not "What will happen to me if I stop to help this man?" but "What will happen to the man if I do not stop to help him?" This is why that man was good and great. He was great because he was willing to take a risk for humanity; he was willing to ask "What will happen to this man?" not "What will happen to me?" (King, 1998, pp. 129-130)

Tales of Protest

The second division of African-American stories includes modern tales of protest (Jones, 1967; Prahlad, 1998). These stories monitor the change in the political climate of African Americans in the United States. While being critical of mainstream society in the United States, as well as African Americans, these stories reveal themes of resistance to social norms. The story topics include man's inhumanity to man, revenge, violence, and self-esteem (Jones, 1967). The theme of man's inhumanity to man generally deals with the treatment of people of African ancestry by people of European ancestry. The stories tell of discrimination, economic deprivation (King, 1998) and injustices in the legal system (Hamilton, 1985). Unlike the stories about discrimination are the injustices meted out by mainstream society. In revenge stories, there is a shift in focus from the docile Negro to an empowered Black person. In terms of self-esteem, there is also a difference in the way the tales unfold. Self-critical stories about skin color and hair texture shift from a perspective of disrespect to self-pride in outwitting White people (Jones, 1967).

Wanda's aunt told a story about what happened to a young White man during the depression:

The man was the son of a lumberyard owner and owned the only place in the area where Whites or Blacks could find a job. The son had a bad habit. He liked walking through the lumber yard during work hours playing the big boss. He would pick up scrap wood and hit whomever he pleased across the arm or back. No one could report his actions or retaliate because they were afraid to lose the only job that was available to them. One night, after his carousing, he was found out alone on a country road. Somebody, or some "bodies", beat him to within an inch of death and left him to die. He was found the next morning as people were going to church. He could not remember who beat him. No one knew. The Kux Klux Klan did not do anything because a White person could have been guilty of the crime. Is it true that no one knew? According to Wanda's aunt, the Black people knew.

FEATURES OF AFRICAN-AMERICAN STORYTELLING

Characters

Idioms, unusual expressions, and folktale characters are distinctive features of African-American storytelling. The list of characters in African-American stories includes saints, sinners, mortals, immortals, tricksters, fools, animals, and "old master" (Jones, 1967). The old master is a character in many antebellum and postantebellum stories portrayed as a White, condescending godfather who looks down on human beings while delighting in owning slaves. The old master is the most despised character, whereas the preacher is the most respected and abused character in this tradition. The preacher is always male and sometimes portrayed as gluttonous, ungodly, woman-chasing, or inebriated (Van Sertima, 1989). In comparison, the trickster symbolizes a longing in the human psyche to be free of oppression (Van Sertima, 1989). Animal characters are usually given human attributes and are used as symbols for events in the plot that mirror the drama of the human world (Jones, 1967). The most common animal characters are buzzards, snakes, and dogs. These symbolize trickery, treachery or deception, and protection or help, respectively (Jones, 1967).

In a story by Hamilton (in Washington, 1990), *Little Girl and Buh Rabby,* Buh Rabby lies to Little Girl in order to eat her sweet peas. Buh Rabby is found out. The next day he is locked in the garden awaiting the return of Little Girl's daddy and punishment for his lie. Buh Rabby is then put into a sack and hung in a thorny tree, but later tricks Wolf into letting him go free.

STORIES OF AND BY BLACK WOMEN

Traditionally, there are more men than women characters in African-American stories. Male dominance is consistent with African tradition, where all storytellers are men, so the legacy continued among African Americans. Therefore, the life of the male represents the life of all African Americans in the stories that have been handed down. Women were usually given supporting roles that included religion and were usually treated with respect. The primary role of storied women was to ensure the mainstay of the home (Washington, 1967). As writers women wrote only about 12% of the documented slave narratives, and these stories are not as well known as those told by men. When women did share stories about themselves, they were not objects of pity. They demonstrate that they were capable of telling their own story, that they were able to change failure into victory, and they resisted and fought back against the effects of oppression. In these stories, women told what it was like to be a female slave (Washington, 1990) from the woman's perspective.

In tales told by Black women storytellers, the characters of mother, wife, daughter, and artist replaced previous roles depicted in slave stories created by men. African-American women became the agents of their own lives after slavery, and the themes of female power, internal strength, relationships with men, connectedness to community, social change, and feminism replaced those experiences, including the docile woman involved in family life (Etter-Lewis, 1996).

Toni Cade Bambara tells stories about women characters who are defined by stereotypes, but are independent, resourceful, self-defining, and self-respecting. In the introduction to her story, *Medley*, Sweet Pea tells her story about a failed love affair:

> I could tell the minute I got in the door and dropped my bags, I wasn't staying. Dishes piled sky high in the sink looking like some circus act. Glasses all ghostly on the counter. Busted tea bags, curling cantaloupe rinds, white cartons form the Chinamen, green sacks from the deli, and that damn dog creeping up on me for me to wrassle his head or kick him in the ribs one. No, I definitely wasn't staying. Couldn't even figure why I'd come. But picked my way to the hallway anyway till the laundry-stuffed pillowcases stopped me. Larry's bass blocking the view to the bedroom.
> "That you, Sweet Pea?"
> "No, man, ain't me at all," I say, working my way back to the suitcase and shoving that damn dog out of the way. "See ya round," I holler, the door slamming behind me, cutting off the words abrupt (Bambara, 1990, p. 356).

STORYTELLING AS A METHOD
OF RESEARCH FOR BLACK WOMEN

Storytelling is a byproduct of African-American life, and the stories that have been created contain themes that reflect the varied experiences of African-American people in America (Jones, 1967). Storytelling has also been used as a means to learn more about factors contributing to the events that affect African-American women's lives. As a form of documentation, storytelling can help impose order and meaning on the life events and interpretation of those situations experienced by African-American women (Emden, 1998). The art form allows them to take their fragmented thoughts, feelings, and beliefs and to combine them into a succinct account that is organized in a chronological fashion.

Analysis of these thoughts, feelings, and beliefs can explain why African-American women behave and think in a particular manner within a specific context. This form of reflection allows African-American women to share their explanation for their actions and insights about their experiences with others.

Etter-Lewis (1996) contended that research with minorities may be problematic, but that the elite and privileged are as exempt from "moral codes-ethics of conduct as those who study [minorities] and become gatekeepers of personal myths" (p. 116). The writer warns that Black women engaged in research about other Black women run the risk of being perceived as indulging in "self-serving research" that will be "ghettoized" because Black women, as a group, are "too specific and too disenfranchised to yield widely generalizable data." Black women, however, are still trying to uncover and disseminate positive information about their lives and thoughts, and they must overcome such negative perceptions of the research that is conducted. Etter-Lewis (1996) asked the question, "Who can better reconstruct the life story of an African American woman than another African American woman?" (p. 116). In answering this question, Black women must find the means to show others that they have and can continue to construct research about themselves and others like them.

Anonymity is an issue in academic research in which Black women become involved either as participants or investigators. African-American women, researchers and participants remind us, need physically and psychologically safe conditions for telling their stories. They are not comfortable relating personal information to a stranger who will, in turn, tell it to another group of strangers. Etter-Lewis (1996) believed that, because African-American women have been exploited by researchers and *do-gooders*, African-American women "have every right not to be forthcoming about the innermost details of their lives" (p. 117). In an effort to remind researchers of their responsibility to the participants in their investigations, Etter-Lewis warned that there is an important issue involving "privileged" undertones/overtones and the notion that researchers are entitled to any and all information about a person's life. Etter-Lewis maintained that we must preserve the personal dignity of our participants, " . . . otherwise we usurp the power of the interviewee's authority and what we have left is . . . coercion" (p. 117).

Black women may be reluctant to tell everything because it is a cultural practice within their community to keep information in the family. They are cognizant of the fact that many times what they have said has been misinterpreted, exploited, or dwells on the negative aspects that make the African-American community look bad (Etter-Lewis, 1996) in the eyes of outsiders. To avoid negative images about their community being disseminated among strangers, Black women simply say good things or nothing at all about their people when they participate in research.

Etter-Lewis (1996) also discussed the issue of alliance between the Black interviewer and interviewee. She stated that the relationship between the two must be one of equality as well as unstructured in design to be the most productive. She maintained that the interviewee is the authority in telling her own story and that the interviewee alone has the power to know, correct, and teach the interviewer. The interviewer, in contrast, must be willing to be a learner who guides the interview process, but does not dictate the direction.

Banks-Wallace (1994, 1998, 1999, 2002), an African-American nurse who also does research, has done extensive work using storytelling as a research method that focuses on Black women. The author asserted that storytelling has a significant function in informing research methodology as well as clinical nursing practice. Storytelling, she said, may be used to advance knowledge about women of African heritage. It is also clear to her that, if we understand more about African-American women, we may be able to appreciate the factors that influence their health decision-making and health-related behaviors. Banks-Wallace (2002) suggested that, to understand the stories of African-American women, it is important to accept the values and experiences that contribute to the composition of each story. She also contended that storytelling has other vital functions in addition to advancing knowledge and understanding of African-American women and their life experiences. Storytelling, the writer believed, has healing, affirming, and emancipatory abilities as well as health-promoting functions (Banks-Wallace, 1998). There are many other researchers, along with Banks-Wallace, who also attest to the healing and affirming properties[5] of storytelling in this arena.

The Functions of Storytelling in Health Research

Six functions of storytelling were identified in a research study conducted by Banks-Wallace (1998) using storytelling as a research method. The functions included contextual grounding, bonding, validating and affirming women's experiences, catharsis, resisting oppression, and educating others. These findings illustrate that the function of stories has not changed over many generations in the African-American culture. The six functions of storytelling are identical to those maintained in the past (Hamilton, 1995; Jones, 1967; Prahlad, 1998) and show the continuity of the African tradition in the present Black culture in the United States.

Kesho Scott's (1991) story, *Elaine,* portrayed how West Indian traditions and culture were passed to the younger generation through the mother in the story. Although the personal characteristics of the character's mother and Wanda's mother are different, Wanda found the story about the novel's character to be quite similar to her own mother's. In both cases, the mothers had strong beliefs about their children. They believed that their children had to be

---

[5]Banks-Wallace (2002), Livo and Rietz (1986), Rybaczyk and Belling (1997), Jones (1967), and Coleman (1989).

clean, smell good, and be decently dressed. Both mothers used "how Whites treat Black folks" stories to emphasize the importance of upholding this ideal. Elaine's mother's stories took place in the West Indies and the United States. Wanda's mother's stories took place in the Deep South and "up North" in the United States. Both women emphasized important rules that their children needed to follow while they lived with them. The mothers maintained a long list of dos and don'ts while they raised their children. The most important rule was not to become the negative stereotype that Whites assigned to Black people. The mothers also maintained that there was a difference between being Black and being a Black stereotype and that their children were not to resemble, in any way, Black stereotypes.

STORYTELLING AS AN INSTRUMENT
OF HEALING AND AFFIRMATION

Stories convey various cultural meanings in the form of values, ideas, beliefs, and feelings. The cultures vary from one country to another and from one state to another in the United States. The cultural forms include civic, religious, ethnic, and personal expressions. Religious culture expresses spiritual and moral values, whereas ethnic culture governs our feelings, values, ideas, and beliefs about language, food, holidays, society, and religion. In the same way that cultural forms express our values, we see that stories reveal our feelings, ideas, and beliefs about everyday life. Tales provide a sense of our personal meaning, identity, and relationship to others (Rybarczyk & Bellig, 1997). Storying about victories over life's obstacles may enhance the self-esteem of minority groups members (Rybarczyk & Bellig, 1997), be cathartic in nature (Jones, 1967), entertain, celebrate, politicize, and serve as a release from frustration and lead to healing.

Those who listen to stories send out affirmations and empathic messages to the storyteller. Relationships that are forged within the listener/storyteller dyad indicate that the listener provides a receptive, nonjudgmental, and safe environment for the telling of life experiences. In a safe and reciprocal setting, the listener takes precautions to protect the speaker from the listener's assumptions and preconceived notions. These notions and preconceptions could distort the listener's reception of the story. It has been observed that storytellers with the same ethnic/racial background as the listener give more richly detailed and personal stories than if the backgrounds of their listeners are different (Rybarczyk & Bellig, 1997).

Acknowledging that differences between the storyteller's and the listener's perspectives may increase misunderstandings, ethnographers who use storytelling as a form of research strongly advise researchers to state that they recognize the differences between listener and storyteller (Livo & Rietz, 1986; Rybarczyk & Bellig, 1997) early on in the relationship. Because differences that exist between one ethnic group and another may hamper the relationship process, both sides of the storytelling team are advised to accentuate their similarities during their journey together.

SUMMARY

The art of storytelling is significant in the culture of African-American people. It is the conduit of customs and traditions. It also has healing and affirming attributes and, therefore, it is an important data-collecting method for collecting research on African-American women. Additional inquiry into storytelling as a data-collection method will be useful to researchers and others who depend on such reports to improve their practice. Written documents that are produced as writers preserve and share the collected stories in Black communities can contribute to Black students' understanding of storytelling and its African-American legacy.

Reading about storytelling helped these authors, Wanda and Joanne, to understand ourselves as writers and storytellers. As we wrote this chapter, we were able to see how the stories we were told as children were part of a culture of traditions handed down from the first Africans to inhabit this country and the Caribbean. Moreover, knowing that the Africans brought to the United States were part of a larger African oral culture increased our appreciation of literacy skills that storytellers represent.

The continuity of Black people's stories throughout time and place is an important consideration as literacy teachers and students piece together the ways in which storytelling uplifts the Black community. Stories have united, connected, and preserved people from Africa who found themselves separated from their motherland for over 400 years. In keeping their stories alive, Africans who were dispersed throughout the world four centuries ago kept their hopes up and ambitions for their children's success in all forms of literacy. It is their legacy of success that we celebrate when we take stories into the literacy classroom and support student development through this ancient tradition.

Understanding how the storytelling tradition inherited from Africa aids literacy and expands a person's ability to communicate fosters appreciation and respect for this ancient art form in literacy journeys. Rather than think of storytelling as a form of culture that can be dismissed because it is principally an oral tradition, we can teach our communities about the ways in which all lives are informed by stories. Literacy teachers can continue to shift attitudes to the storytellers who have taught, celebrated, and admonished us in our daily lives. To acknowledge that stories and storytellers are ways of keeping African culture alive is a step toward better appreciation of the way that Black women are empowered by the form and content of stories. As long as there are women who are Black, literate, and belong to a community, there will be stories to enhance the nation's literacy experiences.

REFERENCES

Abrums, M. (2000). Jesus will fix it after awhile: Meanings and health. *Social Science & Medicine, 50*, 89-105.

Ashing-Giwa, K., & Gantz, P.A. (1997). Understanding the breast cancer experience of African American women. *Journal of Psychosocial Oncology, 15*(2), 19-35.

Bambara, T.C. (1990). Medley. M. H. Washington (Ed.), *Black-eye Susans, midnight birds: Stories by and about Black women*. New York: Doubleday.

Banks-Wallace J. (1994). Beyond survival: Storytelling as an emancipatory tool among women of African descent. *The Womanist, 1*(1), 5-8.

Banks-Wallace, J. (1998) Emancipatory potential of storytelling in a group. *Image: Journal of Nursing Scholarship, 30*(1), 17-21.

Banks-Wallace J. (1999). Storytelling as a tool for providing holistic care to women. *MCN: The American Journal of Maternal/Child Nursing, 24*(1), 20-24.

Banks-Wallace J. (2002). Talk that talk: Storytelling and analysis rooted in African American oral tradition. *Qualitative Health Research, 12*(3), 410-426

Champion, T.C. (2003). *Understanding storytelling among African American children*. Mahwah, NJ: Erlbaum

Coleman, L.G. (1989). Storytelling and comic performance. In L. Goss, & M. E. Barnes (Eds.), *Talk that talk: An anthology of African American storytelling*. New York: Simon & Schuster/Touchstone.

Delpit, L. (2002). No kinda sense. In L. Delpit & J.K.Dowdy (Eds.), *The skin that we speak: Thoughts on language and culture in the classroom* (pp. 31-48). New York: The New Press.

Dupree, C.Y. (2000). The attitudes of black Americans toward advance directives. *Journal of Transcultural Nursing, 11*(1), 12-18.

Emden, C. (1998). Theoretical perspectives on narrative inquiry. *Collegian, 5*(2), 30-35.

Etter-Lewis, G. (1996). Telling from behind her hand: African American women and the process of documenting concealed lives. In R. Josselson (Ed.), *Ethics and process in the narrative study of lives*. Thousand Oaks, CA: Sage.

Greene, E. (1996). *Storytelling: Art and technique*. New Providence, NJ: R.R. Bowker.

Hamilton, B. (1985). *The people could fly*. New York: Alfred A. Knopf.

Hamilton, V. (1995). *Her stories*. New York: The Blue Sky Press.

Jones, B.W. (1967). *A descriptive and analytical study of the American negro folktale*. Ann Arbor, MI: University Microfilms.

King, M. L. (1998). The three dimensions of a complete life. In C. Carson & P. Holloran (Eds.), *A knock at midnight*. New York: Warner Books.

Lannin, D.R., Mathews, H.F., Mitchell, J., Swanson, M.S., Swanson, F.H., & Edwards, M.S. (1998). Influence of socioeconomic and cultural factors on racial differences in late-stage presentation of breast cancer. *JAMA, 279*(22), 1801-1807.

Livo, N., & Rietz, S. (1986). *Storytelling: Process and practice.* Littleton, CO: Libraries Unlimited.

Mattingly, C., & Lawlor, M. (2000). Learning from stories: Narrative interviewing in cross-cultural research. *Scandinavian Journal of Occupational Therapy, 7*(1), 4-14.

McCance, T., McKenna, H. P., & Boore, J. R. P. (2001). Exploring caring using narrative methodology: An analysis of the approach. *Journal of Advanced Nursing, 33*(3), 350-356.

Phillips, J.M., Cohen, M.Z., & Tarzian, A.J. (2001). African American women's experiences with breast cancer screening. *Journal of Nursing Scholarship, 33*(2), 135-140.

Polkinghorne, D.E. (1988). *Narrative knowing and the human sciences.* Thousand Oaks, CA: Sage.

Prahlad, S.A. (1998). African American traditions. In J.M. Foley (Ed.), *Teaching oral traditions.* New York: Modern Language Association of America.

Rybarczyk, B., & Bellig, A. (1997). *Listening to life stories: A new approach to stress intervention in health care.* New York: Springer.

Scott, K.Y. (1991). *The habit of surviving: Black women's strategies for life.* New Brunswick, NJ: Rutgers University Press.

Van Sertima, I. (1989). Trickster, the revolutionary hero. In L. Goss & M.E. Barnes (Eds.), *Talk that talk: An anthology of African American storytelling.* New York: Simon & Schuster/Touchstone.

Washington, M.H. (Ed.). (1990). *Black-eyed Susans, midnight birds: Stories by and about Black women.* New York: Doubleday.

Waters, C.M. (2000). End-of-life care directives among African-Americans: Lessons learned—a need for community-centered discussion and education. Journal of *Community Health Nursing, 17*(1), 25-37.

10

Women and Literacy in Alice Walker's *The Color Purple*

E. Yvette Walters

Women of the Diaspora have carried on the Black oral culture for generations. Long before Black women were allowed to publish, they kept their stories alive through the art of storytelling. When Black women did begin to write and publish, they created works that used the elements of storytelling to impart cultural values. Black women writers such as Zora Neale Hurston, Toni Morrison, Gloria Naylor, and Alice Walker all draw from the orature of African culture to record their histories through their stories.

In telling these stories, barriers, shackles, and obstacles typify an ever-present element in the Black woman's struggle for acceptance, power, respect, love, and, self. Undoubtedly, the most powerful stories are ones about identity; stories that help individuals discover who they are, where they are coming from, where they are, or where they are headed. In *Their Eyes Were Watching God,* Hurston (1978) narrated the story of Janie Stark's quest for self-hood as she struggles to bridge society's expectations of women with her own expectations. Likewise in *Sula,* Morrison (1982) examined the plight of two women who battle to maintain a friendship while developing contrasting individual identities.

The Women of Brewster Place is Naylor's (1980) masterpiece in which seven women attempt to re-create themselves despite their dismal living conditions. In each of their stories, literacy plays an integral role in the Black woman's ability to become self-actualized.

Although the literature simply mirrors the harsh realities of being both Black and female, feminist theory offers numerous perspectives to identify, address, and ultimately solve the problems Black women encounter in a male-dominated society. There are five basic types of feminism, with one focusing exclusively on the plight of Black women. Liberal feminists focus on the rights of individual women. The liberals work to transform traditional beliefs about femininity and masculinity and emphasize individual women's rights to create their own identity. Radical feminists, in contrast, argue that the roots of women's oppression lie in the biological differences between men and women. They work to reclaim women's bodies from male control and to celebrate their life-giving capabilities. Poststructural feminists examine the ways competing language patterns produce notions of gender. The poststructuralist seeks to understand whose interests are being marginalized, silenced, or excluded and to bring change and transformation to those settings. Social feminists believe that race, social class, and gender oppression are interrelated consequences of a patriarchal, capitalist system. The socialists call for a transformation of the social system that will make men and women equal. Black feminism, or womanism, defines African-American women's struggles as issues of race, social class, and gender. Black feminists work to give voice to the experiences of Black women and to take action in the struggle for human freedom (DeMarrais & LeCompte, 1995).

Several studies have been conducted regarding the practical application of feminist theories to women's working lives. In the book *Women's Ways of Knowing*, Belenky, Clinchy, Goldberg, and Tarule (1986) examine the ". . . ways of knowing that women have cultivated and learned to value, ways we have come to believe are powerful but have been neglected and denigrated by the dominant intellectual ethos of our time" (p. ix). Using an intensive interview/case study approach, their study of 135 women revealed five major epistemological categories from which women view reality and themselves and draw conclusions about truth, knowledge, and authority:

(a) silence, a position in which women experience themselves as voiceless and mindless;

(b) received knowledge, a perspective in which women view themselves as capable of receiving knowledge, but incapable of imparting it;

(e) subjective knowledge, a perspective where truth and knowledge are perceived as personal, private, and/or intuitive;

(d) procedural knowledge, a position in which women are actively engaged in learning for the purpose of obtaining and communicating knowledge; and

(e)   constructed knowledge, a position in which women view themselves
        as creators of knowledge while valuing both subjective and objective
        strategies of knowing. (p. 15)

In obtaining the epistemological categories, the book focuses on how women's
self-concepts and ways of knowing are integral to women's struggles to claim
the power of their own minds. In addition, the authors examine how family and
schools both promote and hinder women's development. Although the book
does not center exclusively on the particulars of being both Black and female, it
does offer some universal truths about women regardless of color. This chapter
uses the five ways of knowing (Belenky et al., 1986) to examine the role that literacy plays in the quest for self in Walker's (1982) *The Color Purple*.

> *The Color Purple* was chosen for analysis because Walker is a self-pro-
> claimed womanist: Given its instructive, inspiring story of an oppressed,
> abused, isolated woman who learns to fight back, speak for herself, defend
> other women, "git man off her eye" (204), and make her way in a racist,
> patriarchal world that would deny her subjectivity, agency, and pleasure, it
> is hardly surprising that Walker's *The Color Purple* took the feminist world
> by storm. Or that it has been taken up as a "feminist fable." Or that Celie
> has become a "role model for contemporary feminists," an example of
> woman's oppression and liberation, a symbolic "Everywoman" in both her
> reduction to object and her struggles to become a speaking subject.
> (Kaplan, 1996, p. 124)

SYNOPSIS

The Color Purple traces the evolution of Celie, ". . . who starts out life already a
spiritual captive, but who through her own courage and the help of others
breaks free into the realization that she, like Nature itself, is a radiant expression
of the heretofore perceived as quite distant Divine" (p. 1). From the beginning,
Celie realizes the importance of knowing how to read and write. She says, ". . .
us know we got to be smart to git away" (p. 9). In addition, Celie's teacher,
Miss Beasley, reiterates Celie's thirst for knowledge: "She say as long as she
been a teacher she never knew nobody who wants to learn as bad as Nettie and
me" (p. 10). However, Celie's ability to become self-actualized does not hinge
on traditional notions of literacy, but rather on more in-depth ways of knowing
that extend beyond basic reading and writing skills. As the reader quickly discovers, Celie does not get away. Her formal education ends within the first 10
pages of the novel, thereby forcing literacy to take on a different meaning (i.e.,
survival within the confines of oppression). Hence, Celie is compelled to rely
more heavily on her intuitive, practical, interpersonal, and spiritual forms of
knowing as a means of self-discovery.

SILENCE

The simplest form of knowing is silence. In the epistemological schema, it represents an extreme denial of self and a strong dependence on external authority. Words are viewed as weapons used to divide and conquer people, rather than to connect and liberate them in the silence dimension of knowing. Although she may possess intelligence, the silent woman does not dialogue with self nor does she perform mental acts of consciousness or introspection (Belenky et al., p. 25).

As *The Color Purple* begins, Celie is voiceless. "You better not tell nobody but God. It's kill your mammy" (p. 1). Pa, Celie's stepfather, begins her marginalization by raping her repeatedly with the warning, "You better shut up and git used to it" (p. 1). Even if she dares speak about her condition, Pa warned anyone who might listen, "She ain't smart either . . . you have to watch her or she'll give away everything you own. . . . An another thing—She tells lies" (p. 8). Knowing that she cannot voice her situation aloud, Celie seeks the highest authority possible in trying to discern why she is being demeaned and belittled. "Dear God I am I have always been a good girl. Maybe you can give me a sign letting me know why this is happening to me" (p. 1). Yet the answer does not come, and her situation worsens. In addition to a silent voice, Celie's body is silent. After having two babies by Pa, who sells or, perhaps, kills them, Celie admits, "I don't bleed no more" (p. 5). Unable to reproduce, Celie is barren in every physical way.

After Celie's arranged marriage to her husband, he and his four children continue the oppression. The day of her wedding foreshadows how life with Mr. ____ and his children will be. The oldest son hits her in the head with a rock, and the two young girls accuse her of murder for combing their badly matted hair. Nettie, Celie's sister, encourages her to take up for herself. "Don't let them run over you. . . . You got to let them know who got the upper hand" (p. 16). Celie does not attempt to fool herself. She knows she is powerless even to Mr. ____'s children. Responding to Nettie's plea, Celie says, "I don't know how to fight. All I know how to do is stay alive" (p. 17). Staying alive means keeping quiet and conforming.

Nettie is not alone in encouraging Celie to fight back. Mr. ____'s sister also tells Celie, "You got to fight them Celie. I can't do it for you" (p. 21). Again, Celie answers in the only way she knows: "I don't fight, I stay where I am told. But I'm alive" (p. 21). Celie's inability to associate fighting with survival illustrates her mistaken faith in the supreme authority of other people.

The deep roots of Celie's silence are depicted in other ways as well. When Shug Avery, Mr.____'s mistress, comes to live with them, Celie wants to welcome her, but is terrified to do so. "But I don't say nothing. It is not my house. Also I ain't been told nothing" (p. 43). In another incident, while getting punished for being "stubborn," Celie maintains her position of silence. "I do not cry. I make myself wood" (p. 22). Furthermore, silence is such a major part of Celie's existence that she knows not to think. "I know what I am thinking bout, I think. Nothing. And as much of it as I can" (p. 119). Celie asserts, "I don't know nothing, I think. And glad of it" (p. 120). Despite being completely silenced, Celie knows why the caged bird sings: "This life be over soon, I say. Heaven last always" (p. 40).

RECEIVED KNOWLEDGE

Women who rely on received knowledge think that words are central to the learning process. Yet they have little confidence in their own ability to speak. Believing that truth comes from others, they quiet their own voices to hear the voices of others. Unlike the silent women, who do not view themselves as learners at all, these women feel confident about their ability to grasp the truths received from others (Belenky et al., 1986).

Once Celie has advanced beyond the stage of silence, she relies heavily on what others say and think. Specifically, she looks to others to validate her self-worth. Celie wants to believe in her ability—not because she knows she has it, but because someone else said she does. Not realizing her own capacity for learning, Celie says, "Us both be hitting Nettie's schoolbooks pretty hard . . . I know I'm not as pretty or as smart as Nettie, but *she* say I ain't dumb" (p. 9).

Celie's reliance on other's opinion can also be illustrated through minor tasks. A simple act of choosing a new dress for herself presents a problem for Celie. When Mr. ____'s sister convinces him that Celie needs new clothes, Celie attempts to imitate Shug Avery's style even though the two have never met. "I think what color Shug Avery would wear. . . . Something purple, maybe a little red in it too" (p. 20). She does not find purple; therefore, she is forced to choose a more subtle color, blue, which symbolizes her existence. Still Celie is ecstatic to own a brand-new dress.

Realizing that her life is demeaning, Celie does not actually know that she deserves better. "She say. It's all right, Celie. You deserve better than this. Maybe so. I think" (p. 21). By thinking, rather than knowing, that she is entitled to just and humane treatment, Celie again demonstrates her confidence in someone else's opinions about her.

Celie has many talents, particularly sewing, without comprehending her potential for marketing them. Once Shug sees how well Celie can sew pants, Shug encourages her to make them for other people. Celie is reluctant at first, but does so anyway because Shug suggests it. Even after Celie is making money designing and sewing pants, she still does not believe in herself. She thinks she is just wasting time. "I say, You know, I love doing this, but I got to git out and make a living pretty soon. Look like this just holding me back" (p. 211). Again Shug has to legitimize Celie's sewing as meaningful. "You making your living,

Celie, she say. Girl, you on your way" (p. 212). Finally, the wait is over; Celie is able to exhale.

THE QUEST FOR SELF

Subjective women are characterized by a preoccupation with choosing between the self and the other, acting on behalf of the self as opposed to denying the self, and living through others. In this epistemological scheme, some women become distinctly antimale as they forge new rules and establish boundaries for themselves as well as their relationships. Negative attitudes toward specific men in their past become generalized to all men, whom they perceive as controlling, demanding, negating, and life suppressing. Eventually, their attitude becomes, "I can do it without men." Subjective women perceive themselves as acquiring a voice and a knowledge base from which they can experience the world (Belenky et al., 1986).

Shug is the one who is the catalyst for Celie's transformation into a loving, living self. With Shug's help, Celie begins to feel good about herself. "For the first time in my life, I feel just right" (p. 57). Celie makes this observation after Shug sings a song that she made up just for Celie, "Miss Celie's Song." Regardless of the fact that Shug and Celie sometimes share a sexual relationship, they are more sisters than lovers: "Us sleep like sisters" (p. 141).

After Celie realizes her potential, she becomes preoccupied with acquiring a self. She no longer looks to others for affirmation because she has uncovered the authority within herself. For example, after Celie discovers that Mr. ____ has been hiding Nettie's letters from her, she confronts him. Instead of being belittled by Mr. ____'s derogatory comments, Celie asserts, "I'm pore, I'm black, I may be ugly and can't cook, a voice say to everything listening. But I'm here" (p. 205). None of that matters. Celie has come to accept all that she is or is not, knowing that being whoever she is surely is more than enough. "I am so happy. I got love, I got money, friends, and time" (p. 213).

Celie has assumed her place in the world. Perhaps most important, Celie is no longer compelled to value only the opinions of others concerning how she looks, thinks, dresses, acts, or talks. When Darlene, a woman who helps her sew, tries to change the way she talks, Celie says, "Looks like to me only a fool would want to talk in a way that feels peculiar to your mind" (p. 214). Indeed Celie has moved beyond conforming to the selfish desires of others. Even her cravings for foreign substances have diminished. "Lately I feel like me and God make love just fine anyhow. Whether I smoke reefer or not" (p. 218). Again Celie illustrates her belief in being *enough* by simply being who she is as a human being.

At this stage, Celie has developed a profound hatred toward men, which she has overgeneralized to include God, whom she surmises is a man. She describes God as, "big and old and tall and graybearded and white. He wear white robes and go barefooted" (p. 189). To explain why she has such a negative attitude toward men, Celie says, "Anyhow, I say, the God I been praying and writing to is man. And act just like all the other mens I know. Trifling, forgetful, and lowdown" (p. 187). Celie further maintains, "Take they pants off, I say, and men look like frogs to me. No matter how you kiss 'em, as far as I'm concerned, frogs is what they stay" (p. 235). Here Celie is responding to Mr. ____'s plea that he is a changed man worthy of forgiveness. Celie eventually does forgive Mr. ____, but refuses to remarry him. "I say Naw, I still don't like frogs, but let's us be friends" (p. 284). Celie has fallen in love with herself and can laugh about the past.

THE VOICE OF REASON/SEPARATE
AND CONNECTED KNOWING

Women in the Reason/Separate and Connected epistemological scheme of knowing have encountered situations in which their old ways of knowing have been challenged. Women who use the voice of reason for knowing have discovered that their inner voices sometimes lie. They rely on a mixture of received and subjective knowledge that looks to feeling and intuition for some of the answers, but were external authorities for other answers. Women who use such procedural knowledge pay attention to the objects in the external world, develop procedures for understanding and substantiating opinions, and engage in a conscious, deliberate, and systematic analysis of events. When the procedural woman is silent, it is not a passive silence, but rather a calculated act of reasoning. Similar to liberal feminists, these women try to take charge of their lives in a planned manner (Belenky et al., 1986).

Through reading Nettie's letters and writing her own letters, Celie is able to explore her own consciousness, assert herself against those who dominate her, and even question the nature of God. Because Celie has developed a strong sense of self and a voice, she learns how to use her voice to rationalize her life. Thus, she is driven to examine her past as a means to explain how she came to be. In looking into her past, Celie uncovers some shockingly, dreadful truths. "My daddy lynch. My mama crazy. All my little half brothers and sisters no kin to me. My children not my sister and brother. Pa not Pa" (Walker, 1982, p. 173). Everything about her family that Celie believed to be true is really false. Celie cannot imagine why her life has been consumed with such tragic circumstances given that she has always been a good person.

In trying to make sense of it all, Celie begins to question God: "You must be sleep" (p. 173). Believing that the gracious, just, and loving God to whom she had been praying could not possibly be awake, the same Celie, who would not fight anybody, begins to battle God. "He threatened lightening, floods, and earthquakes. Us fight. I hardly pray at all" (p. 192). At this point, Celie decides to write letters to Nettie rather than to God.

It is not surprising that Celie begins to question the existence of God to move forward with her life because she must comprehend "the why" at this stage of knowing. Words alone are not enough; a redemptive spiritual process is also needed. However, even in battling God, Celie knows that life without God is, perhaps, more miserable than life with Him. "But deep in my heart I care about God. What he going to think. But it ain't easy trying to do without God. Even if you know he ain't there, trying to do without him is a strain" (p. 187). Despite that she does not fully understand, Celie is watching God, looking for answers.

INTEGRATING THE VOICES

The women in this final epistemological position are considered constructivists. They are characterized by their articulate and reflective desire to empower and improve the quality of life not only for themselves, but also for others. Constructivist women realize that, speaking in an authentic voice, they must sort through the pieces of self and reclaim self by integrating intuitive knowledge with the knowledge learned from others (Belenky et al., 1986).

It is significant that Celie first writes letters to God and then shifts to her sister, Nettie. She has come full circle in the final chapter of the novel, addressing her last letter, "Dear God. Dear stars, dear trees, dear sky, dear peoples. Dear Everything. Dear God" (p. 286). The power of language has elevated the semiliterate Celie from a voiceless nonentity to an integrated self with an awareness of the strength of her own voice. She is able, at last, to internalize the belief that, "God is everything. . . . Everything that is or ever was or ever will be" (p. 190). She has also learned that she is part of the universe just as the universe is a part of her: mysterious, wondrous, continually creating and re-creating itself.

Although Shug helped Celie to re-create herself, Celie ultimately learns how to survive alone. "If she come, I be happy, If she don't, I be content. And then I figure this is the lesson I was supposed to learn" (p. 284). Finally, Celie possesses the secret of joy.

CONCLUSION

In life and literature, women cycle through recursive phases of knowing. Silent women are selfless and voiceless, with little awareness of their intellectual capabilities. During the received knowledge and procedural knowledge phases, external truths and other voices prevail as the sense of self becomes embedded in outside roles or definitions. During the subjective knowledge phase, women often turn away from others and deny external authority in their search for self. Constructed knowledge compels women to integrate the voices of the previous phases to reclaim the self and incorporate new ways of reasoning.

Celie, the protagonist of *The Color Purple*, travels through all of the Belenky et al. five ways of knowing. Through her letters—first to God, then to her sister, and finally to everything—we witness as she endures dehumanizing experiences, is moved by another person's love, and ultimately attains sufficient self-worth to survive alone. *The Color Purple* offers some strong implications for further expanding the notion of literacy. For Celie, literacy does not develop from learning to read and write. Formal literacy makes her more knowledgeable, but it does not offer her what she truly needs (i.e., a sense of self). Only when she realizes her connection to the universe is she able to internalize the power of her existence; only then is Celie able to use what she has learned. Through Celie, Alice Walker asserts that knowing one's place within a larger schema enables women to maximize their power, uncover their hidden talents, and discover the God inside. That, perhaps, is the greatest level of literacy— knowing that self is an essential part of all.

REFERENCES

Belenky, M.F., Clinchy, B.M., Goldberger, N.R., & Tarule, J.M. (1986). *Women's ways of knowing: The development of self, voice, and mind.* New York: Basic Books.

DeMarrais, K.B., & LeCompt, M.D. (1995). *The way schools work: A sociological analysis of education* (2nd ed.). New York: Longman.

Hurston, Z.N. (1978). *Their eyes were watching God.* Chicago: University of Illinois Press.

Kaplan, C. (1996). *The erotics of talk: Women's writing and feminist paradigms.* New York: Oxford University Press.

Morrison, T. (1982). *Sula.* New York: Washington Square Press.

Naylor, G. (1980). *The women of Brewster place.* New York: Hyperion.

Walker, A. (1982). *The color purple.* New York: Harcourt Brace Jovanovich.

11

Dysfunctional Literacies of Exclusion: An Exploration of the Burdens of Literacy in Tsitsi Dangarembga's *Nervous Conditions*

Mandi Chikombero

Look what they've done to us . . . I'm not one of them but I'm not one of you.

> – Nyasha in Tsitsi Dangarembga's
> *Nervous Conditions* (1988)

Tsitsi Dangarembga's (1982) *Nervous Conditions* remains one of the most revealing and insightful books to emerge out of Zimbabwe's literary arena. Like any good book, themes continually emerge, and the relevance of the story does not wane. What prompted me to write this chapter, after having read the book on several occasions, was that the work struck a new chord within me. I was in an alien environment that threatened to make me alien even to myself. I read the book, discussed it in a class, and it revealed to me many issues that I observed before, but that suddenly took on new meaning and significance. I realized that Dangarembga had written a timeless classic from which new conceptualizations of the story would continue to emerge.

In this chapter, I discuss some of the ways in which the book makes significant contributions to the understanding of Black women's literacy. Because *literacy* is difficult to define, I try to provide a number of definitions of literacy, identify examples of each in the book, and discuss how the different literacies have various implications for understanding Black women's struggles for acceptance and inclusion in male-dominated societies. To be Black, female, and literate means different things in different contexts. Whether these differences are significant and/or unique is examined here.

RATIONALE

Why *Nervous Conditions*? Why literacy? These questions are important because they help shape the observations that emerge from an analysis of Dangaremba's book as well as answer some of the questions. The experiences of the book's female characters can best be understood when situated within a particular context. The semifictional account provided by Dangarembga in her novel is insightful because it illustrates the social dynamics surrounding women's issues. The importance of literacy in any culture cannot be overstated. Humans are constantly involved in situations that require navigating their physical and mental surroundings. Literacy is an acquired skill that is required for contextual navigation. Different kinds of literacies allow navigation in different situations and relationships. There is, therefore, a need to move from the general understanding of literacy as something that takes place in the academic classroom. Classroom literacy is but one kind of literacy, but it is not the only literacy, and it may not be the most important.

For too long nonacademic forms of literacy took a back seat to academic literacy in the research arena. Research now shows that academic literacy may be influenced by other types of literacies, which may, in turn, impact other literacies. The need to examine other literacies is, therefore, apparent. Although it is now accepted that there are different literacies, some of these literacies have not been studied in depth. Further, the semifictional presentation of these literacies within a particular setting allows for exploration of them and of the relationships they create in regard to gender and race. To better understand the discussions that follow, it is helpful to begin with a brief overview of the context in Dangarembga's work (i.e., a brief history of the southern African country of Zimbabwe).

HISTORICAL CONTEXT

In 1890, the British South Africa Company (BSAC) and the pioneer column raised the Union Jack in Salisbury (now Harare). According to Kahari (1980), this marked both a beginning and an end. It marked the end of precolonial Zimbabwe and the beginning of colonial Zimbabwe. The collision of cultures that resulted from this political change has been the subject of numerous socio-cultural studies and Zimbabwean novels (e.g., Charles Mungoshi's [1975] *Waiting for the Rain,* Dambudzo Marechera's [1978] *The House of Hunger,* and Tsitsi Dangarembga's [1982] *Nervous Conditions*). In some cases, this cultural collision was called *alienation.* Colonial conquest did not come easy for the British. As early as 1896, the people of Zimbabwe rebelled in what has come to be known as The First Chimurenga. The Chimurenga were uprisings against White rule. These first uprisings, however, were temporarily quelled, and Zimbabwe gained independence from the British on April 18, 1980, after a 13-year war for independence.

Today, modern Zimbabwe is a country with a population of approximately 11 million people. The economy is largely agrarian with a rural–urban ratio of 75:25. In terms of academic literacy or the ability to read and write, Zimbabwe has a 90% literacy rate, which is one of the highest literacy rates on the African continent. The literacy rate is 80% for females and 90% for males.

One of the problems haunting Zimbabwe today, as it did in pre-independence days, is that some social inequalities can be directly attributed to colonialism. Social problems stemming from Zimbabwe's colonial past have been the focus of many novels, and Dangarembga's is no exception.

NERVOUS CONDITIONS: THE SETTING

Nervous Conditions is set in the Eastern Highlands of Zimbabwe (formerly called Rhodesia), close to the border town of Mutare (Umtali in the book). The setting is mostly rural and the lifestyle predominantly agrarian. The narrator, Tambu, describes the agricultural lifestyle:

> . . . by the time I was old enough to help in the fields the work was reduced to planting the maize in the years that my father or any visiting male rela-tive who was strong enough found time to use the ox-plough. In the years that they did not find the time, it was digging and planting as usual. After the planting, after the crop had germinated, all through the rainy season until the plants were tall and sturdy, we weeded, using our hands and our hoes. Sometimes it was not only maize but mhunga and rukweza as well. The beginning of the crop year was a busy time. (p. 6)

Substandard housing also characterizes the rural areas. When Tambu returns home for the holidays, she notices the condition of her family's accom-modations:

> This time the homestead looked worse than usual. . . . The thatched roof of the kitchen was falling out in so many places that it would be difficult to find a dry spot inside when it rained. Great holes gaped in the crumbling mud-brick walls of the tsapi, and the hozi was no more than a reminder of shelter. . . . When I went to the pit latrine that was once a good one and built under Babamukuru's supervision and with his finances downwind from the huts, I gagged. (p. 123)

The action in the book occurs almost entirely in the rural area, which is home to the main character, Tambu, and her family. It is important to note that, in the rural areas, the traditional cultural belief system is largely intact. It is in the rural areas that the conflict of cultures emerges and the different literacies of the characters emerge.

Some argue that a semifictional account of literacy and its effects is not useful to researchers. Literature—whether it is fictional or nonfictional—is a reflection of society. An author writes out of a given context for a given context. In this sense, fiction is not fiction, but an angular lens through which to view society. To deny this view is myopic. Dangarembga presented a view of the dynamics of Zimbabwean culture from a unique angle.

LITERACY

Literacy has many definitions, some specific and some broad. Literacy can be defined as the ability to read and write, or the state of being knowledgeable or competent. It speaks to a deep understanding of one's environment and one's ability to exist in and uphold that environment. As Cervero (1985) noted, there is no commonly accepted definition of the term *literacy*. Most definitions point to the ability to function effectively within a certain context. Literacy, therefore and according to Cervero, is "the ability to function within a specific social context" (p. 51). Literacy is relative. Two kinds of literacy are addressed in this chapter: traditional literacy and colonial literacy. Both belong to the category of cultural literacy (i.e., the knowledge and practice of ideas, values, and attitudes of a specific society).

NERVOUS CONDITIONS: THE STORY

It is tempting to say that the story is about Tambu, but *Nervous Conditions* is the story of a number of characters. To understand Tambu and the role she plays requires an examination of some of the other characters who interact with her and contribute to her persona. The story follows Tambu over a number of years during which she leaves her rural home to live at a mission with her uncle,

Babamukuru, who is the mission's principal. In moving from her home to the mission, Tambu encounters numerous changes in her psyche. When the story begins, Babamukuru and his wife, Maiguru, are "been-tos" who have recently returned from England, where they had gone in pursuit of higher education. Later in the book it becomes evident that education in all its forms entails some level of sacrifice. The book examines the social and mental price that comes with academic literacy as well as with social literacy. In some form, all the characters pay highly for the literacy they hold.

TRADITIONAL LITERACY

Traditional literacy refers to all aspects of sociocultural literacies that are examined in Dangaremba's book. Traditional literacy is found within the belief system that remains intact in Tambu's home. The oral traditions, myths, legends, folktales, songs, and dance that Tambu describes are all important parts of this traditional literacy. Traditions are important because they serve as the springboard from which literacy teachings emerge. An example of such oral tradition can be found in the stories and historical accounts that Tambu's late grandmother told.

In traditional literacy, the household is the locus of gender stratification and women's oppression (Schmidt, 1992). Some researchers dispute the stratification notion and claim that the traditional African household is not inherently oppressive to women, but rather that the impact of colonialism played a role in the creation of the gender stereotype. Although there is merit to this argument, Dangarembga painted a picture in which the women who are operating in this traditional literacy are oppressed in a number of ways.

Throughout the book, the women continually pay a price for being female. Their burdens are created and maintained by a traditional literacy that dictates that they are second-class citizens even in their own homes. Tambu's mother, Ma'Shingayi, illustrates this when Tambu yearns to be educated like her brother, Nhamo, who was invited to attend the mission school where Babamukuru is principal. Her mother's response is:

> This business of womanhood is a heavy burden. . . . How could it not be? Aren't we the ones who bear children? When it is like that you can't just decide today I want to do this, tomorrow I want to do that, the next day I want to be educated! When there are sacrifices to be made, you are the one who has to make them. And these things are not easy; you have to start learning them early, from a very early age. The earlier the better so that it is easy later on. Easy! As if it is ever easy. And these days it is worse, with the poverty of blackness on one side and the weight of womanhood on the other. . . . What will help you, my child, is to learn to carry your burdens with strength. (p. 16)

Ma'Shingayi's advice is sensible when viewed from the traditional literacy. Indeed one can argue that Ma'Shingayi's advice is guaranteed to make her daughter literate in the traditional society. Nonetheless, her advice is crippling. It is from this traditional literacy that Tambu yearns to escape. Tambu says, "I decided it was better to be like Maiguru, who was not poor and had not been crushed by the weight of womanhood" (p. 16). Maiguru, incidentally, is Babamukuru's wife, a "been to" who has returned from England, and Tambu's aunt.

In the traditional literacy from which Tambu wishes to move away, women are at the center of reproduction and agricultural production. We see Tambu and her mother constantly working on the land to feed and educate the family even to the point that it begins to take a toll on Tambu's mother's health. Tambu pities her mother on several occasions for the endless work that she does. As a child, Tambu and her sister worked in the fields for the food they ate. They were being trained to play the roles that traditional literacy demands. Indeed Tambu thinks of her young sister, Netsai, as "a sweet child, the type that will make a sweet, sad wife" (p. 10).

As Nzenza (1996) argued, the role of women in this social context varies from that of a passive virgin, to a submissive wife, to a long-suffering mother. Later in the novel, Tambu's mother is forced to make a decision regarding her "wayward" sister, Lucia. Lucia is closest to being the one truly independent woman in the story. Tambu's mother, for example, cannot formulate even an opinion, let alone a decision. Tambu narrates, "Since for most of her life my mother's mind, belonging first to her father and then to her husband, had not been hers to make up, she was finding it difficult to come to a decision" (p. 153).

Passivity is the extent of Ma'Shingayi's adaptation to her role. Throughout her life, she has been forced to assume a role that excluded her from making decisions or from having a say in the home. When Nhamo is invited to attend the mission school, Ma'Shingayi is against the idea, yet her role renders her powerless. Her gendered role excludes her from making choices regarding the education or future of her son. Small wonder that when pressed to give an opinion regarding Lucia, she finally remarks, "Does it matter what I want? Since when has it mattered what I want? So why should it start mattering now? . . . What I have endured for nineteen years I can endure for another nineteen, and nineteen more if need be" (p. 153).

Roles for both men and women are clearly defined in Zimbabwean culture, with each sex being counseled to operate only from within its designated role. It is because of this strict adherence to defined roles that we see Tambu's mother trying to get Tambu to stay within her role. To the mother, neither academic literacy nor education is important because either will alienate a woman from her assigned traditional roles of daughter, wife, and mother. Tambu's father, Jeremiah, is also disappointed in his daughter because she aspires to embrace a different literacy. About her father, Tambu notes:

> He became very agitated after he had found me several times reading the sheet of newspaper in which the bread from *magrosa* had been wrapped as I waited for the *sadza* to thicken. He thought I was emulating my brother, that the things I read would fill my mind with impractical ideas, making me quite useless for the real tasks of feminine living. (p. 34)

Within traditional literacy, Tambu is excluded from education. The traditional literacy excludes and, to this extent, is dysfunctional because it fosters dissension within Tambu. Tambu is not the only one, however, who is faced with the struggle of escaping from traditional literacy. The same literacy, at times coupled with colonial literacy, creates turmoil in Maiguru's mind, resistance in Lucia's world, and confusion in Nyasha's life.

Lucia, arguably, is the one female in the story who comes closest to being truly liberated, yet even she struggles to be included in the social circle that the men form. Like her sister, Ma'Shingayi, she is not educated. Unlike her sister, Lucia is less conforming. At her age, she is unmarried, "sleeps with anybody and everybody" (p. 126), and does not have any children. This lifestyle contrasts with what the culture and traditional literacy dictate. About her aunt Lucia, Tambu narrates,

> Although she had been brought up in abject poverty, she had not, like my mother, been married to it at fifteen. Her spirit, unfettered in this respect, had experimented with living and drawn its own conclusions. Consequently, she was a much bolder woman than my mother. (p. 127)

In the story, Lucia arrives at Tambu's home, is impregnated by Takesure, Babamakuru's cousin, and attributes the pregnancy to Tambu's father. She refuses to leave the home after being told to do so and convinces Babamukuru to find her a job. She forces the family to accept her, leading Babamukuru to remark, "That one . . . she is like a man herself" (p. 171). Takesure describes Lucia as "vicious and unnatural" (p. 145). Lucia transcended the traditional roles that were expected of her. The other women who struggle with the traditional literacies are Maiguru and her daughter Nyasha. Maiguru, as discussed later, is the product of both the traditional and colonial literacies. She too struggles to be included. Her daughter, Nyasha, who lived in England, cannot fit into either literacy.

COLONIAL/MODERN LITERACY

The colonial/modern/academic literacy is yet another type of literacy found in the book. As the story unfolds, it becomes clear this hybrid literacy is not much different from the traditional literacy previously examined. The similarity to the

existing literacy lies in the fact that the motivations behind this literacy and traditional literacy are the same—to exclude. Because of its exclusionary goals,
colonial literacy is also dysfunctional.

The colonial mission was Christianity, Western civilization, and commerce,
which created a divided world in Zimbabwe. As Fanon (1961) contended, the
colonial world is one separated into two parts—colonial and native. The society
presented in *Nervous Conditions* is clearly such a society. Dangaremba's society is a culture in transition. With colonialism came Christianity. Christianity
presented a paradox for Africans because it symbolized a movement away from
the limiting borders of traditional literacy to a preference for the formal classroom as we know it today. It can be said that religious institutions such as the
Christian church were the first institutions to place Africans in a global context.
However, Christianity had nothing of spiritual value to offer colonized
Africans, who, prior to colonialism and Christianity, had their own spiritual
belief systems.

With colonialism came the mission school. Retrospectively, this educational system had little to say to Africans about themselves, yet it was readily
accepted by the colonized people. It was accepted because it symbolized a
breaking away from the old traditions. Tambu yearns to further her education
because, in the book, education is seen as liberating. When the news was broken
to Nhamo that he was going to school at the mission school, his boastful joy
illustrates the hope that the people placed in education, at least for the men. He
boasts to Tambu, "Did you ever hear of a girl being taken away to school? . . .
With me it's different. I was meant to be educated" (p. 49). Nhamo's statement
reveals an excitement about education as well as imbedded values of the culture
regarding men and their expectations in life.

Freire (1972) noted that no educational process is neutral; rather education
is a value-laden exercise. Those who passed through the colonial educational
system learned new values that were not congruent with the ideals they knew
and lived by before their education. Sometimes, as in Nhamo's case, this
process can lead to a transformation. Tambu describes such a transformation in
Nhamo: "All this poverty began to offend him, or at the very least embarrass
him after he went to the mission, in a way that it had not done before" (p. 7).
Worse, "He had forgotten how to speak Shona" (p. 52). In Nhamo's case, the
literacy that he acquired at the mission school created within him the need to
include himself in its culture while excluding himself from the traditional culture. His new literacy and its values were not congruent with the traditional literacy in which he grew up. Although the education from colonial society gives
Nhamo a superior place in his family, it alienates him from the very people who
assured him a special place in their precolonial world. Such is the dilemma that
Maiguru faces and, too, is the challenge with which the young Nyasha lives.

Maiguru, Tambu's aunt and Nyasha's mother, is an educated woman.
Tambu finds out that Maiguru has been educated up to the master's level.
Maiguru tells Tambu, "We both studied, your uncle and I, in South Africa for

our bachelor's degrees and in England for our master's" (p. 101). This information comes as a shock to Tambu, who had never assumed that Maiguru was educated and who is aspiring to be educated. As it turns out, Maiguru's achievements are overshadowed by Babamukuru's not because they are less than her husband's, but because people do not seem interested in knowing about her apart from her husband. Maiguru did not get a lot of encouragement from her family during her education: "Whatever they thought . . . I still studied for that degree and got it in spite of all of them—your uncle, your grandparents and the rest of the family" (p. 101).

Despite her educational success, Maiguru is unable to fully enjoy the benefits of her education. She never gets to spend her hard-earned salary. Tambu notes that "[her] aunt never received her salary" (p. 101). The implication is that Babamukuru, the husband, may be the one who receives Maiguru's salary. Maiguru wishes that things were different. Her education presents a dilemma in that, essentially, she is no different from the other women around her who are uneducated in the colonial tradition. At first, because of her association with Babamukuru, her position in the family and society seems privileged. However, as the story progresses, even Tambu begins to see that, despite her colonial education or maybe because of it, Maiguru remains in poverty. This poverty manifests itself in Maiguru's physical surroundings at the mission. When Tambu first saw the European surroundings, they had awed and inspired her. However, on later reflection, Tambu notes,

> It looked very sophisticated to me at the time. But looking back, I remember that the cooker had only three plates, none of which was a ring; that the kettle was not electric; that the refrigerator was a bulky paraffin-powered affair. The linoleum was old, its blue and white pattern fading to patches of red where the paint had worn off and patches of black where feet had scuffed up the old flooring at its seams and water had dripped from hands and vegetables and crockery to create a stubborn black scum. The kitchen window was not curtained; a pane of glass was missing. . . . Later, as experience sharpened my perception of such things, I saw too that the colours were not co-ordinated. The green and pink walls contrasted harshly with each other and with the lino. (p. 67)

At the relational level, Maiguru's poverty manifests itself in her relationship with her husband, his family, and her children. This relational poverty persists and may have been worsened by her colonial education. Her position in the family came from the fact that she was the wife of Babamukuru; she is essentially the wife of the man whose colonial achievements are viewed with pride by the whole family. Her position does not come from her own individual achievements as a woman navigating in the European culture. Because Babamukuru's position in the family demands that he takes care of everyone,

Maiguru feels this burden. Her relationship with her husband is therefore characterized by her playing the traditional role that is expected of her even if this role is contrary to what she desires. She is forced into a position where she must provide for all of the family's numerous members in one form or another. Her education does not work the way she anticipated. Furthermore, her husband's education is the source of her dilemma.

Maiguru's discontent with her marital status culminates in her temporary leave from her husband and children. Her separation shows that interpersonal relationships were strained as a result of external pressures and demands. There were demands from the extended family—demands that were made of Babamukuru and Maiguru primarily because they were educated abroad. At the very least, because Babamukuru is educated (it appears few know that Maiguru is educated), a strain is placed on Maiguru's relationship with her husband and children.

Before Maiguru temporarily leaves her home, she tells Babamukuru about her feelings regarding her role in the family. The unfairness of the situation hits home for the reader. Prior to Maiguru's leaving, Tambu's parents have been forced into a wedding by Babamukuru. The reason for the wedding is to ward off bad luck because Babamukuru's Christian beliefs do not value any marital unions apart from Christian unions. Babamukuru tells Tambu's father, ". . . yes, Jeremiah, even now, so many years after our mother passed away, you are still living in sin. You have not been married in church before God" (p. 147). Because she sees the ridiculousness of the ceremony, Tambu refuses to attend her parents' wedding, arousing the anger of Babamukuru and causing her aunt Lucia, her mother's younger sister, to visit Babamukuru's home to discuss the situation. This wedding is the last straw for Maiguru. She tells Babamukuru:

> . . . when it comes to taking my money so that you can feed [Tambu] and her father and your whole family and waste it on ridiculous weddings, that's when they are my relatives too. Let me tell you, Babawa Chido, I am tired of my house being a hotel for your family. I am tired of being a housekeeper for them. I am tired of being nothing in a home I am working myself sick to support. And now, even that Lucia can walk in here and tell me that the things she discusses with you, here in my home, are none of my business. I am sick of it Babawa Chido. Let me tell you, I have had enough! . . . And when I keep quiet you think I am enjoying it. So today I am telling you I am not happy. I am not happy anymore in this house. (p. 172)

We see further examples of Maiguru's relational poverty in her lack of communication with her children. Chido is distant from her, choosing instead to spend most of his time away from the home with his friends. Nyasha is a volatile child, disagreeing with everything her parents think, say, or believe. Her relationship with her mother is strained. Nyasha wishes her mother were more independent of her father. She thinks her mother's leaving will be good for her: "She thought there was a difference between people deserting their daughters and people saving themselves. Maiguru was doing the latter . . ." (p. 174).

In a sense, Nyasha wishes to see her mother using her colonial education to the fullest. To Nyasha, education is empowerment, the kind of empowerment that she talks about and that she feels gives her the right to communicate with her parents in the way she does. When her mother returns home after her temporary leave, Nyasha notes, "It's such a waste . . . imagine what she might have been with the right kind of exposure!" (p. 175). Her mother, however, is fighting her own battles for inclusion in the family. Being an educated woman, Maiguru essentially is treated no differently from the other women in the book. Such is the burden that Maiguru carries, and it is this burden that creates an estrangement from her husband and family.

Nyasha presents an extreme dilemma that results from the struggle for inclusion in her family and her parents' traditional upbringing. Nyasha, like her brother Chido, has, in her early, formative years, been raised in England. When her family returns to Rhodesia, she is faced with the task of trying to fit into a society in which she did not live long enough to fully comprehend. Maiguru perhaps explains it best: "They are too Anglicised" (p. 74). One can draw parallels with Fanon (1961), who argued that to take on a language is to take on the culture represented by that language. Nyasha can barely speak the language and does not always understand the behaviors that are expected of her. When she does understand, she refuses to be part of them. When Tambu meets Nyasha for the first time, on her (Nyasha's) return from England, she is struck by the difference in her and laments, "I missed the bold, ebullient companion I had had who had gone to England but not returned from there" (p. 51). Nyasha has learned a different kind of literacy in England. On her return to her original home, she is faced with the burden of her newly acquired literacy and the challenge of fitting into both the traditional literacy and colonial literacy.

Through Nyasha we see the restrictive and exclusive nature of both literacies. Her relationship with her parents, particularly her father, is estranged. Babamukuru wants Nyasha to fit into the role of the ideal daughter. Her assertiveness and impetuousness disturb and anger him. Babamukuru, despite or because of his colonial education, is a patriarch who expects Nyasha to behave in certain ways. His colonial literacy dictates that she act a prescribed way because she is the principal's daughter. His traditional literacy dictates that she act a certain way because she is female. Nyasha resents those expectations and says, "I don't want to be anyone's underdog" (p. 117). Both literacies create underdogs, and Nyasha is aware of this. In the traditional literacy that excludes her, Nyasha insists on inclusion, but on her own terms. The colonial literacy that most of the people revere is seen by Nyasha as inherently exclusive, oppressive, and racist. Babamukuru frequently encourages Nyasha to be more like Tambu. Tambu explains:

> Beside Nyasha I was a paragon of feminine decorum, principally because I
> hardly ever talked unless spoken to, and then only to answer with the
> utmost respect whatever question had been asked. Above all, I did not ques-
> tion things. It did not matter to me why things should be done this way
> rather than that way. I simply accepted that this was so. I did not think that
> my reading was more important than washing the dishes, and I understood
> that panties should not be hung to dry in the bathroom where everybody
> could see them. I did not discuss [the housekeeper's] leave conditions with
> Maiguru. I was not concerned that freedom fighters were referred to as ter-
> rorists, did not demand proof of God's existence nor did I think that the
> missionaries, along with all the other Whites in Rhodesia, ought to have
> stayed at home. (p. 155)

In *Nervous Conditions*, like similar African stories, education is seen as
alienating, uprooting one from one's known environment. Education, particularly colonial education, was geared toward the displacement of the colonized from
familiar surroundings. When she has a psychological breakdown, Nyasha
remarks, "Look what they've done to us . . . I'm not one of them but I'm not one
of you" (p. 201). As a character in Hamidou Kane's (1962) *Ambiguous
Adventure* noted, "The fate of us Negro students is a little like that of a courier:
at the moment of leaving home we do not know whether we shall ever return."
Nyasha has not returned, Maiguru is struggling with her own return, and Tambu
may never return. This again leads to exclusion. This literacy too is dysfunctional. Gender issues further compound the problems of this exclusion and dysfunc-
tionality of the Black woman who is literate.

GENDER

Gender stratification is apparent in *Nervous Conditions,* and the women in the
book attempt to deal with it in a number of ways. Tambu believes that colonial
education will set her free. Her mother believes in the traditional literacy regarding a woman in her place. Maiguru is caught in the middle because she has
learned a hard lesson. Even with her advanced colonial education, she still is not
free. The gender structure of colonialism and the ensuing gender experience are
inherently separationist and hence dysfunctional. The combination of these literacies and gender relations makes for a heavy burden for Black women to bear.
Tambu realizes that part of her exclusion results from being female. In her early
days at the mission, she constantly thought of her mother, ". . . who suffered
from being female and poor and uneducated and black . . ." (p. 89). When she
sees a colonially educated woman such as Maiguru still suffering, she realizes
that a big part of the problem is femaleness. She frequently thinks of Nyasha's
"rebelliousness":

Babamukuru condemning Nyasha to whoredom, making her a victim of her femaleness, just as I had felt victimized at home in the days when Nhamo went to school and I grew my maize. The victimization, I saw, was universal. It didn't depend on poverty, on lack of education, or on tradition. It didn't depend on any of the things I had thought it depended on. Men took it everywhere with them. Even heroes like Babamukuru did it. And that was the problem. You had to admit that Nyasha had no tact. You had to admit she was altogether too volatile and strong-willed. You couldn't ignore the fact that she had no respect for Babamukuru when she ought to have had lots of it. But what I didn't like was the way all the conflicts came back to this question of femaleness. Femaleness as opposed and inferior to maleness. (pp. 115-116)

Gender is not the only confounding factor in the dilemma that the characters experience in *Nervous Conditions*. Race also presents an issue that further complicates the characters' situation.

RACE

The colonial experience in Rhodesia was inherently racist. Tambu experienced the racism that Nyasha read in her books when she attended school at Sacred Heart. At Sacred Heart, the student dorm rooms were separated along color lines. In a sense, some of the frustrations that the characters experience in the story can be traced to colonial Rhodesia's racist and classist system. On a larger scale, the characters in Dangarembga's story are all fighting for inclusion in a society that has disinherited and relegated them to an inferior position. The cumulative effects of the racism, when examined alongside the exclusivity of the literacies discussed, create discontent in characters like Nyasha. The characters, some perhaps unconsciously, are struggling for inclusion. Babamukuru's and Maiguru's education, for example, is a search for social inclusion. They command awe from their peers because people see them as a couple that has moved closer to inclusion in the larger White-controlled society. When Nhamo goes to the mission, he compares Babamukuru's and Maiguru's luxury with the material lifestyles that the White Rhodesians enjoy: "Not even the Whites . . . not even the Whites themselves could afford it!" (p. 61).

Thematically, the success story of Babamukuru is a continuation of the oral history that was passed onto Tambu by her grandmother. The grandmother talked of how she had struggled to raise Babamukuru and his siblings after she was widowed. She had taken the young Babamukuru to the missionaries to get him educated: "For my grandmother, being sagacious and having foresight, had begged them to prepare him for life in their world" (p. 19). This act is clearly a search for inclusion.

Nyasha, however, sees the racist practices of the system. She is discontented with the material she learns at school. She realizes that they are all victims of the racist system in which they are living: "Do you see what they've done? They've taken us away. Lucia. Takesure. All of us. They've deprived you of you, him of him, ourselves of each other" (p. 200). The literacy that the colonial system brings was ultimately as exclusive as the traditional one and may perhaps compound the problems raised by the traditional literacy. Each literacy, therefore, becomes a burden that must be borne by those who live within that literacy.

THE BURDEN OF LITERACY

Tambu's mother, Ma' Shingayi, sums it aptly for us: "This business of womanhood is a heavy burden. . . . And these days it is worse, with the poverty of blackness on one side and the weight of womanhood on the other" (p. 16). The literacies present a burden that the characters in the book must carry. For Babamukuru, the burden of colonial and traditional education is to be the provider of his family even at the expense of his wife's happiness. For Maiguru, the burden is accepting the fact that she is a highly educated modern woman who, on the surface, may appear to be living a life vastly different from Ma' Shingayi; yet, when all is removed, is still as unhappy and as unsatisfied as Tambu's mother from the rural society. Maiguru's burden also is to provide Nyasha with direction to succeed in a colonial world, the very Nyasha who believes her mother is a failure. Nyasha's own burden is to find a place where she can belong for she fits with neither the British culture, the traditional culture, nor the colonial culture. Tambu's burden is to negotiate a middle ground between the various literacies. Her mother's burden is to balance her attempts at protecting her daughter with efforts at encouraging Nyasha to aim higher.

CONCLUSION

The two literacies in Dangaremba's story, traditional and colonial/academic, are exclusive, and they are dysfunctional within the national setting in which they operate. This is not to say, however, that there is no way for the novel's characters to get the most from all the literacies. Dangarembga's tale is a painful yet revealing story about Black people's struggle for resolution among the challenges presented by the conflicting literacies. *Nervous Conditions* is also a hopeful story. In presenting the two literacies and the burdens they bring to the book's characters, Dangarembga offers counsel regarding the need to find the middle ground, which becomes a path to inclusion of all literacies. Tambu represents the middle ground in *Nervous Conditions* because she survives the transition from traditional literacy and makes her way in colonial/academic literacy without sacrificing her sanity or her soul. Nyasha realizes this middle passage is the ideal that she also should strive to achieve in her fragmented life. In a letter she writes to Tambu while Tambu is away at Sacred Heart school, she alludes to this longing, ". . . I am missing you and missing you badly. In many ways you are very essential to me in bridging some of the gaps in my life" (p. 196). The middle ground that Tambu represents (i.e., the bridge between the colonial/academic and traditional literacies) may be the primary lesson inherent in the struggle for new worlds that are based on *inclusion*, rather than those societies based on separation or rejection of people, particularly Black women, dictated by particular literacies.

REFERENCES

Cervero, R.M. (1985). Is a common definition of adult literacy possible? *Adult Education Quarterly, 36*(1), 50-54.

Dangaremba, T. (1982). *Nervous conditions*. Washington: Seal Press.

Fanon, F. (1961). *The wretched of the earth* (Trans.). Harmondsworth: Penguin.

Freire, P. (1972). *Pedagogy of the oppressed* (Trans.). Harmondsworth: Penguin.

Kahari, G.P. (1980). *The search for a Zimbabwean identity: An introduction to the black Zimbabwean novel*. Gweru, Zimbabwe: Mambo.

Kane, C.H. (1962). *Ambiguous adventure* (Trans.). London: Heinemann.

Marechera, D. (1978). *The house of hunger*. London: Heinemann.

Mungoshi, C. (1975). *Waiting for the rain*. London: Heinemann.

Nzenza, S. (1996). *The reconstruction of womanhood in African literature*. Unpublished doctoral dissertation, University of Melbourne.

Schmidt, E. (1992). *Peasants, traders, and wives: Shona women in the history of Zimbabwe*. London: James Currey.

12

Reel Women: Black Women and Literacy in Feature Films

Joanne Kilgour Dowdy

Critical film literacy is an important component of any literacy student's tool-box for survival in our media-saturated society. Beach and Myers (2001) suggested that we ask students to look into the way that symbols (i.e., words, actions and pictures) help create systems that mediate our world as we experience it. Literacy teachers who want to encourage a variety of communication skills in their students also look to verbal, visual, kinesthetic, and aural arts to facilitate their students' success in the language arts classroom (Harste, 1994; Reiff, 1992; Doig & Sargent, 1996). Being a Black woman who is literate in writing, acting, and videography, my interest in the literacy levels of Black women informs the way that I look at films and read novels and other literature that include the stories of Black women. It is with this lens, looking for what literacy affords women of color in our society, that I encourage students in my classrooms to analyze videos by using their critical literacy faculties.

Given that there is no "material difference" (Brown, 2002) in the lives of Black people in the United States in the last 100 years, I find it imperative to invite students into the world of critical analysis of films that include Black characters. I have found that, when we give students the tools that allow them to step back from the story structure of a film (i.e., beginning, middle, and end), they untangle themselves from the emotional effect of the writing and cine-matography. In this space of critical observation, not the stance of a naive con-sumer, they gain an important experience in the art of looking at films to learn about their society and its values (Fiske, cited in Alvermann & Hagood, 2000). In the development of an understanding of the perceived value of the lives of Black people in our society, as presented in the successful films promoted by film producers, students come to interrogate many of the attitudes and habits they take for granted as citizens who view films in this country.

"Passion Fish" (1992), "Wit" (2001), "The Color Purple" (1985), "Losing Isaiah" (1995), "The Josephine Baker Story" (1991), "Clara's Heart" (1988), "Sarafina" (1992), "Music From the Heart" (1999), and "Eve's Bayou" (1997), were released to cinemas across the country over a 16-year period. Each film offers an interesting view of the lives of Black women as perceived by the writ-ers of these films. They also show the way in which these women interact with White society in the writers' imaginations. I describe each of the nine films and analyze the implications for Black women and their attainment of different liter-acy levels within the world described by the script. I use the critical lens that I have developed through teaching this method to students. Because the literacy level of each Black woman's character who appears in the films is not always explicit, I make certain assumptions about the persona and the level of formal education that she has attained based on the work that the character performs in the story.

In much the same way that the books by Alice Walker (1984), Tsitsi Dangaremba (1988), Merle Hodge (1981), Paula Giddings (1984), J. California Cooper (1984), and Darlene Clark Hine and Kathleen Thompson (1998), allow the readers the opportunity to glimpse the lived experience of Black women with different literacy levels, movies provide an opportunity to witness the everyday experiences of literate Black women within certain sociocultural con-texts. Our imaginations, however, must be engaged to fill out the picture, so to speak, based on the minimal facts the authors provide in books and films. As *readers* of the film or book, we must create a fictive reality that embraces the social limitations within which Black women have had to organize their lives over the last three centuries (Dowdy, 2001; Harley & Terborg-Penn, 1997). Because Black women still live within the barriers that mainstream American society organizes through decisions made on the basis of skin color, language, financial background, and educational preparation (Gregory, 1999), it is some-times difficult to construct the social circumstances within which a Black female character is depicted in a movie.

Like a picture, a film is worth a "thousand words." Books of photographs about Black people and culture help evoke past eras.[1] We can also learn about

---

[1]Moutoussamy-Ashe (1986), Thompson and Mac Austin (1999), Willis-Braithwaite (1988), and Winfrey (1998).

fashion, social trends, politics, educational norms, religious mores, history, and family relationships within the given epoch that a film depicts. These historical documents help build a case for character sketches when teaching students to analyze films with Black female roles. The movies described next demonstrate how a writer and a movie production team can communicate information about time and circumstances—things that are not communicable through printed words. Characters enacted by leading Black actresses (i.e., Goldberg, Woodard, Berry, and Bassett) also allow a glimpse into the window of the actress' experiences as literate women. Through the actresses' interpretations of the Black women they depict in the mainstream film industry, we garner evidence of the legacy about the value of education in the Black community's history.

Why These Movies?

In my search for feature films with Black female leads for use in the classroom, I have come to rely on the box office appeal of leading actresses. This is because movies with popular female leads are seen by many students and, therefore, are easy to find in video rental stores. The movies also act as a barometer in terms of the way in which mass audiences celebrate or denigrate the ideas in storytelling that mainstream filmmakers offer to the public. By bringing these movies into the classroom, I build a bridge from the known world of student film viewing to a new world of analyzing films through a refined lens. The students and I join in a "treasure hunt" for details and evidence that prove a case about women and literacy that we build together. Although some of my ideas and the background research on the history of Blacks in film in the United States are not always palatable to my students, they begin to build a repertoire of analysis tools that make it easier to communicate their interpretations as well as their challenges to my reading a film as text.

Choosing films that span 16 years in the industry brings a variety of discussion points to the classroom. We not only have an opportunity to look at the way characters are represented by fashion and communication styles, but an opportunity to discuss the economic reality that makes it possible for a certain type of film to be produced in one era and not another. These discussions lead students to research in politics, economics, religion, education, and artistic values, and then to write about their perceptions of a film's value within these contexts.

The Politics of Location

My interrogation of the word *Black* has been informed by a conversation with Dr. Lindsay Pentolfe-Aegeter. In her reference to "Altherusserian ways in which we are 'interpellated' to occupy various 'subject positions'" (i.e., those identities marked by race, gender, class, culture, ethnicity, sexuality, spirituality, religion, nationality, regional identity, rural or urban background), she directed my attention to the power that is the root of all politics of identity. As Pentolfe-Aegeter stressed in our conversation, the fact that "rules and roles create social expectations" and lead us to believe in the "natural" order of things, bring us to an understanding of the "politics of location." We are all a combination of identities, and each of our "selves" wields a certain level of power, or lack thereof, that is dependent on time and place.

An example of this shifting locus can be seen in professor Pentolfe-Aegeter's life. When Dr. Pentolfe-Aegeter lives in Zimbabwe, her English accent allows her many privileges that the dark-skinned Africans of her home country are not given. However, when she is in London, England, her accent sounds foreign to the English residents, and therefore she is less likely to be treated with respect. She is, in fact, made to understand by the English that she is an alien and, therefore, of another, lower class than her English associates. Her white skin, Eurocentric features, and claim to being a descendant of a White British couple cannot shield her from the reality of her lack of power in that English location.

In another instance of the politics of location, one of the doctoral students in my "Black Women and Literacy" class asked what was to be done with the White South African priest who said that he was proud to be an African American. Was it simply a matter of birth by Africans and immigration to the United States that made one African American? The White priest certainly had no power within the Black American contexts due to his white skin and lack of cultural orientation of Black people on this side of Africa.

What is one to do about the fact that being dark skinned and Black, in the African-American sense, gives one more privileges in some parts of the Black American community than in others? When can one claim to be Black and be totally sure that a personal notion of the meaning of the word will be universally accepted by those outside your community? When can one say that one was powerful, literate, Black, and a woman of African descent in the United States?

These questions are indications of the kind of analysis that a politics of location rubric can engender in a classroom. The rubric gives everyone involved a vocabulary to use and develop as they analyze the levels to which their stereotypic notions affect their perceptions of people in certain circumstances who have certain skin tones. The students' conversations are always lively and revealing of the kinds of symbols that inform each student's worldview and their reading of the markers of race, class, sex, and literacy attainment.

Literacy as a Lens

A discussion with my doctoral students in the "Black Women and Literacy" class in the fall of 2002, led us to some interesting claims about the attributes of those whom we believe are Black and literate. The students represented different fields of study, including communications, literacy, curriculum and instruction, educational foundations, and health education. The racial composition was six Black women and one White woman. Their observations of the way in which literacy functions in the lives of Black women were based on their personal experiences as well as those of the Black women who have been students in their classes.

These students raised some interesting notions about literacy, including the reflections that literacy is connected to technology, navigation, certain ways of knowing, negotiating successfully through life, understanding, reading, manipulating information, using information for discriminating, maneuvering, attaining advanced education levels , and expressing oneself articulately.

More important, they found that an examination of the term *illiterate* gave even more information about the values and symbols associated with a literate person. One who is deemed illiterate, according to my doctoral students, is supposedly "unable to function in mainstream society, lacking in (education) credentials, having minimal verbal and communication skills, unable to decipher, having low intelligence, being ignorant, and unable to read." Within the vernacular of Black culture, they suggested, such a person would be deemed *simple*.

A later discussion with an independent filmmaker led me to understand that a scriptwriter also has a rubric for creating and judging a character's literacy level. He included in his list of literacy attainment symbols the descriptions of "people that she kept company with" or "the fact that she had intellectual conversations" about love affairs. The writer also talked about the lifestyle that a character was shown to have, the fact that a college degree might make someone conservative, and that a character who "has aspirations beyond the regular nine to five" job has more literacy than one who is a homemaker. These are broad generalizations about the subject, but they helped me understand the breadth of the notion of literacy in a filmmaker's mind, its attendant qualities, and the way these ideas lead to symbols on the screen. A writer could summon a character with these literate traits, I reported to my students, by simply choosing a costume, dialect, and location with people to communicate information about literacy level.

The class realized through discussion that an examination of literacy terms means that a character can be literate or illiterate depending on the situation in which he finds himself. A student who was assessing another in terms of their literacy level not only talked about the number of years spent in traditional schooling, but was also assessing the kind of social interaction the person had been exposed to in her lifetime. The resulting evaluation would be based on the symbols of worldly wisdom and fashion sense that the person under question exhibited; that identity was usually due to a combination of book sense (i.e., formal schooling) and common sense (i.e., the knowledge acquired from mixing with a particular social group and learning to identify with their values and experiences).

In the evaluation of the literacy levels of the Black women in the feature films discussed next, I tell my students that I make a judgment based on the kind of book sense or "school literacy" (Fingeret, 1991) that the characters exhibit in the plot and the symbols of literacy that the scriptwriter has included as a kind of shorthand for the viewer. The audience looks at the film expecting to understand the type of literate person that the filmmaker intends to represent in the plot. I explain my understanding of the women characters as Black people by pointing to the fact that they are the only persons of obvious African descent in the movies. The women are usually dark skinned and, if not, are identified with African-American cultural symbols that make it easy for the viewer with a background in popular movie watching to identify the characters as stereotypes from the Hollywood pantheon of historical images (i.e., the mammy, sapphire, nurse, or cook; "Toms, coons, bucks, or mulattoes"; Bogle, 1999).

The descriptions of the films and the literate Black woman's role in the plots offered next are necessarily short because the lives are represented in such a sketchy manner. The shorthand involved in summoning the character's life is deft and appropriate for the importance of the role in the scheme of the story. I tell my students that I press my imagination and commonsense knowledge about Hollywood stereotypes into the job of describing the story line and a Black character's role to enlighten their attitude to my perspective on the given evidence of Black, female literacy levels in the plots.

"Passion Fish"

"Passion Fish" is a story about a White actress, Mary McDonnell, who is paralyzed in a car accident and decides to return home to Louisiana to recover. After several bad experiences with live-in nurses, she finds herself a Black nurse, played by Alfre Woodard, to care for her. As the story unfolds, the nurse (Woodard) is exposed as a recovering cocaine addict who needs the job to convince her father that she can take care of her only child. Ms. Woodard can barely keep herself under control within the tense relationship that develops between herself and her crippled employer. It is revealed that Woodard did not finish her nursing program, and she begs her employer to let her continue doing what she knows about caring for paraplegics so she can keep her job. The two women develop a makeshift agreement that brings some semblance of peace to the house and ensures that each does not take advantage of the other's weaknesses.

I explain to my students that Woodard's character is designed to fill the stereotypic role of the understanding "mammy," who leaves her own child to take care of her crippled White mistress. It is also revealed that the mistress has developed a drinking problem. At the end of the film, both women are resigned to their life together as two recovering addicts in need of each other's support, and the crippled mistress tells Woodard that she must "learn to cook."

What kind of literacy does one need to function within the world created by the film? Did Woodard really need to finish nursing school to do the work of a caretaker? She is marooned in a country town with no Black people around and no family to support her as she recovers from her addiction. We never see her writing or reading during the film. She goes into town and becomes involved in an affair with a man who has several ex-wives and children by each of them. She chooses a relationship with him over complete isolation and to ease the reality of living with an alcoholic employer. Her book sense is not utilized in this story; rather it is sidelined for the common sense that she brings to the situation.

"Eve's Bayou"

In "Eve's Bayou," starring Samuel J. Jackson and Lynn Whitfield, viewers are treated to a different version of the same social arrangement. In this film, Lynn Whitfield is the Black stay-at-home mother of three children. Her husband is a physician and the stereotypic alcoholic. Her mother-in-law is the live-in "help" who allows her to cope with her husband's philandering. We cannot discern what level of formal education Whitfield has attained because we do not see her engaged in activities other than cooking, hosting a party at her house, visiting a soothsayer in the marketplace, and chatting with her sister-in-law (a clairvoyant who tells people's future by holding their hands). All the women in "Eve's Bayou" are Black, and none appears to have jobs that take them outside the household.

Apart from the education that is necessary to run a doctor's large house and entertain guests, it is hard to imagine what kind of literacy Whitfield is supposed to have attained before marrying and raising her children. It seems that her role in life is to wait on her husband and children, pray for the end of the agony called a marriage, and look pretty. Once more, book sense takes the back row in this story of Black women placed in a location where they have little economic power.

"The Josephine Baker Story"

The "Josephine Baker Story" offers a different picture of Black women and their literacy. This is the story of the poor Black girl who worked her way up to riches and fame in France. She won the Croix de la Guerre for her underground work during World War II, and the story is an inspiring chronicle of the "rags to riches" saga. Against the odds of racism in the United States and exoticism in Paris, Lynn Whitfield as Josephine Baker paints a credible portrait of a woman determined to make a better life for herself and the 12 children she adopted. Again, however, viewers are confounded in a search to determine the level of literacy that prepared Ms. Baker for her rise to fame in the performing arts. Clearly she was a good dancer, comic, actress, and singer. She started her own business in Harlem and went on to be named the "richest woman in the world" following a tour of Europe as a performer. Yet what exactly did she learn in school? Who were her teachers "on the boards" during her stage life? Did her business managers teach her everything, or did she guide them in making decisions that were profitable to her solo career? What did she do about her reading and writing skills as she scaled the walls of social acceptance in White society? The movie has only one scene where Whitfield writes, and this picture comes in the beginning of the movie. The scene shows the actress writing in her journal, which supposedly forms the basis of the story that reveals her life. Josephine Baker's biography, the one that informs this movie's text, says that she dropped out of school at an early age to earn a living.

"Losing Isaiah"

A film that provides an interesting window into the portrait of Black women who have attained some measure of literacy in their lives is "Losing Isaiah." This film features Halle Berry and Meryl Streep as two mothers who vie for first position in the baby "Isaiah's" life. Streep is a social worker of some 15 years' standing. Berry is a crack cocaine addict who abandons her baby in an alley to get a hit of cocaine to feed her habit, rather than care for her screaming baby. What do we find out about Berry as she works her way through a rehabilitation drug program and earns the right to keep her baby? At the time, she can barely read a children's book. When she does read, she is too heartbroken to finish the assignment because it reminds her that she did not take care of herself when she was pregnant with Isaiah. She did not eat fresh fruit and vegetables and exercise enough to produce a healthy baby, she tells her counselor.

Clearly, Berry is an unfit mother because she is barely literate, works as a maid for someone else's children, and depends on a nonprofit agency to provide legal assistance when she tries to find and keep her baby. She cannot win Isaiah's affection when he comes to live with her because he has bonded with Streep. At the end of this Black versus White saga, we are left to consider the ill effects of low literacy in a Black woman's life. When students used their analytical tools to examine the message about literacy in the lives of Black women, they found themselves questioning the chances Berry had of maintaining contact with Isaiah if she did not improve her level of book sense. Book sense, they concluded, was also essential in maintaining any parity in her relationship with Streep.

"Wit"

Emma Thompson is the lead in "Wit," a story about a literature professor who dies of ovarian cancer. Her only friend during her drug-assisted journey is the Black nurse, "Sue." It is the Black nurse who informs Ms. Thompson that the doctors have not found a cure for her rare cancer. Furthermore, Sue is the one who recommends that her patient decide on the way she wants to be treated when her heart stops beating. Does she want a "code blue," which means resuscitating her heart, or does she prefer to die and be left alone? It is Sue who makes sure that Thompson's wishes are carried out when her heart does stop beating, even though a doctor calls in the code blue squad. Near the end of the illness, the doctors stop treating the patient like a human. Thompson can neither hear nor answer them near the end of her painful illness, yet Sue continues to rub cream on the patient's hands.

There is a revealing scene in the movie, which the students in the "Black Women and Literacy" class expose with their critical analysis tools. In one conversation, Sue and her patient are talking about the effects of a drug, and the patient asks if it will make her "sophorific"? No, says Sue, but it will make you "very sleepy." Thompson laughs and then explains that the word she used means "to make you sleepy." Sue admits that it was "stupid" of her not to know that and then joins her patient in laughter.

The doctoral students asked, how do you become a nurse who is given the responsibility of a patient with a rare case of cancer and not know the meaning of sophorific? What does it say for Sue's character, the only Black person in this drama, and her literacy level if she can administer powerful drugs and respect her patient's last wishes by stopping a blue code when the patient dies? What is the implication of a lesson that Thompson's character imparts to the Black nurse who is dismayed about the pecking order among the medical staff? We know the nurse's low status because she is ignored when she informs the rescue staff that the patient does not want to be resuscitated after her heart stops. The Black nurse, my students deduce, is invisible in her role as caretaker, and book sense is of no value in this story line.

"The Color Purple"

"The Color Purple" brought Whoopi Goldberg tremendous fame and fortune. She portrays a young woman who was raped by her father and bore him children for many years before finding out that he was not her father, but rather her stepfather. She learns to read and write when her sister comes to visit her in her husband's home and finds her living in shambles. Goldberg is obviously dominated by her autocratic husband. By hanging signs on items in the kitchen space (i.e., window, pot, plant, etc.), Goldberg begins to recognize print as a symbol system that can be read. She does not progress beyond this rudimentary level of literacy according to the account of her life given in the film. Later in the movie, a business is set up so that she can sew clothes and earn enough money to live independently.

Goldberg's portrayal of a woman who "makes a way out of no way" is both compelling and informative. The students observed that there are many ways to be functional in the world without reading and writing skills. They also observed that a woman who is not literate is controlled by a dominating man's influence and/or a creative female lover's dictates. Goldberg returns to her husband's farm at the end of the movie, teaching him to sew and enjoying the company of her neighbors. But does she write her story or teach others to write so that they too can change their lives in the way she did when she became literate? Does her literate sister play a bigger role in Celie's life after she recovers from her experience with domestic violence? As the students understand the realities outlined in the film, they see there are limited signs regarding the benefits of book sense for the Black leading lady in this drama.

"Clara's Heart"

"Clara's Heart" enters the world of a Jamaican woman who, after meeting a vacationing White woman, immigrates to the United States as a housekeeper. The White woman, performed by Kathleen Quinlan, has recently lost her baby, and she finds Clara, played by Whoopi Goldberg, a refreshing voice in her world of depression and self-pity. As the housekeeper, Clara moves in and literally takes over running the White woman's house. Her charge, a young White boy, is suspicious at first and resistant to her presence in the home. Over time, Clara wins the young boy over, and she becomes the child's only loving presence among the adults who people his world. The boy learns Jamaican songs and speaks Jamaican with Clara and her friends. When his mother and father decide to divorce, he decides to move into Clara's apartment.

Once again the viewer has no clue regarding Clara's literacy level based on the work she does in the house. Apart from fixing and serving meals, entertaining the young boy when his parents are busy with their romantic liaisons, and giving advice to the boy's mother, the viewers are left to construct their own biography of this Black woman's literacy. Clara has a suitcase full of old letters that have been returned to her. Therefore, we imagine that she can read and write. But what is the level of her literacy attainment? What does she aspire to become given the world to which she is exposed in this film? Does she want to own her own business like her friend who is a beautician? Is she going to enter the medical field? We may infer as much because, at the end of the movie, Clara is observed teaching a Jamaican folk song, *Brown Skin Girl*, to a group of children at a hospital. Does book sense play any role in Clara's future, the students wonder?

"Music From the Heart"

Meryl Streep stars in "Music From the Heart," a story about a violin teacher who establishes a music program in East Harlem. The program is successful due to the support of the community and the financial backing of rich performers who volunteer to give a benefit concert at Carnegie Hall. Angela Bassett is the Black woman who plays the literate school principal who has the vision to employ Streep as a permanent substitute teacher in the first year of Streep's career. Unfortunately, Bassett is not influential enough to reverse the budget cuts that the Board of Education mandates when Streep is at her peak in the citywide violin program. Bassett is savvy enough, however, to support Streep. The school principal goes out of her way to enlist parent support for a fundrais-ing event that attracts the attention of the *New York Times* and other newspa-pers. Common sense is depicted as Bassett's strong suit in this role.

The viewer wants the school principal to be the beacon of hope for the inner-city children in her care, but she is depicted as powerless in the face of the political structure, which makes Streep the heroine in this movie. Education, the plot seems to say, will only get you so far in this Eurocentric society. A violin program in East Harlem is as likely to flourish as an acre of corn on Fifth Avenue without the support of White patrons. Because of the exotic nature of the music program, combined with the feisty attitude of the music teacher, pro-fessional musicians sign on to support the teacher in her quest to bring classical music to the inner city. Literacy, in the Black woman's hands, is trumped by the wider political pressures: being poor, Black, and underserved by an economic system that creates challenging situations for Black children. The doctoral stu-dents who analyzed the literacy issues in the film reminded me that if Streep's character had no violins with which to start her Harlem music program, the chil-dren would never have had an opportunity to make music. The students under-stood that White social and economic power were the winners in this plot, instead of book learning.

"Sarafina"

"Sarafina" was originally a stage play. In the movie version, Whoopi Goldberg does her turn for education and "liberation theology." As a teacher in a South African school, Goldberg's character assumes the responsibility for delivering a nonstandard curriculum so that she can encourage her Black students to think critically about their country's political structure. She crafts classes that make a joke out of the textbook's version of the history of South Africa. Because she is obviously loved by the children in her class, she becomes the prime suspect when a school building is burned.

Goldberg delivers a convincing portrayal of a politically aware secondary school teacher who is committed to telling the truth as she sees it. She inspires her student, Sarafina, to make sacrifices that will improve the way of life in her school and town. Sarafina, however, is left to her own devices after Goldberg "killed herself." Goldberg's death occurred while she was detained by the police for disobeying the law by teaching nonsyllabus topics. The Black, literate woman who began the movie as a shining star in the children's lives, a music teacher who encouraged students to create their own stories and to sing them in a concert, was erased from the screen and the children's future. Literacy neither serves Goldberg nor the children in this violent portrayal of pre-Mandela South Africa. The class noted that Sarafina told her story to the world as a high school dropout.

A Cross-Case Analysis

It is important to recognize that these nine films—from 1985 to 2001—offered lucrative jobs for the Black women who were fortunate enough to win the lead roles. It is also important that their images appear on the boxes that hold the videotapes in stores. This picture symbol on the videotape box can be used as another opportunity to dissect the explicit message that movie producers want to sell to consumers. In essence, I tell my literacy class, a person shopping for a movie is being told that a Black woman has the lead and that the story is about a low-literate female. The graphic with the Black woman's image also tells the story that it is no small feat for a Black woman to achieve this high market value in the commercial film industry. Where would we be in this discussion, I ask my literacy students, without the performances of Lynn Whitfield, Whoopi Goldberg, Alfre Woodard, Halle Berry, and Angela Bassett? Commercial film has trained us to expect a reality where a Black life is included as an incidental fact in the storytelling of a White scriptwriter. Understanding the way Black women fit into the schema of White society, I remind my students, is another kind of literacy code that we must unpack when we view films by mainstream filmmakers.

In our cross-case analysis of these Black women's roles, we can learn much about the way in which literacy facilitates the life of a woman of color in the White world painted in the stories. School teachers, drug addicts, performing artists, wives, maids, and nurses all get a chance to say something on behalf of the world of Black working women who people the lives of White society. How do the Black characters find themselves in these jobs that are described in the plots? They serve White people in some capacity and are rewarded according to the sacrifices they make to earn a living under existing socioeconomic structures. In these women's lives, is book sense a means to a better lifestyle or a future with socioeconomic privileges? Such are the kinds of questions that students must begin to answer to use their own critical skills.

In "Eve's Bayou," Whitfield is depicted as a doctor's wife and an unhappy homemaker. However, she is the paragon of virtue regarding the issue of raising her children. Her payoff is an opportunity to live in a big house and have her in-laws' support when she struggles to make sense of her alcoholic husband's womanizing. What is the economic advantage of her literacy level? Based on this plot, she gets a home, children, husband, and property that are the envy of her friends and neighbors. In a sense, Whitfield gets a social existence that the character of Josephine Baker gets in the life portrayed by Whitfield (i.e., wealth and comfort that are, nonetheless, dependent on other people).

Goldberg in "Sarafina" and Bassett in "Music From the Heart" present another view of the rewards of literacy among Black women. Goldberg wins the love of her students and becomes a martyr. Bassett participates in a game that allows White professionals to keep inner-city schools alive and thriving in the face of severe budget restraints. The rewards for these Black teachers are the intrinsic satisfaction of serving their communities within the limiting circumstances that White political leaders create for them. Such *super women* are not attractive advertisements for young girls who are looking for role models with literacy credentials that lead to success. Unlike the movie stars who play the martyr roles, Black women portrayed in the films are the ones who challenge the "establishment" and do not receive financial rewards for going against social expectations. Rather, the Black characters are blessed with access to a special status that is best described as a cut above poverty level.

The maid or nurse stereotypes presented in "Clara's Heart," "Passion Fish," and "Wit" are no more inspirational than the previous films from the point of view of meaningful literacy in the lives of Black women. In the final analysis, what does Clara win when she is finished with her White sponsor's son and moves on to teaching children at the hospital? Is her pay better? Is her own son restored to her? Is her husband on his way back to their marriage after many years of silence and estrangement? We cannot answer these questions from the film, but we do know that Clara continues to care for other people's children. Caring for others' children is the job that her family values and education win for her. Nonetheless, she continues to be a single Black woman making her way in a White world.

"Passion Fish" constructs a symbolic relationship between the Black protagonist and White antgonist that appears permanent at the movie's end. Alfre Woodard stays on with her White alcoholic employer at the end of "Passion Fish." Woodard has a safe place to recover from her drug habit, plus a country home that fosters her child's sense of security. Woodard's White employer controls the relationship by reminding her that she is a recovering addict with no place to live and because she has no nursing degree, no job prospects. Woodard's future seems bleak in one respect, but encouraging in another. She now has a home that is safe and an employer who is completely dependent on her. Woodard functions as the "boss," as it were, and makes decisions that positively impact her life and her employer's existence. The two women, one Black and one White, form a *republic* of their own seemingly in the middle of nowhere. The caretaker–patient relationship is, according to the movie's author, a vision of equality: two *cripples* looking out for each other in a hostile world that could easily consume both if they returned to their addictive habits.

"The Josephine Baker Story" offers the most interesting view of a Black woman's prospects as a literate citizen. Whitfield portrays a hard-working, family-conscious, ambitious Black woman. She climbs the rough side of the White acceptance mountain to reach a life of fame and fortune. What does she do with her level of access to the rewards of the White world? She begins adopting children faster than she can earn the money to pay for raising them and maintaining her French country castle.

Whitfield works and calls the shots within her world, therefore she exists on a different level than the other Black characters under discussion. She begins the movie by penning her memoirs to her children, "to set the record straight." She knows her outsider status as an independent business owner will not serve her well if she is penniless and ostracized. She loses her second husband because of her headstrong belief that she can maintain the lifestyle that she has come to expect as a wealthy woman. Planting strawberries in her fields is one strategy she devises to bring in extra income for the upkeep of the household. Yet the strawberries do not survive the winter, and she does not follow the advice of her White husband, a successful musician who works for her, and ends up losing everything.

What is the outlook for Whitfield/Baker in this situation? When she is evicted from her castle, she returns to the stage to make money to maintain herself. She sends her 12 children away to stay with her friends and her husband so that the children will have a home and food. Relying on the reputation she established as a member of the French Resistance during World War II, she makes a comeback before she dies—penniless. Her hard work both on and off the stage earns her a reputation, but does not support her through the difficult times she endures during the last years of her life. Would she have been more successful with a high school certificate? A college degree? References from former White employers at the European theaters where she performed? Viewers are left to guess at the end of the movie because Ms. Baker left behind only her recorded music, photographs, children, Croix de la Guerre, and films. Such were the products of her literate mind. Her literacy level, consequently, must be evaluated on the basis of her legacy in the entertainment industry and in the home she gave to orphans.

Implications

Students of Black women's history and Black women's literacy in the United States have to search in many places to piece together the story of a people's struggle to learn to read and write. Historically, Blacks in this country earned their literacy skills at the threat of death (Hine & Thompson, 1988). The story is not well documented for the entire Black population, and certainly it is more remiss with respect to Black women. The case of Grandeson (Davis, 1983), a Black female slave who took in 12 slaves at a time and taught them to read and write in hiding before emancipation, is a legend in the annals of African-American literacy and should be introduced to all students of literacy. Literacy classes should also be told the history of the women who came to the southern states to educate the newly freed Black people (e.g., Anna Julia Cooper and the Forten sisters; Giddings, 1984) after slavery ended.

Literacy students should also be assisted in making connections to contemporary times through such examples of literate Black women as Dr. Lisa Delpit (1996, 2002), Chicago-based educator Marva Collins (1992), and Dr. Johnetta Cole (Sister President; 1997). The lives of these Black women are a living part of the legacy of Black scholarship that has always been a component of the Black tradition in the United States. These contemporary women scholars have climbed beyond the double negative of color and institutional racism in their respective fields and have earned merit for their efforts (Epstein, 1973).

When students are introduced to films, such as the nine discussed in this chapter, it should be noted that there is little evidence of the advancement that Black women have made in the educational field since emancipation in 1865. Teachers can indicate that many women in America have come a long way since they were granted the right to attend school alongside their North American brothers (Hourigan, 1994.) It is also important that students know that Black women always had the privilege of studying with Black men. Early in the history of Black literacy, Black men and women learned together on the underground railroad as well as in the secrecy of the slave owners' homes.

If literacy classrooms facilitate discussions that help students explore how children exposed to commercial TV and film are denied experiences that characterize the people depicted in "Sarafina" or "Passion Fish," it will help foster positive changes regarding the history and presence of Black literacy in our society. Younger students could possibly say that they wanted to "be" Halle Berry because she gets paid a lot of money to "act illiterate" (i.e., look like a drug addict, struggle to read a child's story book, and "make nice" with the White social worker who has won her young child's heart). We need a process of research and reporting that answers questions about what literacy would look like in the minds of people critiquing Hollywood's portrayals of Black literate women. A community project could supplement the learning process by interviewing people from different backgrounds about how much literacy training they believed an actress like Berry or Goldberg needed to be successful in Hollywood. This kind of reality check could go a long way to making a difference in the choices that students make when they are in school and want to make the best of their academic choices.

The work by Foster (1998) provided a model for using films as a means to enhance language study in middle school, high school, and higher education. By structuring classes so that films afford our students a vantage point on history and social contexts, we create a means for them to develop a critical lens for interpreting movies. Showing films in the community, whether it is in schools, theaters, or community buildings, is imperative for training students to analyze the stereotypes propagated by mainstream scriptwriters. As literacy instructors, we should interrogate the norms for literate Black women as established by Hollywood and other producers of popular culture with our students. By putting films in a historical context, we inform the pedagogy that our community inherits.

Important also is a discussion about the operant social forces that keep many Black women in subservient positions. Illuminating the structures that protect and support those with Eurocentric values, education, and tradition helps students analyze the value system that makes the film industry a powerful vehicle in educating the masses. A classroom experience used by Dr. Pentolfe-Aegeter is one way to create space where the politics of location, multiple identities, and content that provides a means for revealing the way in which power operates in our lives. Dr. Pentolfe-Aegeter directs students to figure out who they are and what power they wield at any given moment. The exercise leads to conversations about the sociopolitical hierarchy that governs our daily choices. These discussions can then lead to writing assignments and research projects involving politicians and power brokers within the community and beyond (Dowdy, 2003).

It is not enough to say that Hollywood's treatment of Black women is lacking in scope and depth. Instead we must show how Black history disputes the notion that Black women have not been exposed to a cultural milieu that upholds education. Assigning students books that address the experiences of Black women who lived their lives as literate citizens is an important part of any serious campaign against such misconceptions. Books by Lerner (1972), Gregory (1999), Igus (1991), Larson (1992), Krass (1988), Sterling (1984), Andrews (1986), Child (1987), and Taylor (1991) provide teachers and students with an array of historical material regarding the journey of Black women toward literacy in this country.

Teachers of literacy can also use Hollywood movies to train students to subvert the explicit and implicit messages conveyed to them. By using work such as Baines and Kunkel (2000) to develop students' multigenre expressions of knowledge, films can be turned back on themselves and, therefore, encourage students to question the norms created by Hollywood. Poems, letters, murals, pottery, sculpture, multimedia installations, drama, and video documentaries can depict the themes about issues raised in movies, and particularly those films discussed here. Rather than shrink at the stereotypes of Black maids, teachers, nurses, and entertainers, both students and teachers can research and develop story lines and symbolic products that arrest the negative messages about women of color that are perpetuated through these movies.

As Lena Horne said, regarding her role in the evolution of Hollywood's history of employing Black talent (Buckley, 2002), we must "keep the door open" for other forms of artistic expression from our youth. The dramatization of the life stories about the lead actors and actresses who keep the name of Black artistry alive in Hollywood serves many purposes. Not only does the drama provide an outlet for young actors, designers, musicians, and production specialists, it can also give history teachers and performing artists a chance to work together to develop a positive image for literacy among young people. As many Black leaders have exemplified, the combination of book sense and common sense is always a stellar mixture, and such educators in drama as Brown-Guillory (1990), Holder (2000), and Perkins (1991) can be beneficial to the cause of enhancing the image of the literate Black woman.

CONCLUSION

The doctoral students in the literacy class were aghast at the similarities among the films studied, although there are 16 years between the earliest (1985) and most recent (2001) films. The students were, as literate Black women and a teacher of literate Black women, dismayed about the paucity of descriptors used to represent the world of hard-working, intelligent, and talented women. One student indicated through her challenge to my analysis of a mother figure in one of the films that there was some truth in the stereotypes depicted in the stories. What was disconcerting to the student, however, was that the repetitive images and symbols employed by the filmmakers to represent the world of the Black working woman led viewers to believe that the United States was populated only by poor, dependent, low-literate Black women. What do such ideas mean to people living outside the United States who depend on the movie industry to create and sustain conceptions about Americans?

To ensure that students attain and use critical perspectives in assessing Black characters in mainstream films, literacy teachers must incorporate and analyze film in their curricula. Likewise students must be invited to ask questions such as: How many films exist on the market? How do films portray Black women in a positive role? What proportion of positive stories include a literate Black woman as a significant character? What is the ratio of exceptional Black films to the rest of the films produced by the mainstream film industry? Finally, how do we classify the levels of literacy represented in these movies to understand the logic at work in these profitable creations?

Such questions are the beginning stage of a thorough investigation into the ways film symbols can be used to expand our students' literacy within this communication genre. Because we are a society immersed in TV and screen productions, it makes sense that we would use these symbols to enhance students' education. Teachers can challenge students to reach beyond the entertainment aspect of these films and create additional works that explore a wider variety of Black experiences.

When literacy classes encourage students to write stories about Black women—the women who teach, broadcast the news, lead colleges, fly with astronauts, and operate banks—we will be on the way to undoing the damage that negative film images have contributed to our society. We can then say that our pedagogy has moved beyond being critical to making constructive changes in the way that Black women are represented in movies and the way that critical analysts use such symbols to enhance their worldview. We can use the lessons learned from our experience with popular film to build a bridge to learning more about the history of African-American women and celebrating their contribution to our society and the world.

REFERENCES

Alvermann, D.E., & Hagood, M.C. (2000). Critical media literacy: Research, theory, and practice in "new time." *Journal of Educational Research, 93*(3), 193-206.

Andrews, W.L. (Ed.). (1986). *Sisters of the spirit.* Bloomington: Indiana University Press.

Beach, R., & Myers, J. (2001). Hypermedia authoring as critical literacy. *Journal of Adolescent & Adult Literacy, 44*(6), 538-546.

Baines, L., & Kunkel, A.J. (Eds.). (2000). *Going bohemian: Activities that engage adolescents in the art of writing well.* Newark, DE: International Reading Association.

Bogle, D. (1999). *Toms, coons, mulattoes, mammies, and bucks.* New York: Continuum.

Brown, E. (2002). *The condemnation of Little B: New age racism in America.* Boston: Beacon.

Brown-Guillory, E. (1990). *Their place on the stage: Black women playwrights in America.* Westport, CT: Greenwood.

Buckley, G.L. (1989). *The Hornes: An American family.* New York: New American Library.

Child, L.M. (1987). *Incidents in the life of a slave girl: Written by herself* (H.A. Jacob and J.F. Yellin, eds.). Cambridge, MA: Harvard University Press.

Cole, J. (1997). *Dream the boldest dreams: And other lessons of life.* Marietta, GA: Longstreet.

Collins, M. (1992). *Ordinary children: Extraordinary teachers.* Charlottesville, VA: Hampton Roads Publication.

Cooper, J.C. (1984). *A piece of mine.* New York: Doubleday.

Dangaremba, T. (1988). *Nervous conditions.* Seattle: Seal Press.

Davis, A.Y. (1983). *Women, race, and class.* New York: Vintage Books.

Delpit, L. (1996). *Other people's children: Cultural conflict in the classroom.* New York: The New Press.

Delpit, L., & Dowdy, J.K. (Eds.). (2002). *The skin that we speak: Thoughts on language and culture in the classroom.* New York: New Press.

Doig, L., & Sargent, J. (1996). Lights, camera, action. *Social Studies Review, 34*(3), 6-11.

Dowdy, J.D. (2001). Carmen Montana, the General Education Diploma, and her social network. *Journal of Literacy Research, 33*(1), 71-98.

Dowdy, J.K. (2003). *GED Stories: Black women and their struggle for social equity.* New York: Peter Lang.

Epstein, C.F. (1973). Positive effects of the multiple negative: Explain the success of Black professional women. *American Journal of Sociology, 78,* 912-935.

Fingeret, H.A. (1991). Meaning, experience, and literacy. *Adult Basic Education, 1*(1), 4-11.

Foster, H.M. (1998). Reading and writing in the shadow of film and television. In J.S. Simmons & L. Baines (Eds.), *Language study in middle school, high school, and beyond* (pp. 167-189). Newark, DE: International Reading Association.

Giddings, P. (1984). *When and where I enter: The impact of black women on race and sex in America.* New York: Bantam.

Gregory, S.T. (1999). *Black women in the academy: The secrets to success and achievements.* Lanham, MD: University Press of America.

Harley, S., & Terborg-Penn, R. (Eds.). (1997). *The Afro-American woman: Struggles and images.* Baltimore: Black Classic Press.

Harste, J. (1994). Visions of literacy. *Indiana Media Journal, 17*(1), 27-32.

Hine, D.C., & Thompson, K. (Eds.). (1998). *A shining thread of hope: The history of Black women in America.* New York: Broadway Books.

Hodge, M. (1981). *Crick crack, monkey.* Portsmouth, NH: Heinemann.

Holder, L. (2001). *Renaissance women: Five plays.* Bloomington, IN: 1st Books Library.

Hourigan, M. (1994). *Literacy as social exchange: Intersections of class, gender, and culture.* Albany: State University of New York Press.

Igus, T. (1991). *Book of black heroes: Vol. 2. Great women in the struggle.* East Orange, NJ: Just Us Books.

Krass, P. (1988). *Sojourner Truth: Antislavery activist.* Danbury, CT: Grolier.

Larson, C.R. (1992). *An intimation of things distant: The collected fiction of Nella Larsen.* New York: Doubleday.

Lerner, G. (Ed.). (1972). *Black women in White America: A documentary history.* New York: Random House.

Moutoussamy-Ashe, J. (1993). *Viewfinders: Black women photographers.* New York: Writers and Readers.

Perkins, K.A. (1991). *Black female playwrights: An anthology of plays before 1950 (Blacks in diaspora).* Bloomington: Indiana University Press.

Reiff, J.C. (1992). *Learning styles: What research says to the teacher.* Washington, DC: National Education Association.

Sterling, D. (1984). *We are your sisters: Black women in the nineteenth century.* New York: W. W. Norton.

Taylor, M. W. (1991). *Harriet Tubman: Antislavery activist.* New York: Chelsea House Publishers.

Thompson, K., & Mac Austin, H. (Eds.). (1999). *The face of our past: Images of Black women from colonial America to the present.* Bloomington: Indiana University Press.

Walker, A. (1984). *In search of our mother's gardens.* Orlando, FL: Harcourt, Brace.

Willis-Braithwaite, D. (1998). *Van Der Zee: Photographer, 1886-1983.* New York: Harry N. Abrams.

Winfrey, O. (1998). *Journey to beloved.* New York: Hyperion.

13

To Be Black, Female, and Literate: A Personal Journey in Education and Alienation

Leonie C. R. Smith

Education, we are told, is the key that opens the imaginary door to success. Education, therefore, is supposed to uplift us from misery—to improve our economic situation in life. However, the path to acquiring an education and advanced academic literacy is fraught with difficulty, and opening the door to success comes with a price. My own journey to becoming a multilingual literate Black woman began on the island of Antigua, an island in the Caribbean, the place of my birth. For me it seems that becoming educated was not a choice, but my destiny. My education, whatever shape it took, would be a life-long process and would become a tool with which I could do the necessary activist work in my community.

GROWING UP BLACK, FEMALE, AND LITERATE IN ANTIGUA.

I am the youngest of 11 children born to my parents. My father grew up on an estate that totaled more than 300 acres of land. He was an intelligent boy who had to drop out of school in third standard to help his family work the land. Both of my paternal grandparents were illiterate, meaning they could not read or write, and their illiteracy caused the family to be victimized by an obeah woman.

This woman persuaded my paternal grandmother to sell her the estate by convincing her that her children would rob her, and she "paid" my grandmother for the land with bags of flour for her bakery and a $5 bill. My grandmother, being unable to read, had accepted a promissory note without understanding its contents, and the result was the loss of her estate. Perhaps the victimization of my grandmother was the driving force behind my father's decision to dedicate his life to educating his children and others.

Growing up as a young black girl in Antigua was mostly a pleasant experience. My parents were very intelligent people who, because of their family situations, were unable to complete their education. I believe that education held such importance to my family precisely because my father witnessed his mother's victimization at the hands of a woman who was more literate. My father's family had money and with the snap of a finger it was gone, and the end result was a struggle for survival. I witnessed parts of this struggle during my childhood. We were not dirt poor, but with 13 mouths to feed and only one income, things were difficult. My mother worked outside the home prior to becoming a wife and mother, but after marriage she became a homemaker. My mother was a savvy homemaker; being a talented seamstress, she made our clothes instead of buying them. She also earned money sewing for others in the community. To feed her family, she grew fruits and vegetables in her garden and baked her own bread. By the time I was born, my father had already retired from his trade as a plumber and had been raising livestock and farming crops. The two oldest children—my brother, a policeman, and my sister, then a high school teacher—spent much of their earnings supporting the family. Looking at my family's past, I realize that I came from a family of survivors, and the resilience that permeated throughout our family would prepare me for the life battles to come.

Like Tee, the main character in Merle Hodge's (1970) *Crick Crack Monkey*, I too lost my mother at a very young age. I was barely 5 years of age when she died. She was a very kind and loving individual, and everyone loved her. She bore 11 children throughout her reproductive lifespan; she was always pregnant, and her body never had a chance to recover. I do not know how mother died. No one knows really because autopsies were not done back then. I remember that she went to the hospital one day, she stayed about a week, and then she died. I visited her on a Sunday afternoon while she was in the hospital. We talked about the cut on my right index finger wrapped like a sausage in a Band-Aid. I remember my mother asking me for a hug and kiss; being the shy child that I was, I refused. I have always regretted my failure to comply with her wish. Perhaps she knew something that I did not. Perhaps she knew that those few moments together would be our last. I too realized that she was leaving for good as I stood and watched her body laid out in a wooden coffin, dressed in white, with her hands crossed over her stomach, but somehow her departure did not seem final until I watched with hysteria as she was lowered into her grave and covered with dirt as the mourners sang "Abide With Me" to the accompaniment of Uncle Neville's accordion.

My father attempted to raise the younger children on his own, but given that he worked while my mother raised the children, he did not know what to do with four little girls all under the age of 13. My father was also struggling with the depression resulting from the loss of his wife of 28 years, and he was too sad to take care of his children. He became an emotionally absent parent. The older girls took care of the younger ones. My eldest sister, who was studying in Jamaica to become a nurse, and my eldest brother, provided financial support to the family.

My family's house burned down the year following my mother's death. It was some time in 1981, and we were all asleep in the house while it was engulfed in flames. A passerby saved our lives when he banged on the front door screaming, "Mr. Smith your house is on fire." My father woke us and got us out of the house. We did not own a telephone, so we used a neighbor's phone to call the fire department, which was located in All Saints Village several miles away. We would have been dead by the time they finally arrived. The house could not be saved, and everything turned to ashes and charcoal. Fortunately, no one was hurt.

My family relocated to All Saints Village, where I attended J.T. Ambrose Primary School (formerly All Saints Village Primary School). Although I was born and raised in Swetes Village and I lived a stone's throw from the village school, my siblings and I were sent to school in the neighboring village because our mother feared that the Head Mistress at our village school would mistreat her children. As a result, I walked many miles going to and from school during my childhood.

After our house burned, my family relocated several times. We lived with different relatives in two villages over a 2-year period until my father was able to buy another house. We finally moved into our new house, a yellow three-bedroom wooden house, which was placed in the exact spot where our old house was located. I lived in that house for several months before moving out after a fight with one of my older sisters. As I reminisce, I can only laugh now, at the thought of my 8-year-old self packing my bags and telling my father that I was going to live with Aunt Mary, one of my maternal aunts who lived about 2 miles down the road. My father did not object, and I stayed with Aunt Mary for 3 years before moving to New York at the age of 12 to live with my eldest sister. In 1984, just four years after my mother's death, my father immigrated to the United States, where he remarried, leaving his children behind.

In reexamining my childhood experiences, I find it remarkable that, amid the chaos of the death of my mother, the fact that my entire family almost perished in a burning house, and temporary homelessness, my schooling was never interrupted. As a child, I was encouraged to attend school and to do well. Literacy was valued in my family.

The classes were divided into As and Bs in primary school, from Infant 1 (Kindergarten) to Junior 5 (6th or 7th grade). The A classes were for the students who were considered to be academically gifted, and the B classes were for those students who did not fare as well academically. I remember always being in the A classes, and I always came in first, second, or third place within the class. In primary school, there was a certain rivalry among students in my class—we were always in competition with one another for the top three positions. School was always easy, it was life that was hard, and my life seemed to be one struggle after another.

I was never discouraged from pursuing an education as a child. I was never told that there were limitations to what I could achieve. I was free to dream, and in my dreams I could become anything I wanted to be. I was born in a country where the majority of the citizens were Black. Hence, I never had the opportunity to observe the denial of education to myself or my peers on the basis of race. I was always encouraged to read and write. My father, who had to truncate his own education to help his family work the land, understood the need for formal education. Therefore, it was expected that his children would be educated in schools, that his genius would not go to waste.

My father was a mathematician, and his dream was to become a school Head Master. Although he did not complete his formal education, he continued to educate himself and others. He taught adult literacy classes in the community and preached in the church. My mother also passed on the importance of education as a vehicle to becoming independent and self-sufficient. Perhaps this was due to the fact that she relinquished her independence and access to her own money when she married. She was transformed from a single working woman to a wife and mother. The value, the need to be educated, independent, and self sufficient was passed down to me and my sisters with the hope that we would in some way get the education that our parents never had the opportunity to complete, and thereby enhance our capacity for self-sufficiency. My life long pursuit of education and academic literacy is a stepping stone on my way to independence. It is in essence a fulfillment of the stifled dreams of my parents.

Looking back, my primary school education in Antigua was decidedly British. Antigua gained its independence in 1981, a year after I began my schooling in the public education system. Although Antigua was an independent state, it educated and continues to educate its citizens according to British values. As Mistron (1999) stated "when the values taught in school conflict with reality children may suffer a damaging loss of identity and self esteem" (p. 2).

For a short time, perhaps at age 3 or 4, I attended Teacher Georgette's Nursery School until I was old enough to attend primary school. I attended J.T. Ambrose School for 7 years—from age 5 to age 12. I do not recall learning anything about the enslavement of Africans in the Caribbean. In fact, I do not recall learning anything about Caribbean history other than the geography of the other islands and a few things about the Arawaks and the Siboneys, the original inhabitants of Antigua. My primary education was focused mainly on mathematics, science, language arts, social studies, and home economics. There was nothing in my schooling that focused on my Blackness or my African past; whatever history lay behind me was completely negated.

I was taught British English in school and I spoke patois at home with family and friends. I was always able to switch back and forth between the two languages with ease. Even at such a young age, I knew when to use each language. I knew that if I spoke standard British English in my community, I would be accused of trying to "yank," yet the use of standard English was expected in school and other formal settings. As a child I had neither the opportunity nor the time to question what I was being taught in school, and so it had or appeared to have had no bearing on my identity as a Black woman. I was an Antiguan. Unlike Tee in *Crick Crack Monkey* (Hodge, 1970), who disintegrates and endures not only an identity crisis, but also cultural alienation because of her early education, I was apparently unaffected. It was not until I immigrated to New York that my identity as a Black person came into question. The question was, where and how do I belong in this new setting? What does it mean to be Black in America?

LEARNING TO BE BLACK, FEMALE, AND LITERATE IN AMERICA

In 1987, I entered the seventh grade a few months after moving to Brooklyn, New York. Moving to New York signified a new horizon—a chance to move beyond the confinements and limitations I faced in Antigua. By limitations I mean that, on completion of secondary school, the career opportunities for girls were traditionally female roles and limited in scope. My options were limited to becoming a teacher, nurse, or secretary, and my career interests lay elsewhere. I viewed my new life in New York as an opportunity to expand my career possibilities, but my excitement was coupled with trepidation. I was in a strange and new place, with an even stranger climate and people. New York was a cold place in more ways than one. The people were unfriendly and suspicious if you greeted them. I was shocked by this response because it was considered impolite in my Antiguan culture to pass your neighbors without greeting them. The children in school were not very different from the adults.

I first began to feel isolated during my schooling in the New York City public school system. This isolation began with my removal from my homeroom after I received a poor score on a seventh-grade reading test. Let me preface this by saying that my schooling in Antigua nurtured my critical thinking and writing skills. I was used to writing essays and giving detailed explanations of my thought processes. I was introduced to multiple-choice questions for the first time in the seventh grade. I was given the Degrees of Reading Power test, and when I scored a whopping 29 I was immediately demoted. I was removed from an already average class and placed into a class of even lower academic standing. I had never seen a multiple-choice test before, and many of the topics were unfamiliar to me. I was wronged in several ways. First, I was placed in a class based on my age and my status as an immigrant. (I have always believed that I should have been placed in a higher grade and a class that was more academically challenging. In fact I believe I should have skipped the seventh grade altogether.) Second, I was placed in a class with students who were not of the same academic caliber as I. There were SP classes in my junior high school; these were honor's classes where the work was reportedly more challenging. I was a member of the Arista National Honor Society, an academic honor society for students with grade averages above the 85th percentile, yet I was never given the opportunity to accept this challenge. I had been an excellent student in Antigua, where the course work was more difficult than that of my seventh-grade curriculum in New York, yet I was placed in a class that underestimated my academic abilities. Third, my reading and academic abilities were now being judged on the basis of a reading test that was culturally biased in several ways. For example, the test provided several answers for each question. In Antigua, I was taught to write essays in answer to a question. The test denied me the opportunity to explain myself, as if to say that my thoughts were unimportant. Much of the material in the reading exam was also describing things that were out of my experience, so I did not have the benefit of making up answers based on my common sense.

There were questions about things such as alpine skiing, which had no relevance to me. Growing up in Antigua, I had never seen or heard of snow, let alone alpine skiing. Yet I had to answer questions about subject matter of which I had no concept, and I was subsequently labeled *illiterate*. It angered me to be labeled as someone who could not read especially because I had been reading since the age of 3. I had to learn a lot more than the material on the page if I was going to become literate in the American sense.

After I was demoted, I refused to attend school until I was put back into the class where I was originally placed because I was starting to make friends. I worked out a compromise with the then assistant principal; I would attend an after-school reading program in exchange for placement in the class where I began my education in the American school system. With the help of the after-school tutors, I was able to familiarize myself with the multiple-choice reading test and was able to improve my score by 50 points the next year. For the remainder of my time in Gladstone Atwell Junior High School, I excelled in school once I got over the hump of transitioning from British English to American English both in the written and spoken forms. I even discovered that I had a talent for learning and mastering foreign languages. I learned to speak French in the 2 years I was at Atwell Junior High, and I performed so well on the citywide exams I was accelerated to third-year French by the time I entered high school.

Looking back, I would have slipped through the cracks had I not been bold enough to advocate for my formal education. As a literate Black female child coming from a foreign country, my literacy, and consequently my intelligence, was called into question based on my reading score on a culturally biased test.

The difference in learning styles and the context of my literacy education were never taken into account. It never occurred to this assistant principal that someone like me, raised in the Caribbean and educated under a different system, would respond differently to U.S. testing methods.

In addition to the academic education I received during my early years in the United States, I also received a social education. I had moved from Antigua, where my skin color or my race was a nonissue, to Brooklyn, New York, and I had to learn what it meant to be Black in the United States. Because New York had large numbers of Caribbean immigrants, I spent much of my primary and secondary schooling surrounded by Caribbeans of different backgrounds. It was comforting for me because I felt somewhat out of place—like an alien in a foreign land among North Americans. Black American children made fun of the way I spoke, the color of my skin (I was much darker than I am now, having spent my life in Antigua beneath the scorching heat of the sun), and the shape and size of my eyes. For the first time in my life, I felt different. I was now a dark-skinned, foreign-born Black girl with "frog eyes" and an accent. Through observation of the girls who were sought out for dates, I learned that light-skinned Black girls with hazel eyes were the brand of Black girls preferred by boys in the United States. There was a mixture of American and Caribbean Blacks, Latinos, Jews, Asians, Indo-Caribbean, and Middle Eastern students in my school, and the light-skinned Latina and Black girls were the favorites. Without a doubt, the boys pursued the light-skinned girls with long hair. It was an eye opener for this Antiguan girl. I had never experienced this firsthand in my country. Most of the people around me were of similar dark skin tones, but in retrospect I have observed many Caribbean women, even in my own family, who bought into this White ideal of beauty through their use of *Ambi*, *Skin Success*, and other products to lighten their skin and *Revlon* relaxers to straighten their hair. I had also heard stories of the uproar in my mother's family, which took place when my light-skinned mother married my dark-skinned father.

As early as the seventh grade in the United States, I was given signals that dark skin was unattractive, and this sentiment came from other children. Unlike Tee, in Hodge's novel, I did not internalize this color prejudice that I was observing. I simply focused on my studies and the friends that I had at the time to get on with my life. I did not run out and get hazel contact lenses, which were in at the time, as my classmates did, nor did I covet them. I did not try to lighten my skin. I do admit, however, to occasionally passing an ironing comb through my hair to make it straight, and for that family members accused me of trying to look like an East Indian. It was quite preposterous. I have never in my life suffered from a color complex. I accepted the color of the skin with which I was born, and I understood that I would live with this skin color for the rest of my life. I had no desire to change my chocolate-shaded skin that would later yield so many compliments. My "frog eyes" would later become a source of admiration from people who thought my eyes were shaped like almonds; they called them "bedroom eyes."

Another source of alienation for me was my accent. Indeed I had a thick Antiguan accent, and my pronunciation was markedly different from those New York accents around me. I sometimes mixed Antiguan patois and standard English when I spoke, and sometimes I could not be understood by my New York classmates. I remember a teacher once asked about the ingredients for a tossed salad and I volunteered "cucumba," and no one knew what I was talking about until the teacher replied, "Oh, cucumber," and then there was a roar of laughter. I was also unfamiliar with important dates in North American history. I confused the Antiguan Independence Day with the American Independence Day, and one day when the same teacher asked for the date of Independence Day, I proudly said November 1, 1981. That answer was met with the strangest of looks, as if I were indeed from another planet. My ignorance of American history was glaringly clear and another source of my feeling of alienation.

I socialized mainly with Caribbean Blacks; some had immigrated to America and others had been born in America. Coming from a country where Black people are the majority, it was strange to be in a country where I was now a minority. To fit in with other children in school, I began to assimilate into the Black American culture around me through music and language. I began to listen to Rap and R & B, and I learned to speak and dress like Black Americans. Given that my sister was raising my two older sisters and me as well, she could not afford to buy a lot of clothes for us. She made some of my dresses and bought the rest. True to their nature, the children made fun of me for wearing churchy-looking clothes. They also made fun of my sneakers and my clothes because they were not name brand. In one instance, I was greeted by a Black American girl of Caribbean parentage with "What's the name of your shoes" rather than "Hello." I quickly learned that my lack of interest in materialism was a trait that differentiated me from my African-American counterparts in school. Being a child then, I naturally felt some degree of shame about the rejects that I wore. *Rejects* was the name Black American children gave to sneakers or shoes that were not name brand. I was mature enough to realize, however, that buying expensive things was beyond my control. I was glad to have shoes and clothes to wear because there were many people who were less fortunate than my sisters and I. In Antigua, I was used to playing barefoot in the countryside. I only wore shoes to school, church, or town. I had nothing to complain about as far as I was concerned.

I realized that I was different from my peers in many other ways. I was a motherless child, an orphan, and I was more mature than most children my age. Knowing that I did not have parents to give me everything pushed me to seek the best out of life, to fight for myself, to get an education so that I could be self-sufficient. After 2 years in junior high, I graduated with the highest average in eighth-grade social studies in my entire junior high school, and I walked away with numerous awards. Funny for an immigrant girl who was labeled illiterate at the beginning of her U.S. education career.

I was recruited from junior high school to the Gateway to Higher Education Program, an honor's program that at the time existed in five high schools in New York City. The program sought to increase the number of minority students going into careers in science, medicine, and technology by introducing them to a rigorous dose of math, science, and technology during the high school years. My high school experience was certainly more pleasant than my junior high experience. I went through high school with a cohort of about 30 students from varying ethnic and cultural backgrounds, most of whom were African American or Afro-Caribbean. I was isolated from the other 2,500 students in high school in that I was chosen for this honor's program. I was pegged as one of the academic elite within the school. I was more motivated and ambitious than the average student at my high school, and I was being groomed for success. When I entered high school, I was reunited with some of the students from the honor's classes in junior high, and throughout high school I consistently outperformed these students in every subject with the exception of mathematics and graduated with a high school ranking far above them.

The alienation I experienced in high school was a complex one. I, like the rest of my Gateway peers, was "outed" as a smart kid. We were given the moniker "GEEKWAY" by other students. We were teased, but I never took the teasing seriously. I was proud to be a geek. Being a geek meant being motivated to do more than just get by in life. I never attempted to downplay my smartness. It was a gift I inherited from my parents, and it would afford me the privileges and opportunities they never had. I knew that if I used my intelligence in the right way and took advantage of the opportunities before me, I would "go places in life." I finished high school in the top 1% of my graduating class, ranking sixth out of nearly 500 students in the graduating class, and I embarked on a journey that would forever change the rest of my life.

After high school, I enrolled at Hamilton College, a private predominantly White upper middle-class miniature Ivy League institution located in the Adirondack Mountains of Central New York. During the final years of my high school career, I began to realize that I would need a first-class education to compete in America. Naively, I thought I would only be afforded such an opportunity by attending a predominantly White institution. Finding ways to get money was a constant in my thoughts. I was an orphan. My sister was raising me, and although I was expected to go to college, I was not sure where the money would come from. We were a middle-class family. My sister had a good-paying job as a nurse, but three of my sisters were in college when I was about to start, and I thought I would never get a scholarship to a historically Black college. We were not rich, but we were not poor enough, and I was not an American citizen, so I did not qualify for any of the scholarships available to African-American students. I was under the impression that unless you were "dirt poor," getting a full scholarship was out of the question. At 17 years of age, I was fully engaged in evaluating my options for financing a college education. I knew that a PWI would provide a generous financial aid package that would allow me to attend college without incurring a ridiculous amount of debt. I also knew that I would have to borrow money, but getting a scholarship meant that I would not have to borrow the entire amount that it would cost to pay for the 4 years. My feeling at the time was that I needed to experience interaction with different people, particularly White people, to function effectively in American society.

I was extremely naive on entering college, and I was utterly unprepared for the racism and ignorance that I encountered. Beckham (1988) stated that alienation, lack of involvement, marginalization, overt racism, insensitivity, sexual harassment, and discrimination tended to characterize the campus experience, classroom, and curriculum for students who are different. Moreover, such students tended to feel like outsiders or "strangers in a strange land" (Beckham, 1988). This quote was a most accurate summary of my college experience because I had experienced all of the above and more.

Intense loneliness and isolation marked my years at Hamilton College. I often sat in my dormitory room contemplating my existence and wondering what I was doing in a place like that; questioning what possessed me to leave the diversity of New York City and the security of my family and friends. I traveled 280 miles to get the first-class education I believed would give me a leg up in the world, only to be met by racism, ignorance, and utter rejection. Had it not been for the legacy of my parents and my raw determination to succeed, I believe I would have dropped out. After my first semester, I wanted to run away to someplace where people would not judge me by the color of my skin, where they would not despise me because of it.

In the documentary *A Litany for Survival,* Audre Lorde (cited in Griffin & Parkerson, 1994) said that battling cancer was like battling racism. My experience at Hamilton College was a struggle for survival, a fight to succeed in my academic endeavors. I was one of a handful of Black students at Hamilton College, and with great difficulty I tried to forge a way for myself in science. I found that with each step, I was knocked down right back to square one. I left high school believing that I would become a medical doctor. I was one of the smartest kids in my high school, and yet I was struggling in this predominantly White college.

My problem was not academic, yet this is one of the many ways in which it was manifested. The real problem was the extreme difficulty I had coping with racism. It was foreign to me, and I had no clue how to deal with it. Hamilton College exposed me to the "cancer of racism," and for this battle I was ill equipped. I could not comprehend how White students could sit next to me in class, converse with me when the class assignment necessitated it, borrow my spare pen if they needed one, and then ignore me once class was over. This was incomprehensible to me.

It was unbelievable that I was expected to show team spirit as a member of the track team. I was a short sprinter on the women's track team my first year in college. I was one of two Black women and three women of color on the team. I often felt uncomfortable and unwanted as a member of the team. In fact I did not feel that I was really part of the team. I was simply the talent, the little Black speedster who would win points for the team, and I felt the pain of knowing it was all that I represented. My teammates could not see beyond my skin color. They spoke to me during practice and cheered me on during meets, but once I exited the field house I no longer existed. After the meet, they no longer knew who I was. They walked past me on the path with their noses in the air or their eyes fastened to the ground, staring at the perfect arrangement of bricks on the pavement. It was curious to observe them going through these exercises. They avoided making eye contact with me, and when they did they feigned friendliness. After a year and a half, I quit track and field my sophomore year. I was sick of feeling like an outsider. I would not, could not run for them and pretend to be unaffected by the racist attitudes that prevailed among the members of the track team.

Sadly, I had the same experiences within the classroom. I was often the only brown face in my classes, and I felt compelled to represent Black people or make sure we were not being misrepresented. I was often expected to be the expert on Black issues, but I was only capable of presenting my perspective. I was still getting acquainted with being Black in America, and I did not know enough about Blacks in America to be an expert. I rarely left classes with new friends. My classmates worked on projects with me, they asked for my comments on papers, and they too would later walk by me as if I was a nonentity. At times, when working in groups, they would ignore my ideas and later reclaim them as their own. I was invisible to them. Yet I imagine that it must have been difficult to miss a brown face in a sea of whiteness. A White woman in one of my French classes once told me that she did not know me because "we did not speak English in class." The statement was enough to make me cackle.

Some professors taught to exclude, and this was especially true in the sciences. The science classes were always large and lecturing was the preferred style of teaching. There was a lot of information to process, and it was often difficult to imagine the molecules spatially in my general and organic chemistry courses. Structural models were sometimes used to illustrate a point, but if you did not comprehend the material the first or second time, you often felt stupid. The teaching methods seemed to be designed to weed out the students who "did not belong," and it was often the students of color who were failing. Many of these students dropped out of science course work or changed their field of study altogether. Sometimes there was an attempt to remedy the problem by offering tutoring, but without altering the style of teaching this was not worth the extra effort. The head of the chemistry department acted as the gatekeeper to the higher level courses; he decided who would go to medical school and who would drop out. According to Smith, the experience of involvement or alienation can directly or indirectly affect the performance and success not only of students, but of faculty and staff as well (Smith, 1991). I was extremely distracted by the social issues such as racism that plagued my daily existence, and my academic performance, especially in chemistry, was affected.

Professors did not seem to hold the same high expectations of Black students or other students of color as they did for White students; consequently, they were not as supportive as they could have been. In fact one of my chemistry professors felt compelled to tell me "how fortunate I was to be at Hamilton College since I was from the inner city." He did not feel that the college was lucky to get a bright Black student.

It seemed that a grade of D was what was expected of Black students, and anything above that was suspect. In my junior year, I took two semesters of organic chemistry. I was doing poorly, and I had gotten some help. However, when I began to do a bit better, I was accused of cheating. I confronted the professor, who replied, "I don't know what old exams are floating around out there" or something to that effect. In the meanwhile, there were many White students who were often observed programming chemical formulas and hiding notes in their calculators. I still wonder how many of them were accused of cheating. I stopped taking science courses after this class. In fact I was so sick of my college environment that I applied for a leave of absence and I got out of the country.

I went to Paris, France, with Wesleyan University, where I spent a semester studying at the University of Paris IV (La Sorbonne) and at Reid Hall, a consortium of American colleges in Paris. It was helpful getting away from the small-town environment of Clinton, NY, especially because it meant I only had a few months left until graduation. But there was racism in Paris too. My host mother, or shall I say landlady, because that was the only role she played in my development, was an elderly White woman from Bretagne (Brittany) in western France. She seemed nice, and we got along well until she accused my British Nigerian friend, who was studying law at the University of Paris-Assas, of stealing. She began daily tirades about "you Africans" and our "fatalism, having too many children," and that she did not understand "why we come to France to study." The woman, Madame C., did not want me to eat fish out of her china dishes; rather she preferred that I use paper plates. She also did not want me to use her doving pot, which, she felt compelled to tell me, came from Germany. She seemed to be under the impression that I was someone who was not used to anything refined, that I was some kind of barbarian who had never seen a china plate let alone a doving pot. I ate on china plates on a daily basis in America, we had doving pots there too, I wanted to explain on many occasions. I was paying $500 per month to rent a small room in her apartment with kitchen privileges, yet she would tell me, "*Il faut pas faire un grand repas tous les jours*." She told me that I did not need to cook every day, adding that I could have cold cuts for dinner. Her son even instructed her to put me out of the apartment so that she could go on Christmas vacation in Bretagne. Toward the end of my stay, she began an early morning tirade about my Nigerian friend being a prostitute, drug addict, and murderer. I left the apartment abruptly without eating my breakfast and, as a result, suffered from an attack of hypoglycemia and fainted, hitting my head on the cement floor of a cathedral while on a field trip with my class. I realized that I was essentially paying this landlady to be harassed toward the end of my stay in France.

I lived in a sheltered world before Hamilton College. I knew nothing concrete of racism. What I knew of racists was what I saw on the TV screen—it happened to other people, not me. My baptism into racial conflict in America was therefore second hand. On matriculation at Hamilton College, I began to feel or at least relate to what those people whom I was seeing on the TV screen experienced. The cancer of racism infected academics; it infected sports, social life, and every aspect of my being. It metastasized to my bones, it reached my heart, and it almost got to my soul. It ate away at me, tore me up inside for 4 long years.

For all my college years, I had to struggle to attain this academic education that is supposedly available to all, accessible to anyone regardless of race, creed, religion, sex, ethnicity, and all the other divisions that society names. Yet I had to fight to get it. I had to suffer to get it. Like Lorde's battle with breast cancer, homophobia, and sexism, my battle with the cancer of racism, sexism, and classism, along with the ignorance of my identity in the culture of the United States, left me worn out. It almost destroyed me. I had bouts of emotional breakdowns. Sometimes I thought I was going crazy. College was supposed to be an exciting experience, but instead it left me with a damaged psyche. My experience left me slightly broken, but not bent out of shape. My battle with the cancer of racism eventually made me stronger, and it helped me speak up and defend those who are incapable of defending themselves. It has also helped me define myself, on my own terms, and I think that clinging to my Caribbean identity is what saved me.

When I read the novel *Crick Crack Monkey,* it transported me back to my childhood days in Antigua. The book juxtaposed Black and White, rich and poor, town and country, self-rejection and prideful identity, academically educated and socially educated to illustrate how formal literacy alienates Tee, the main character, from most of her family. I was able to relate very well to her experiences as an outsider as she became more educated at school. Like me, Tee was a young dark-skinned Black girl from a Caribbean island. Her mother had also died when she was very young, and her father moved to England, leaving her with his sister, Tantie. When Tee wins a scholarship to St. Anne's School, she goes to live with Aunt Beatrice, her maternal aunt, so she can attend the school. Through her experiences at Aunt Beatrice's house and those of her early school days, Tee becomes a fragmented, marginalized other in the life of her aunt, cousins, and father's family.

Prior to attending high school, Tee looks forward to the experience. She is idealistic and filled with fantasies of the transformation that will come about as a result of learning to read and becoming educated. She tells us:

> I looked forward to going to school. I looked forward to the day when I
> could pass my hand swiftly from side to side on a blank piece of paper
> leaving meaningful marks in its wake; to stare nonchalantly into a book
> until I turned over a page, a gesture pregnant with importance for it indicat-
> ed one had not merely been staring, but that the most esoteric of processes
> had been taking place whereby the paper had yielded up something stared
> at. (p. 22)

Tee is initially thrilled at the thought of becoming smarter and the advantages to
be gained from learning from books. She identified school with gaining an
immense amount of knowledge from books, but the fantasy soon collides with
reality when the kind of academic advantage she receives drastically differs
from her experience in a new social situation.

I had the same feelings of excitement and idealism before I entered college.
Like Tee, once I got there, I realized that the dream of social promotion was
markedly different from the reality I experienced. Much of Tee's education centers on learning about White people, and she begins to draw comparisons
between her reality and what she is being taught, and she begins to feel alienated from her inner self. For me, it was being in the midst of White people who
negated my existence by ignoring me that caused me to feel alienated. Like Tee,
I sought a White education because I believed it would afford me certain social
privileges. Yet with the advantages of that first-class education came a price—
my self-esteem, my confidence, my concentration, and sometimes my sanity.
No one had prepared Tee or me for that fact of our existence as educated Black
girls living in a predominantly White society.

In his essay, *The ABCs of Alienation and Re-Integration*, Bill Clemente
(1997) stated that education can best be described as a double-edged sword,
because it promises social and intellectual elevation, but often at huge costs.
Just as Tee's idealized notions about learning clash quickly with the reality of
her aunt and uncle, Mr. and Mrs. Hines, who couple religious instruction with
the students' lived experience, my idealized notions about learning how to interact with White people clashed with the reality of being snubbed because of my
race and socioeconomic status. Unlike Tee, who becomes alienated from her
culture and her language because of her education, I held onto my culture and
language precisely because of the educational environment where I lived. While
Tee imitated the speech and mannerisms of the British, I spoke patois with my
Caribbean friends and wrote poetry in patois. I also took courses in Africana
Studies to learn about the people of Africa and the African Diaspora. I did not
attempt to assimilate into the White culture and values around me; I held firmly
to my own, the Antiguan culture that had been my shield, my backbone. My
strong sense of Caribbean identity was my suit of armor. It helped soften the
blow of racial conflict, but it failed to protect me completely from the alienating
effects of being an immigrant Black woman and becoming educated in an over-
whelmingly White environment. Yet it is that sense of Caribbeanness that

helped me stay connected to my roots through my connection to other Caribbeans on campus.

Much like Tee's education, my own education was more social than academic. For, like Tee, it is in the educational setting that I learned about racism, classism, and prejudice. Hamilton College was a place where there was a reinforcement of a system of privilege and exclusion based on race and economics. This exclusion was most noted in the existence of the "Black" table in the dining halls. Most of the Black people and other students of color tended to sit in one area of McEwen dining hall. McEwen was the most diverse of the three dining halls on campus, and so we would eat at this hall no matter where we lived on campus—we walked the distance to be around people who looked like us and understood our experiences. I occupied a curious space at Hamilton College because I was marginalized and privileged at the same time. I was privileged because I was getting a first-class college education reserved for a select White few, but I was also marginalized because I was a dark-skinned Black female, I was poor by comparison to the majority of my White counterparts, and I was an immigrant. In a very short time, I became the racialized Other, a subalternized Third Worldish thing with an accent. It was mind boggling during my whole time on that campus. At the height of her marginalization, Tee says,

> I wanted to shrink, to disappear. I felt that the very sight of me was an affront to common decency. I wished that my body could shrivel up and fall away, that I could step out new and acceptable. (p. 107)

Tee begins to realize that the only thing that matters in her new surroundings is skin color and class. She begins to feel she is unacceptable as she is and has "a death wish" of sorts, where she hopes to shrivel up and reemerge as something new—presumably light skinned or White. Did Tee's desire to reinvent herself parallel my need to escape from Hamilton College and change myself for something new and less repulsive to White people? No, I did not feel that way. I never wanted to change myself. After one semester, I was ready to quit. I tried to join the Army, but changed my mind after I realized that military life was not for me. I returned to school, and I found refuge in writing poetry, listening to music, and spending time with my close network of girlfriends. I turned my angst, frustration, and disappointment into poems in which I was free to express myself as I wished.

My education was indeed a double-edged sword, replete with positive and negative aspects. It differentiated me from the people in my neighborhood and from my childhood friends. I was once accused by a friend from junior high school of sounding like a White girl when I returned to Brooklyn after my first year of college. He had not gone to college. In fact he was still struggling to finish high school. Most people in my neighborhood had not been to college, many of the residents in the area were on public assistance, while I had a middle-class upbringing. I had more educational and class privilege compared with the people in my neighborhood who were faced daily with the fear of death and deprivation. However, in the upper middle-class White world of Hamilton College, I was relegated to the position of an unwanted stepchild. My position was one of powerlessness and discomfort. I became well aware that Black people and other people of color were not wanted on campus. This was certainly evidenced in the racial harassment perpetrated against the most vulnerable students of color and the intense hatred that permeated the college campus. I also had to deal with sexually harassing notes left on my dormitory room door by drunken White boys. My isolation was affirmed by one of my White friends and teammates from the track team who told me that I "did not fit in here." After all I was a dark-skinned Black woman with braids in my hair living on a campus of white-skinned people with blond hair and blue eyes. The college education I received taught me that people are valued and treated accordingly, not based on character, but the color of their skin and the number of zeros following the dollar sign in their bank account. White, rich, heterosexual, able-bodied and American was the standard at Hamilton College. To me it seemed that intelligence, character, or who you were as an individual were irrelevant to the people in my classes. However, if you were Black and rich, you were acceptable if you were willing to alienate yourself from the other Blacks on campus.

As a young literate Black woman pursuing an education in a predominantly White institution, I was exposed to the ugliness of racism and classism where White skin privilege was the rule. In a number of ways, I was repeatedly told that my skin is of the wrong hue, that I did not belong, but I was determined to get the academic education for which I came and I was not going to allow anything to stand in my way. I joined cultural organizations such as the Black and Latin Student Union, La Vanguardia, and Asian Cultural Society to learn about other cultures, and I forged strong friendships with Black women and other women of color at Hamilton College. I was especially close to women of Caribbean origin, and I found strength in those relationships that helped me cope with the strain of navigating my way through an educational maze. I had a support system of five amazing women who entered college at the same time as I, and to this day we are still a source of support for one another. After graduating from Hamilton College in May 1997 and being jobless, with my pricey diploma, I went back to college. I spent the Fall 1997 semester at Brooklyn College taking calculus, hoping to find my way back to the path to medical school. Some personal dilemmas forced me to withdraw from the class, but the upside is that I took the time to apply to the Master of Public Health Program at Hunter College in New York City, and I began working on my master's in Spring 1998.

I completed my master's degree in Public Health in 1999, two years after I graduated from Hamilton College. I still aspired to be a doctor, and I had hoped to use my public health background as a stepping stone to medical school. I was still experiencing the aftershock of my experiences at Hamilton College, but I was living in New York City again, and so the first tier of my graduate school experience was buffered by the tremendous diversity around me and having my friends and family nearby. After 4 years at Hamilton College, I learned to harden myself, and therefore the racial issues that plagued my life then were almost absent from life in graduate school. I focused solely on my studies. There was one professor, however, in my master's program, a White woman, who I felt had racist tendencies, but I remained largely unaffected by her attitude—and it showed up in the way that she ignored the needs of Black graduate students. I once sought her advice on my course of study and I was completely dismissed. Although she was the program coordinator, she acted as if she did not have time to be bothered with me. I was not alone in my experience because other Black students had also complained about her attitude. My eldest sister, who also took graduate courses with this professor, relayed a similar story about her attitude toward Black people in the classes she taught. I graduated with honors. Shortly thereafter, I became a mother, and I took a 2-year sabbatical from academics. During my pregnancy, I applied to a PhD program in Health Education and Promotion, and I was accepted to Kent State University, where I am now juggling work, academics, and single motherhood with my 3-year-old daughter.

Kent State reminds me of my undergraduate experiences because it is also predominantly White, and once again the number of brown faces around me is minute. The isolation now is that of being a young educated Black woman and single parent, chasing a doctorate degree on a White campus and trying to navigate my way through this maze without the benefit of guidance and mentoring. These days I am no longer preoccupied with being Black on a White campus. I have come into my own, and being a single Black female parent is simply a fact of life. The shock of living among White students has worn off, and the naivete about the way in which they react or do not seems to have faded. Here I have seen and experienced the same racism that nearly crippled me in my undergraduate years, only this time I am more than equipped for battle. Ten years have passed since my first real encounter with the ugliness of racism, and other people's ignorance no longer consumes me. With my daughter at my side, I remain focused on the task at hand—getting my PhD.

REFERENCES

Beckham, B. (1988). Strangers in a strange land: The experience of blacks on white campuses. *Educational Record, 68*(4), 69(1), 74-78.

Clemente, B. (1997). The ABCs of alienation and re-integration: Merle Hodge's *Crick Crack Monkey*. In S.W. Gilbert, D. Perez, & C. Macias (Eds.), *Sincronia*. University of Guadalajara Jalisco, Mexico.

Griffin, A.G., & Parkerson, M. (1994). *A litany for survival: The life and work of Audre Lorde* [Videotape]. New York: Third World Newsreel.

Hodge, M. (1970). *Crick crack monkey*. Portsmouth, NH: Heinemann.

Mistron, D. (1999) *Understanding Jamaica Kincaid's Annie John*. Westport, CT: Greenwood.

Smith, D.G. (1991). *The challenge of diversity: Alienation in the academy and its implications for faculty* [Electronic version]. Retrieved November 4, 2002, from http://www.ntlf.com/htm/lib/bib/ diversity.htm.

Author Index

Subject Index

A

The ABCs of Alienation and Re-Integration, 196
Academic failure, blame for, 109
Aesthetics, 45
Affective aspects, of adult literacy, 22
Affirmative Action legislation, 59
African-centered affirmations, 103
African-centered worldview, 103, 110
African Diaspora. *See* Diaspora
Africans, as first storytellers, 119
Aid to Dependent Children (ADC), 29
Aid to Families With Dependent Children (AFDC), 28
Altherusserian ways, 165
Ambiguous Adventure, 158
American Association of University Women, 41
Anderson, Marian, 4

Angelou, Dr. Maya, 3, 27
Anxiety, 71
Attention deficit hyperactivity disorder (ADHD), 71
Auditory information, processing into long-term memory, 72
The Autobiography of Malcolm X, 93
Axiology, 45

B

Baldwin, James, 93
Bambara, Toni Cade, 130
Becraft, Marie, 53
Bethune, Mary McLeod, 2, 53
Bethune-Cookman College, 54
Birney, Sunny-Marie, 7
Black and on Welfare: What You Don't Know About Single-Parent Women, 27-36
recommendations, 34-35

CPSIA information can be obtained at www.ICGtesting.com
Printed in the USA
BVOW071916050613

322544BV00001B/5/A